LIVE AT THE CONTINENTAL

LIVE AT THE CONTINENTAL

BOOK ONE: BETTE, BUNS and BALLS

The Inside Story of
the World-Famous Continental Baths

As Told by Its Founder
Steve Ostrow

Copyright © 2007 by Steve Ostrow.

Library of Congress Control Number: 2007902213
ISBN :   Hardcover   978-1-4257-5101-2
           Softcover   978-1-4257-5099-2

All rights reserved. No part of this book may be reproduced or transmitted in any form or by any means, electronic or mechanical, including photocopying, recording, or by any information storage and retrieval system, without permission in writing from the copyright owner.

This book was printed in the United States of America.

*Note . . . that the author Steve Ostrow has designated that all his net proceeds from the sale of this book go to the Chulah DeJan Foundation for AIDS Research.

To order additional copies of this book, contact:
Xlibris Corporation
1-888-795-4274
www.Xlibris.com
Orders@Xlibris.com
35329

Contents

July 1969 9
Prologue   April 1968 11
Can We Talk? 13

Chapter 1   Let's Start with Me 15
Chapter 2   The First Lady of the Baths 19
Chapter 3   Freedom Sucks 23
Chapter 4   The Proposition 27
Chapter 5   The Discovery 31
Chapter 6   A Broadway Opening 37
Chapter 7   The Entertainer 44
Chapter 8   A Star Is Born 49
Chapter 9   The Count 56
Chapter 10   Decriminalized 60
Chapter 11   A Kiss Is Still a Kiss 65
Chapter 12   Stardust 67
Chapter 13   Fire Island 71
Chapter 14   Dreams 78
Chapter 15   Captain Hook 83
Chapter 16   The Visit 87
Chapter 17   Mr. X 91
Chapter 18   The Continental Kibbutz 94
Chapter 19   Doing the White Thing 99
Chapter 20   Captain Cooked 101
Chapter 21   Jess 103
Chapter 22   "Could It Be Magic?" 107
Chapter 23   Bette, Buns, and Balls 112
Chapter 24   Close Encounters of the Third Kind 116
Chapter 25   Friends of the Family 121
Chapter 26   Putting on the Ritz 127

Chapter 27	It's Rudy! Men, Tarry!	131
Chapter 28	Fire!	139
Chapter 29	The Golden Girl	141
Chapter 30	The Ritz Continental	146
Chapter 31	Room Service	148
Chapter 32	Decadence	151
Chapter 33	Queen for a Day	157
Chapter 34	Stuttgart	159
Chapter 35	Legends	163
Chapter 36	Twinkle, Twinkle, Little Stars	172
Chapter 37	The Key to the City	175
Chapter 38	Triple Play	181
Chapter 39	The Met Comes to the Baths	187
Chapter 40	High Noon	193
Chapter 41	Winter Is Nigh	201
Chapter 42	The Last Dance	209

Epilogue 215
Disclaimer and Acknowledgment 217
Ostrow's List 219
Index 223

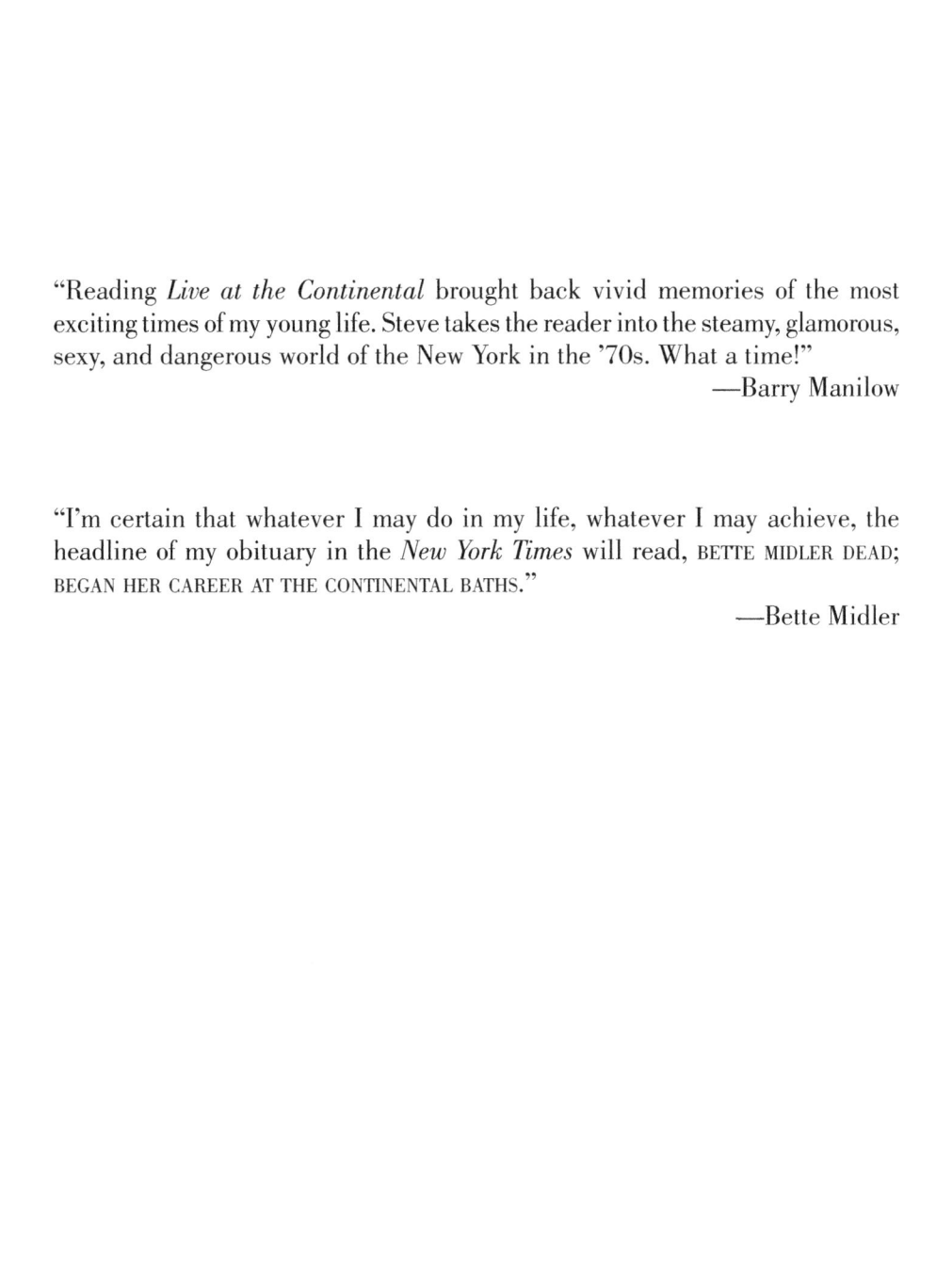

"Reading *Live at the Continental* brought back vivid memories of the most exciting times of my young life. Steve takes the reader into the steamy, glamorous, sexy, and dangerous world of the New York in the '70s. What a time!"
—Barry Manilow

"I'm certain that whatever I may do in my life, whatever I may achieve, the headline of my obituary in the *New York Times* will read, BETTE MIDLER DEAD; BEGAN HER CAREER AT THE CONTINENTAL BATHS."
—Bette Midler

July 1969

Suddenly, from behind a tacky gold curtain, a burst of energy in the form of a short, rather busty redhead converged on the towel-clad audience, igniting the damp surroundings. Two hours later, having devoured, consumed, and otherwise ingested the mass of New York's most blasé and sophisticated genitalia, having led them from one frenzied climax to another and then spat them out, the curtain came down. But a new era in the gay life of New York—and perhaps the world—had been ushered in.

The Ansonia Hotel

Prologue

April 1968

The old Ansonia Hotel at 2109 Broadway is one of New York's grandest edifices. It covers the whole block front on Broadway from Seventy-third to Seventy-fourth Street and rises seventeen giant floors high, with a wrought-iron winding staircase boring right through its center. Each of its magnificent apartments has a stone balcony with elaborate gargoyles and figureheads carved on the lintels underneath the huge windows.

I usually entered on the Broadway side for my singing lessons but one day happened to be coming down Seventy-fourth Street, where I spotted a strange outcropping that I mistook for a side door. It protruded from the building wall, rather like a subway entrance, and had a covered tin canopy, very art deco. Trying to enter through this newly discovered portal, I was stopped by a boarded-over, rusted metal doorway. *How mysterious,* I thought.

I asked Solomon, the doorman, whom I had come to know from my many visits, what was behind the doorway. He told me that it was a deserted health club. Wow, a deserted health club, just what I was looking for. I pressed him for the name and telephone number of the owner of the building, a Mr. Jacob Starr. A fast call and Mr. Starr agreed to meet me that very afternoon.

Starr's office, located on the third floor of the hotel, was a large round room with immense bay windows looking out onto Broadway. There, hardly visible behind a magnificent mahogany desk, I saw a short balding, gray-haired man with a cherubic round pink face and thick spectacles. He must have been about eighty-five years old at least, but the eyes behind the glasses were bright and alert. He gestured for me to sit on the antique chair fronting the desk.

"So what's your idea?" he asked, with a pronounced Yiddish accent.

I said that we were looking for good open space to set up a men's health club and spa, describing the plan in detail, to which Starr replied, "And women? What about women?"

"No women," I said. And looking at me as if I were crazy, he asked, "So what makes you think you will make money from this?"

I told him we had market researched the project and were convinced we could make it go. Never once did I mention that it would be a gay club.

Starr then picked up the telephone and, growling some unintelligible sounds into it, summoned his son-in-law Allen to show me the space.

We took the elevator all the way down below street level and emerged into a cavernous space clouded with musty-smelling dusty air.

Once my eyes got accustomed to the gloom, I could see that the space was enormous, almost a city block square, with an immense depression at its center covered in junk and mud. Allen saw me staring and said it had been the swimming pool.

A swimming pool! Lights went on in my head. No gay baths had anything but grotty little plunge pits. I immediately had visions of fantastic-looking guys, all nude, frolicking in the pool.

The walls surrounding the area were muddied, but one could make out glimpses of blue and white tile underneath the slime. It had the makings of a Roman amphitheater; all it needed were the gladiators.

We then climbed up a flight of stairs to the second floor of the club, which was at street level. Here there was nothing but open space, which, together with the downstairs, probably measured about forty thousand square feet.

Proceeding to the next level, there was a sign that proclaimed the Jewish Men's Hashiva Club. Allen unlocked a door that opened into a huge room with a stage. He said that the Hashiva Club still met there on Sunday afternoons. They were paying a retainer fee on the unused premises, which was why it had remained unrented.

By the time we returned to Jacob Starr's office, my mind was in a whirl. It was all I could do to stammer to Jacob Starr, "Is this space available?"

"Available?" Jacob Starr said. "It's been available for fifteen years."

Can We Talk?

Three of the most significant cultural events in the shaping of our gay culture took place, almost around the same time, over thirty years ago. Stonewall in June of 1969, the birth of the I-won't-take-it-any-longer generation; Woodstock in August of the same year, which saw the melding of all gender identities into a new specie, the love child, also known as the hippy generation; and in September of 1968, the Continental Baths, an arena where society's miscreants could come together and, through immaculate conception, conceive a whole new generation who would celebrate their uniqueness by calling themselves "gay": no longer "queer," no longer "faggot," no longer "bent," no longer an abomination.

The new gay man that would evolve would recognize that, rather than being a perversion, he was simply another version. For if mainstream society was to recognize and worship God's omnipotence, then how could he have fucked up at least 10 percent—according to Kinsey—of the time, accounting for at least six hundred million of the six billion inhabitants of this planet?

With this newfound freedom, gay people rejoiced and celebrated themselves. In 1970, on the first anniversary of the Stonewall riots, there was a small commemorative parade on Sixth Avenue. After a few years, it had grown enormously and moved to Fifth Avenue, then becoming a major annual event in the city's calendar.

In the spring of 1971, the first gay rights bill was introduced into the New York City Council. But even with the backing of the then mayor John Lindsay, it failed to pass. It was legal to be homosexual, but you just didn't have any rights. So once again we took to the streets.

The abandoned docks on the waterfront became sex palaces at night, and Christopher Street became the gay main street leading to Valhalla. One after the other, gay bars and shops started to open in Chelsea, north of Greenwich Village, and also on the Upper West Side, in proximity to the Baths. We were no longer low profile. But the new gay lifestyle wasn't confined to sex and dance bars. It soon went further and became a drug culture.

Thanks to Dr. Timothy Leary, LSD came into vogue, together with Quaaludes and angel dust. Amyl nitrate, originally a patent medicine for persons with angina pectoris, became a must to enhance orgasm. At that time, it was sold as boxes of capillary tubes of liquid wrapped in cotton and encased in bright yellow mesh, twelve in a box. After crushing the phial between your thumb and forefinger, you would press it against your nose and inhale the vapors. (Incidentally they were manufactured by Burroughs Wellcome, the same pharmaceutical company that now makes AZT.)

In the arts, the musical *Hair*, celebrating the hippy lifestyle, opened on Broadway to sellout crowds. Bob Dylan, Joan Baez, Richie Havens, and the Rolling Stones were soon replaced by the glitter rock of David Bowie, Iggy Pop, and the New York Dolls.

In the discos, it was the OJ's and the Supremes who were topping the charts. With the advent of DJs, gay bars, freed from the Mafia—now that they didn't depend on the Mafia-owned jukebox industry—became a booming business with celebrated DJ heroes.

Bottled beer was out, and the new innovation—pop-top cans—were in vogue. The standard gay uniform was Levi's 501s, T-shirts, and army jackets. Leather bars became commonplace. Gay restaurants serving quiche-type food sprang up everywhere. The movie *Sunday, Bloody Sunday* played to packed houses.

Dr. Howard Brown, the former New York City health administrator, came out publicly after he left office and founded the National Gay Task Force in 1973. And then, in 1974, the APA (American Psychiatric Association) voted to remove homosexuality from its list of pathological disorders. We were gay, and it was okay. The gunfight was over. And everybody came to the Continental corral to party.

How the Continental was created and who were the protagonists are integral to the relating of this story. When you came to the "Tubs," as it was to be affectionately nicknamed by the Divine Miss M, you came to see the people, not concrete walls.

And so I will now set the stage and introduce you to the players. But remember, they are real people . . . just like you.

Chapter 1

Let's Start with Me

So how did a nice Jewish boy from Brooklyn come to be the founder of the world's largest and most famous gay bathhouse?

All I ever really wanted to do as a kid was sing. I had never even heard of a bathhouse. But there was to be a series of fateful events that would lead inexorably to the Continental.
The first was brought on by my joy as a teenager in taking singing lessons. But when my father became ill with terminal cancer I had to stop, as there was no money to pay for such a luxury. Then I learned about the Henry Street Settlement, a charity-subsidized performing arts center where well-known artists donated their time. It was the catalyst for my maiden voyage over the Brooklyn Bridge to Manhattan where I auditioned and, crude as I was, was accepted as a voice student and assigned to a Professor Benjamin DeLoache.
Professor DeLoache was of English and Southern aristocracy, a giant of a man with a noble bass baritone voice to match. "Sing on a cushion of air," he would say. Soon he invited me to take private lessons at his home, a wonderful flat on the top floor of the majestic old Dakota apartments on West Seventy-second Street, the same building where *Rosemary's Baby* and John Lennon were shot, one with camera and the other with a gun, all of which was only two blocks away from where the Continental would be some twenty years later.
I remember how intimidated I felt on my first day when I was greeted by a liveried doorman who directed me to the lift, an immense, elaborate birdcage, operated by a rather severe and formal uniformed gentleman, who transported me to Professor DeLoache's attic loft. As I lifted the brass knocker, the huge mahogany door swung open. There stood Professor DeLoache, all ruddy-complexioned six feet four of him, topped with a shock of white hair,

swathed in a large baker's apron and carrying a rolling pin. He was making yogurt, homemade corn bread, and hopping John for lunch. I politely sat down and did my best with the bread and yogurt, but after learning that hopping John was tripe and steamed onions and that tripe was the intestine of a pig, I settled for a scone with freshly made cream and strawberries. Mercifully the lesson then began.

An avid cook, Professor DeLoache was also a gentleman, connoisseur of all things artistic and tasteful. His sister was married to the very famous and elegant Australian baritone John Brownlee, star of the Glyndebourne Festival and the Metropolitan Opera Company. The professor himself was engaged to be married to one of New York's leading socialites. He was to teach me manners and the ways of the world as well as voice and took great pride in introducing me to his friends as his protegé. It was perhaps the professor who had the greatest influence in expanding my horizons. Till then my outlook was quite provincial, certainly nothing that could have predicted how international destiny would force me to be.

After about a year and a half, the professor was appointed head of the music department at Yale University. In this position, he was able to grant two complete music scholarships each year to those who he felt were deserving and qualified. When he offered me one of the scholarships, I was overwhelmed with joy and gratitude and raced all the way home to tell Mom the good news.

"Guess what happened?" I exclaimed, bursting into the house. I can still remember my mother's face clouding with tears instead of reflecting my joy. My elder brother Marshal was by this time hospitalized, having suffered a nervous breakdown after Dad's protracted death; and the scholarship would mean that she would be left all alone, with no source of financial support other than her part-time job. There was nothing in the world I wanted more than to go, but I couldn't leave her to fend for herself and my brother.

With that sacrifice, my entire life shifted course. Professor DeLoache went off to his new assignment, and I was left with my dreams unfulfilled, but then again, had I gone to Yale, there would probably never have been a Continental Baths. The Lord works in mysterious ways, his wonders to perform.

Along with my social skills, my sexual awareness was also developing, albeit rather ambiguously. I felt very sensual whenever I would think about or see naked bodies, male or female, but I never attributed any deep meaning to this. There had been times when as a kid delivering orders on my bicycle, I detoured past the Reiss Park swimming hole where teenage boys skinny-dipped, jumping off rocks into the water with the sun glistening off their lithe bodies.

I also was intrigued by the girlie magazines of the times: *Hustler*, *Playboy*, and so on, and indeed, had a whole collection of *Sunlovers Nudist* magazines, which I found exciting. Both in school and at play, it was common practice for us boys to masturbate together over girlie magazines. It gave us a nice feeling of camaraderie.

In those days, the male body appeared chiefly in nudist "health" magazines or weight lifting magazines, which featured the likes of Steve Reeves (Mr. America) or Charles Atlas, posing in skimpy briefs. But there was one magazine, *Physique Pictorial*, that went so far as to feature athletic young men in highly suggestive poses, with fishnet draped over their private parts. For fully nude photos, you had to send away to England, which I did surreptitiously. I remember looking forward to those discreetly packaged airmail envelopes that would contain the latest in male physique beauty, always in black and white.

Still, I had little opportunity to explore my early sexual stirrings as I worked long hours during the week contributing to the family. It wasn't until I was twenty-one and working for the Beneficial Finance Company as a collector that I was relieved of my burdensome virginity.

Every Friday night, after the cash was balanced, all the "finance executives," together with Barry Cross the manager, would go out to an Italian restaurant in the neighborhood. There we would have a meal, a few beers, a good Chianti with dinner, and, generally, a good time. Barry in his away-from-office mode could be quite a raconteur, for, living in a hotel room in New York, he led what to us was a very cosmopolitan life. Occasionally we would hear him talking on the phone to his various paramours in dulcet tones we were unaccustomed to from this martinet.

But I was still shocked one Friday when, by chance, sitting next to Barry at the restaurant he leaned over to me and, in a very confidential sort of whisper, said, "Hey, Steve, how would you like to get laid tonight?"

Turning every color in the rainbow, I stammered with as much aplomb as possible, "Sh . . . sure, Barry, why not?"

"Leave everything to me, kid," he replied.

Till that night, although I had been on dates and enjoyed heavy petting and kissing and much fondling, I had never experienced actual intercourse with man, woman, or beast. People were much more innocent in those days. Needless to say, the rest of the meal was a blur until everyone else said their good-byes and Barry made a telephone call. Then we got into his car and drove to the Upper East Side, where we pulled up at a very fashionable-looking apartment building. The uniformed doorman escorted us into the elevator, and when we reached our floor, Barry rang an ornate brass bell outside an apartment door.

Lo and behold, a voluptuous blonde lady, completely swathed in diaphanous white garments, greeted us. Barry gave her a great hug and then, turning to me, said, "Well, he's all yours now, Veronica. Be gentle." Then pressing something into her hand, he turned and departed through the door.

Veronica took a long look at me and then proceeded to guide me into a very comfortably upholstered chair, saying, "Hi, honey, would you like a drink or something?"

"Oh, just a glass of water will do," I replied, as I really didn't think I could handle anything else just then.

Once the glass of water arrived, I gradually became aware of the enormity of what was happening. I felt like running out, but I knew that would get back to Barry. There was also no denying that I was feeling a sense of expectation and excitement that was quite overpowering. I knew that I would stay.

While I was sipping my water and contemplating all this, Veronica put some lush music on the record player and drew me into the bedroom. It was like a set out of a motion picture with a four-poster canopied bed covered with silk damask cushions of all sizes and shapes and all done up in white. There was a thick white carpet covering the floor, and the whole room gave you the feeling that you were floating on a cloud.

Before long, there I was in all my glory, with Veronica savoring my erection in her painted mouth. She was soft and white and curvaceous and *very* talented. It wasn't but a few moments when I experienced a tidal wave of feeling and a rush of adrenaline and God knows what else . . . then it was all over.

Chapter 2

The First Lady of the Baths

By now, my brother was recovered and home; and, still convinced that my life's calling was to sing, I answered an audition call for the Bel Canto Opera Company, a sort of off-Broadway opera company for up-and-coming young singers. I auditioned for the company by singing "Chella Mi Credo" from Puccini's *La Fanciulla del West* and was accepted and then cast as Rodolfo, the poet in Puccini's *La Bohème*. The tragic heroine of the opera, Mimi, who dies from consumption in act 4, was to be played by a girl with the rather austere name of Anna Regina. Ms. Regina—which translates to Queen—turned out to be a tall, statuesque young lady with long shining brown hair and a rather classically beautiful face and body, all of which she demurely hid behind glasses and thick, loose wool sweaters. Blessed with a photographic memory, she could flick the pages of the score and perfectly retain the music and the text. Having no need to study, she would constantly try to engage me in idle conversation, which I found quite annoying as I was struggling very conscientiously to master the Italian dialogue.

At each rehearsal, Anna seemed to curve herself closer to me. Her sweaters, which grew progressively sexier, showed clearly the seductive curves of a full-bosomed body sitting atop a splendid pair of long and shapely legs. I began to experience a confusing contradiction of feelings: annoyance at her interrupting my concentration between scenes and a powerful attraction.

Finally I took a stance and, looking squarely at her wide-set brown eyes, which, together with her high cheekbones and pert nose, reminded me of Grace Kelly, said exasperatedly, "Look, Anna, I *really* have to study between scenes if I'm going to be ready by performance time. So suppose we don't talk now, but after the rehearsal's over, we go to a café somewhere."

Anna in delight replied, "Sure, Steve, that's fine."

So that night, after rehearsal, we made our way down through SoHo to a local café. Anna told me she lived uptown and that she worked as a secretary for Revlon. I didn't know at the time that she was Charles Revson's personal secretary and took dictation in French at 120 words a minute.

As it turned out, there was a lot more that I didn't know about Anna Regina, and a lot more that she didn't know about me.

* * *

The six weeks of rehearsal for *La Bohème* flew by, and it was soon opening night, a magical stage debut that I will never forget.

Anna made a most *simpatica* and tragic Mimi, with a limpid voice that had a quality reminiscent of Licia Albanese, the reigning Met soprano, at her best. The two of us soared through Puccini's amorous act 1 aria and duets, followed by the festive and youthful ardor of the second act's Café Momus scene. Then came the impassioned third act snow scene. By the time the tragic death scene in act 4 was over, there was nary a dry eye in the house, and Anna and I both knew we were born for the stage. Overjoyed with the success of the performance, Anna and I made our way out of the tiny dressing room area to be greeted by our friends and relatives. Amidst the guests were a distinguished-looking tall man and a strikingly handsome woman whom Anna shepherded me over to, introducing them to me as her mother and father. Suddenly I recognized the gentleman as John Reed King, the most famous and well-known TV and radio personality of the '60s. Anna Regina's real name, I found, was Joanne English King! And the girl who I thought was just another struggling artist like the rest of us turned out to be not only a Scarsdale debutante whose family lived in a semimansion replete with maids, housekeepers, cooks, and gardeners, but a "King" rather than a "Queen." Not to mention that Joanne—and in fact each member of the family—had their own horse! Feeling betrayed and embarrassed at Anna's deception, I made up my mind that I would not talk to Anna, Joanne, or whatever her name was, except when our performances required it.

Over the next six months, however, we were cast together in various operas, often playing romantic leads and having to simulate great love and passion for each other on stage, night after night. In time that passion came to seem real, and I began to think that I would either have to part company with Joanne or get married.

Married! I didn't even know if I was in love. After all, what was love? But I was now twenty-seven, and almost every other girl I had been with had bored me to tears. Joanne, by contrast, was beautiful, talented, and, while rather highly strung, was very exciting. When I talked about it to Mom, who had met Joanne at one of our performances, she said she liked her, but after all she was a shiksa, and how could I marry out of the religion?

Not wanting to lose her, I invited Joanne to a Sunday barbecue at our house in Brooklyn. She arrived in a long summer frock with dozens of crinolines flouncing out the skirts, high-heeled shoes, upswept hair, gold earrings, a floral parasol, and white gloves. She was the epitome of femininity, a *Vogue* cover girl; my mother and brother loved her. So one night, after rehearsals, we drove under the Brooklyn Bridge and parked. As we sat watching the glittering lights of the city and the shimmering waves lit by the moonlight, I handed Joanne a *little* black box. When she saw the *little* engagement ring inside the *little* black box, she screamed with delight. I asked her to marry me. She said yes. And our lives would change forever.

* * *

Once the announcement was made, I was summoned to appear before Joanne's mother, Jeanne Reed King, a formidable presence of a woman, at her Scarsdale mansion. After some cursory questions and polite responses to my saying that my family was middle-income Jewish and that we lived in Brooklyn, Mrs. King looked at me sternly and in quite regal tones said, "Really, Steve, we don't know enough about you to have any objections . . . yet." Somehow though, I must have passed muster, for at the end of the questioning, she said that Joanne was admittedly a very highly strung girl; but if she loved me—conceding that she obviously did—then I would have a loyal companion forever. "She'll always be your best friend," her mother said.

And so we were to wed. Joanne's mother wanted a large wedding at St. Patrick's Cathedral in New York, and as I was not a formally practicing Jew, I didn't mind getting married in a church. But Joanne wanted a simple private wedding. John Reed King took me aside and said, "Steve, I'll give you ten thousand dollars if you elope with Joanne."

Joanne was all for that, but I didn't want the money. Much as we could have used it to start out with, I didn't want to disappoint Joanne's mother entirely. So a compromise was made for a wedding in Scarsdale, at the Church of the Immaculate Heart of Mary. It was a fabulous affair, with the cream of Scarsdale society present in their gowns, jewels, and furs. My brother Marshal was my best man. We ate and drank and sang until it was time for the limousine to take us to the airport for the flight to Florida for our honeymoon.

In Florida, we checked into the just-built Carrillion Hotel, a quite spectacular edifice, but our wedding night was a catastrophe. Joanne changed into several layers of white lingerie and seemed to take an interminable amount of time in the bathroom, making me more and more apprehensive and impatient.

Finally, when I could wait no longer and embraced her for what was to be our bridal consummation, Joanne panicked and asked me to wait out on the balcony. Reluctantly, as you can imagine, I complied.

After what seemed to be hours, I finally lost my patience and, grabbing the balcony door to let myself in, found to my amazement that Joanne had locked me out.

It had taken every nickel I had and all my credit cards to pay for the ring and the honeymoon, and by the time we were married, I was $10,000 in debt. *Maybe I should have taken John Reed King's offer after all,* I thought.

But the trauma of that first night finally wore off, and a kind of warm intimacy started to grow between Joanne and me, although I never did get the impression that Joanne really enjoyed sex. But she was affectionate and warm in her own way, and we built on that.

Chapter 3

Freedom Sucks

In 1961 I resigned from Beneficial Finance Company and with the help of some private investors formed the Freedom Finance Company based in Staten Island, the fatal and final step that would lead to the Continental. In five years' time, Freedom became the largest independent finance company in New York State. I was the executive director and worked around the clock, building the business. We were turning over millions of dollars' worth of loans each year.

I developed a great staff at Freedom Finance Company. Carol my receptionist was tall, about eighteen, with the largest breasts I had ever seen. This, on top of a waspish waist and long black hair, made her a real knockout. Gabe, my assistant manager, and Marie, who was my cashier and his fiancée respectively, were to become real good friends with Joanne and me. Two or three others made up the crew. And *then* there was Harold.

Harold was originally hired as a file clerk but had progressed to collection assistant. Harold was about twenty-one, with straight dark hair, doelike brown eyes, was very fair complexioned, and had a kind of dreamy mystique. Although he could be very businesslike, it was obvious that Harold was *different* and that he liked me. But we kept it very proper. We were all hardworking and efficient, but we were *also* fun.

With things going real well at Freedom, I soon got another bright idea. All loan companies at that time were restricted to making loans in the state they were licensed in. But the wording of the law provided that the loan be closed in the office under the company's license (a law that has since been changed). It occurred to me that if we mailed out loan applications to customers in whatever state and then processed them and issued cheques by mail, this would be "closing the loan" in our office *under* the license. We would be obeying the letter of the law, but all of the United States could then become our potential market.

That's exactly what we did, and the loans poured in. We were the envy of every other loan company in the country, for no one had had the balls to try to revolutionize this staid business. Freedom Finance quickly grew so big that we were working with a brokerage firm to prepare a prospectus for a stock issue on the small board.

Then, on the morning of February 16, 1966, my whole world came crashing down. At 10:00 AM, six large Federal Postal trucks surrounded the office. Dozens of uniformed marshals pushed their way in. In a moment, I was notified that I was under arrest and handcuffed to my desk.

As I watched helplessly, they confiscated the entire contents of the office. Then I was carted up, thrown into a truck, and, after a harrowing ride, was incarcerated in a cell in the infamous "Tombs" in Manhattan.

The procedure of being booked is a harrowing one if it has never happened to you before. You remain in handcuffs until the proper officer has time to tend to you. All the while you are sitting alone in a dark detention cell with no facilities at all.

Finally a plainclothes detective approached me, released me from the handcuffs, which by now had painfully bruised my wrists, and proceeded to dip my fingers in a smelly oily ink solution. He then pressed my thumb and fingers onto a form card and, after taking my photo, told me that I was allowed to make one phone call. I called Joanne, and luckily she was in. I told her to get in touch with Reuben Gross, an attorney and the son of Samuel Gross, our biggest investor, and tell him what had happened.

It didn't take very long then for Joanne to arrive. She said that she had reached Reuben, and he was making the necessary arrangements to try and get me released. Joanne was so infuriated at what had happened that I was afraid that the police would arrest her too. She was ranting at the officers in charge, and I think that they would really have locked her up if Reuben hadn't arrived soon with an order of release from a magistrate stating that I was to be released on my own cognizance, pending a trial.

I was charged with eleven counts of mail fraud, each offence carrying a sentence of five years, meaning that if convicted, I could face a potential of fifty-five years in federal prison.

At this time, Joanne and I were living in Matawan, New Jersey. We now had two kids, Maria and Scott, and had bought a brand-new Levitt house, complete with fireplace, garage, garden, and patio. We were considered to be the pillars of our suburban community, and I was even president and cantor of the local reformed Jewish temple, which I had helped establish. Together with me, Joanne was very active and even considered converting from Catholicism. But the day that I was arrested, the *Matawan Journal* devoted its entire front page to photos of me being led away in handcuffs, with glaring headlines: LOCAL FINANCE EXECUTIVE ARRESTED FOR MAIL FRAUD.

So here I was, with two children and a wife to support, disgraced in the community where I lived and released under a bond that required that I not leave the states of New York and New Jersey until charges were laid and the trial was concluded.

The problem now was how to find a way to make a living while under the threat of imprisonment.

That answer came sooner than I thought one day shortly afterward when I was reading the business section of the *New York Times*. It was in the form of a boxed ad that said,

> Investors wanted
> to open a men's health club and steam bath.
> Enq Walter Kent.

The ad intrigued me. I called the number, and a jovial-sounding man answered. After some trivial pleasantries, we agreed to meet in the Lower Village, at a coffee shop at twelve noon the next day.

Walter had described himself as a stocky, slightly balding middle-aged man. When I arrived promptly at twelve, he was nowhere in sight. In my usual impatience, I paced around and finally decided to go to the men's toilet to relieve myself before taking off.

While I was doing my thing in the urinal, I noticed the short, stocky, rather balding man next to me who was also taking a pee. In a quiet tone, I said, "Walter Kent, I presume?"

"Are you Steve Ostrow?" he asked. And I realized then that I had not described myself on the telephone.

Walter had obviously been waiting for me but didn't know whom to look for. And so, in that urinal, at 12:05 PM on Wednesday in 1968, the Continental was born.

For Strathmore Man
Love of Good Music Led to Opera

By LARRY LAMB
Evening News Staff Writer

MATAWAN TOWNSHIP — "It has all the pathos of a drama," said Stephen A. Ostrow describing his own youth and entry into opera.

Ostrow, who lives at 42 Ivy Hill Drive in Strathmore, has a varied background in opera and has performed with several New York opera companies and radio station WNYC.

True to tradition, Ostrow was born in Brooklyn and worked as a boy to help support his family. He spent his spare money on operatic recordings while other youths went to the Saturday matinee.

MUSIC EVER PRESENT

"Opera was played in the house — and I think that's important," Ostrow explained. "My father sang a great deal at home, but never as a professional. Music was ever present.

"The greatest influence in developing my interest in opera was recordings. Instead of collecting baseball cards like the other kids, I collected operatic recordings.

"I saved my money instead of going to the movies just so I could buy more records."

As his burgeoning interest swelled, he began to look for someone who could help him develop his voice. Through the help of a friend, young Ostrow, only 14, was led to a young girl in Brooklyn who was studying music.

She taught him for a short time, but when she won a Fulbright Scholarship and left for Europe he was left without a teacher.

Undaunted, Ostrow went to the Henry Street Settlement where he studied under Benjamin DeLoauche, who is now Dean of Music at Yale University.

OFFERED SCHOLARSHIP

DeLoauche was impressed with the fleding artist, and when he left Henry Street for Yale he offered Ostrow a full scholarship at the university.

However, Ostrow's father died, and he was forced at 16 to remain in Brooklyn and "get the family back on its feet."

When the disrupted family was solid again, he went to Alfredo Martino, renowned artist of the time, and sought help.

"Martino asked 'Are you prepared to give me five years of your life?' and I did," Ostrow said.

Under Martino's supervision, Ostrow developed his tenor voice. He has performed with the Opera Art Company and Community Opera Company, both of New York.

About six years ago he was appearing almost weekly on WNYC when operatic excerpts were presented. He has performed in La Boheme, Rigoletto, Cavalleria Rusticana, La Traviata and Tosca.

While playing in Tosca, he met his attractive wife, Jo-Anne. Mrs. Ostrow has also studied opera and was playing the lead opposite him when they met.

GAVE UP CAREER

"I gave up opera for housekeeping and raising a family," Mrs. Ostrow explained.

She has performed with New York companies including the Broadway Grand Opera Company.

The Ostrow's 15-month-old daughter already shows a keen interest in music.

When asked why people either like opera or don't, he explained that the arts which combine to form opera will determine a person's attitude toward it.

"If you are exposed to opera enough," he claimed, "you will enjoy it."

OPERA SINGER: Stephen A. Ostrow of Strathmore-at-Matawan has been studying music since his boyhood in Brooklyn. He has performed with several New York opera companies and on the radio.

Chapter 4

The Proposition

Walter was a mild-mannered, affable kind of guy. He was of medium height, rotund, and balding. I guess he looked much like everyone's favorite uncle. The kind that somehow you trusted from the onset.

After tidying up in the washroom, we made our way out to the coffee shop and sat ourselves down in a vacant booth.

Walter told me that he ran a coin-operated shoeshine machine business. Apparently he owned machines that he placed in various locations and then periodically collected the money from them. It seemed like a rather prosaic kind of business, and I didn't really see the connection between that and a steam bath.

We chitchatted around for a fair bit, getting to know each other but still being rather guarded, not really revealing too much about ourselves. Finally I said, "Okay, Walter, what is this really all about?"

He looked at me obliquely and said, "Well, I've got a lot of gay friends, and they all tell me that there is really no place safe and clean for them to go and have a good time like they have in some other countries, so I figured opening up a men's health club and steam bath would be a great idea."

I thought to ask him what *having a good time* meant but didn't want to appear too naïve, so I let that digest for a while before asking him if any baths existed now.

Walter said yes, that there were places like the St. Marks in the Lower Village, the Everard Baths on Twenty-eighth Street, and also a place in upper Harlem that catered to black people; but they were all rather unsavory operations. He had done the research and found that opening a basic steam bath would cost about $15,000. He was prepared to put up $5,000, with the rest of the money coming from one or two other partners.

The prospect seemed quite interesting if not overly exciting, so we exchanged business cards, and I went off to do a little investigation of my own.

I decided to start at the St. Marks Baths, located, fittingly enough, on St. Mark's Place in the lower East Village. The sign out front called it the World-Famous Russian Baths, and I'm sure that at one time it had been a very legitimate public spa for Slavic immigrants and their families. But as I walked up the concrete stairs to enter the four-story stone building, the people leaving the Baths looked anything but Russian.

The clerk in the wire-cage reception booth looked at me disdainfully and muttered, "Five dollars for six hours." Then shoving a ratty towel and a key toward me, he buzzed me into a room that was so dark that I could hardly see where I was going. As my vision cleared, I could see all manner of strange people—black people, white people, brown people, yellow people—all bedecked in nothing but towels around their waists.

Making my way to a door marked Locker Room, I shed my clothes and became one of the towel people myself. Wearing nothing but a towel is like losing your identity and persona. It takes a bit of getting used to but does invite a new sense of freedom and excitement.

Now properly attired, I set out to explore the St. Marks Baths from the bottom up. The basement housed the Russian Baths, the steam room, a sauna and showers and toilets, all grey with grime. The water in the plunge pool and the spa was a murky brown. Repelled, I ascended a flight of dimly lit stairs leading to a room that could only be described as a dormitory. There, some three dozen rusted iron cots with torn hair mattresses played host to men in all stages of dishabille. Some of the cots held two and three men engaged in various types of sexual activities that I couldn't make out. On others men actually slept, or pretended to. I was beginning to understand what *having a good time* meant. But the whole scene was enacted under a ceiling of chicken wire mesh, infested with spiders spinning their webs, and all manner of rodents scurrying about.

I quickly left and made my way up the stairs to the next level. This floor seemed to contain little cubicle rooms, some with their doors open and some closed. As I passed through the narrow corridor, I could make out shadowy shapes of men of all ages, types, and colors, lying on cots in provocative poses in the open rooms. The stench of the unclean mattresses, blending with the odor of feces and urine, was overpowering.

I then climbed the last set of stairs, which led to a dark room with no furniture, no lights, no windows: just a sweaty mass of human flesh all intertwined in and out of themselves and other people. This, I later found out, was the aptly named Orgy Room.

Feeling dirty and claustrophobic, I was hurrying to find my way out when I passed a room with an open door in which a very handsome young black man, not more than twenty, I would say, was propped up on his cot. When he flashed a wide smile at me, I stopped in my tracks to stare. He made no movement or gesture to either invite or ignore me, but I couldn't resist that beautiful smiling face. Hesitatingly, I took a few steps into the room. Still no movement, but the finely etched ebony body glistening with sinew and taut muscle drew me irresistibly. With two more steps, I was inside the little cubicle; and at that point, he reached over with his outstretched foot and kicked the door shut.

The next hour was spent in one of the most savagely intense sexual experiences I have ever had. There seemed to be no limit to the lust we felt for each other, the pleasure we derived from our bodily contact, or the sexual ways we found to express it.

Afterward, exhausted but feeling wonderfully fulfilled and relieved, we began to make conversation. His name was James, and he was a student of architecture from the Deep South. He was staying with his aunt and uncle in Upper Harlem and was having a tough time, both with his studies and his homosexuality, which he had to keep secret from his family. I told him I was married and had a daughter and a son. He listened without judging as I told him about myself. We spent what was left of the afternoon in each other's arms, and then it was time to go.

Now I could understand the attraction of such a place, even with the spiders, dirt, rodents, and surly help: a beautiful experience had been shared by two people who probably could not have met under any other circumstances in a city that still looked upon homosexuality as being illegal. Had we enjoyed each other as we did in any other place, we could have both landed in jail if caught. That was gay life in New York City in the '60s.

* * *

That night I told Joanne about the Walter Kent proposition, explaining—without going into the details—that I had already checked out one of the existing bathhouses. She seemed quite keen on the prospect. When I told her that there was another bathhouse called the Everard Baths on Twenty-eighth Street, she said, "Why don't we check it out together?"

I sort of laughed and said that I didn't think that was possible unless she had a sex change, but why didn't we case it from the outside to determine how much business they did? Joanne seemed excited about it, and so one evening soon, off we went in the car.

The Everard Baths was located on West Twenty-eighth Street and Broadway, not too far from the garment center. We parked our car discreetly about fifty feet from the building, on the opposite side of the street. Our plan was to stay in the car to clock the number of people entering the establishment per hour. It was about eight thirty in the evening of a weeknight, so we didn't expect it to be too active. We had just shut off the engine and turned off the lights when we noticed a man walking toward us. As he approached the Baths, he looked furtively in all directions, presumably to see who was watching, and then, seeing no one, darted across the street and through the doors. No sooner had he executed this procedure than another man came from the opposite direction and performed essentially the same ritual. And so it went on for as long as we stayed, with the pace only quickening as midnight approached. By 11:30 PM, we had clocked 180 men slipping into the Baths. One person per minute!

Thinking that the heavy traffic had been a fluke, we came back every night for a week. Never did the count go lower than one person, on average, per minute. We even clocked it in the daytime, and even then the average was never less than a man a minute. Joanne and I both agreed that this was indeed the business to go into.

I then called Gabriel, who had been my assistant manager at Freedom Finance, and briefed him on the business opportunity. I was very frank about the nature of the business as Gabe was very straight but by no means naïve. We had also been in some small landholding ventures together and had built up not only a friendship but a trust.

There are many ways to go into business. You can either fulfill a need or create a desire. *But if a business can create a desire that fulfills a need, how can you lose?* I thought.

We met with Walter Kent in an Italian restaurant called Joe's on Eighth Street in the Village. Walter described to Gabe the expenses of setting up the business, and I filled in with what we could expect to see as gross income, my calculations being based on the survey that Joanne and I had done. If ratty, dirty holes that hadn't been cleaned in years could prosper, then it seemed to me that if someone opened such a business and treated gay people like customers, providing proper service and clean facilities, they would have to do fabulously.

It was agreed that we would set up a fund of $15,000, $5,000 each, with all three of us sharing equally in the responsibilities and the profits. We were all to canvass the city for a location, and as soon as a suitable place was found, we would start rolling. Taking turns at possible names, we came up with some real whoppers. In the end, we decided to go with something discreet rather than descriptive: the Continental Baths and Health Club was the unanimous winner.

Chapter 5

The Discovery

Around the time of my meeting with Walter, Lauritz Melchior, the great Danish Heldentenor and another of my idols, announced that he had created the Lauritz Melchior Heldentenor Foundation, whose mission it would be to sponsor a young singer who had the necessary attributes to become a full-fledged Wagnerian Heldentenor. The Heldentenor voice is a rare combination of baritone and tenor and only begins to come into maturity in one's midthirties. Since Melchior's prime had passed, no one had come along able to take on the Wagnerian repertoire with the command and prowess of the great Dane.

The foundation planned to stage auditions for one year, starting in New York and then continuing throughout the world, finishing with a final competition of the few selected successful aspirants back in New York at the conclusion of the year's search.

After reading about it in all the papers, I thought, *What the heck, why not go for it?* So after asking around, I engaged the renowned accompanist Gerry Kondouris to help me learn the German repertoire. And guess where Maestro Kondouris had his studio? In the Ansonia Hotel, one of the great buildings of New York, located at Seventy-fourth Street and Broadway where both Caruso and Chaliapin had at one time maintained residences.

Thus, it was that one day I stumbled upon the boarded-over door and, like Alice going down the rabbit hole, discovered the underground realm that would become the center of my life, the Continental Baths.

When Walter and Gabe saw the space, they were as convinced as I that our search had come to an end. We had come up with odd areas of unused space in various parts of the city, all of which would have required tremendous installation costs for plumbing and facilities.

But here was a ready-made health club, complete with swimming pool, albeit requiring a major cleanup and restoration. The location was great; the West Side was undergoing a tremendous resurgence and was starting to be in vogue. The new Lincoln Center complex that took up Sixty-sixth to Sixty-eighth streets had been part of the catalyst.

We were all eager to get started, and it was put to me to make a deal with Jacob Starr. Starr was an old-line Jewish businessman who had come up the hard way having made his millions through acquiring downtrodden properties, restoring them, and then making the most use possible out of them. He had only recently taken control of the Ansonia, and I'm sure it irked him that the club area had been unused for so many years, being secured only by a token payment from the Hashiva Club. Our timing couldn't have been better.

Being a pretty good businessman myself, I sized Starr up and decided to let him take a fatherly approach, as if he were guiding us. I said that we were novices in the business, and did he think we could afford to set up the operation on our limited budget of $15,000? Or did he think we should seek more up-to-date premises?

He guffawed and, beaming paternally, said, "All you need is to work! Are you so afraid to get your hands dirty?" He said he would take care of the Hashiva Club and also all the electrical and plumbing work if we dug out the pool, cleaned up the place, and put in our own installations. It so happened that Starr also owned a construction company and had dozens of workers sitting around doing nothing.

I said, "Well, in that case, how much would the rent be?"

He asked how much business we expected to do.

"We estimate a gross of about $250 a day, based on an average of fifty people paying a $5 entrance fee."

The old man paused and said, "Well, I let you have the place for a thousand dollars a month."

I thanked him but replied that that was more than 10 percent of our gross income and counteroffered, "How about $10,000 a year net, including heat, water, and garbage removal?"

Starr looked at me and grinned, enjoying the bargaining process. Pulling out a box of Cuban cigars, he handed me one and lit one up himself. "Of course," I said, "we'll need three months' rent-free lead time."

Biting on his cigar, Starr growled, "Watch out now how you push me."

"Okay. We'll sign a three-year lease."

"Five years," he countered.

I went one further. "Five years with option to ten."

Starr relaxed back in his swivel chair so that only his smiling face, cigar, and glasses were visible. "You got a deal, Ostrow. Go away now."

Walter and Gabe were jubilant over the deal. We immediately began sketching out plans for a sauna, steam room, locker room, snack bar, TV room, cashier and receptionist's area, upstairs dormitory, and community room, and to make it all look wholesome, a basic gym room. We also planned for fifty eight-by-ten-feet cubicle rooms to start with. These were to be outfitted with built-in resting platforms covered in easy to clean vinyl.

We divvied up the jobs, and one of mine was to somehow tap into the gay community and spread word of the new bathhouse. Sending out press releases to all the gay outlets I could find, among them a gay activists association, a magazine called *Michael's Thing*, and of course, the *Advocate*, which was the national gay periodical, it wasn't long before I received a call from a Michael Giametta, the creator of *Michael's Thing*, a brassy young man, full of moxie. Michael and I came to an immediate understanding and developed an advertising and editorial strategy that would emphasize that this was to be the first gay operation in the city of New York that was to be run for gay people *by* gay and gay-friendly people. Every other operation seeking the gay trade was then owned and operated by distinctly ungay and unfriendly people whose only interest was to exploit a vulnerable minority group.

Next I met with the leaders of the gay activist group. Once they were convinced of our good intentions to serve the gay community, they committed themselves wholeheartedly to supporting us and spreading the word. The *Advocate* too agreed to give us editorial coverage and support in return for our advertising.

Meanwhile, Walter had called the contractors in, and we were receiving bids on the construction. But thanks to the gay activist group, the cleanup process became a community effort, with volunteers digging out the pool and scrubbing down the walls and floors. It seemed that for every task that came up, there was a ready pair of hands to do it. There was no question that our small budget would never have been able to accomplish even a fraction of what the volunteers were managing to do. It wasn't long before what had resembled the bowels of a coal mine was shaping up as a clean and appealing space, ready to receive the accoutrements that would turn it into a bathhouse. We could feel the excitement building up in the community as the word was spread not only by the press but by the guys who were working on the project.

Gabe for his part was contacting the various city agencies to arrange for whatever licensing was required, but strangely enough, no one seemed to know what a bathhouse was licensed as, and so we decided to proceed and worry about it later.

The cleanup at the Baths had progressed well, but the construction had bogged down completely. Walter was a nice guy, but nice wasn't getting things done, and the tradesmen were stepping all over him. Walter didn't know how to get rough; but I, on the other hand, having had excellent tutelage from Barry Cross as a collector, knew how to shake things up. It was apparent that if we were to get this place open, I would have to step in and take over the situation. I felt very strongly now that the Baths was going to be a success and that I needed to give it my full attention.

The day finally came when all the basics were ready: everything freshly painted, clean, and operational. We had a very friendly crew in place, and our policy that customers were to be greeted and escorted to their rooms was revolutionary for a bath operation in the '60s. Finally we announced an opening date and gave out flyers in all the local gay bars. The gay press were to send their news staff to be on hand, and it had the makings of a landmark event.

Then in the middle of all our preparations, we received an anonymous call that stopped us dead in our tracks. The unidentified caller said, "This is a tip-off. You guys are going to be raided by the vice squad the day you open," and then hung up.

Gabe, Walter, and I had all been working in the office when the call came in. Walter was pale as a ghost, and Gabe looked as though he had just seen one. Emptying the office of staff, we sat down for a policy meeting.

Walter and Gabe were scared and wanted to delay the opening. I couldn't really blame them, but having come so far, I wasn't about to give up. Then too, I was potentially facing fifty-five years in prison from the federal mail-fraud case, which was still pending. So I didn't have much to lose.

Recognizing that Walter and Gabe would suffer more from any notoriety than me, I offered them the opportunity to pull out. They both jumped at the chance to have me buy out their shares but still wanted to be a part of the operation. And so it was agreed that I would become the sole operating officer of the company, with Walter becoming a paid manager and Gabe a part-time assistant manager. All I had to do now was raise the funds to cover their stakes.

I had scraped the bottom of the barrel to raise the original $5,000 as we had taken a loss in the panic selling of the Matawan house. After running up all my credit cards to the limit, I was still short $5,000. The last thing that I wanted to do was to borrow money from family, but I couldn't let this opportunity slip away. The very same night that I told Joanne of the predicament, she got on the telephone with her father, John Reed. After a brief explanation, she put me on with him. "Dad, I think it's a great opportunity. Can you help me with a short-term loan of $5,000?"

There was a long silence; and then John Reed quipped, "Steve, you should have taken that $10,000 I offered you to elope. We both would have come out better. Yeah, sure I'll help; send me ten postdated checks for $500 due monthly, and I'll wire the money to your bank."

I thanked him profusely and hung up the phone.

And so it came to be that I was the sole owner of the still-unopened Continental Baths, financed by a Scarsdale debutante and her socialite family.

* * *

Walter, Gabe, and I had agreed to keep the threatening telephone call confidential; but somehow word leaked out. Now I felt that I had no choice but to get the whole thing out in the open and to offer the entire staff the chance to defect, with no questions asked.

Their response was unanimous: no one wanted out. In fact, the threat galvanized everyone into action, and opening the Baths had now become more a mission than just a commercial exercise. It was 1968: homosexuality was still illegal; two men dancing together, illegal; consensual sex for two adult men in public or private, illegal.

And yet here was a bath operation embracing all of the above, getting ready to publicly open its doors. The word was that you didn't open such a business in the city of New York unless you either had all of the right people in your back pocket or were a member of organized crime, in which case they were there anyhow. Without either or both, you would soon be shut down by the police or snuffed out by the Mafia.

Being so naïve as to believe in good over evil, and determined to fire a salvo in the battle for gay rights, there was nothing that was going to stop me from opening, especially with my committed crew, who now looked to me as their leader and champion.

The Ansonia Hotel another view

Chapter 6

A Broadway Opening

We announced to the gay press that we would open for business at 6:00 PM on September 16, 1968, which happened to be my birthday, and that to celebrate we would serve a full roast chicken buffet to all customers that night, free of charge.

As early as noon, a trickle began; and then men of all ages, sizes, shapes, and colors started to line up at the door under the tin canopy on Seventy-fourth Street—at 230 West Seventy-fourth Street, to be exact. By 3:00 PM, the line stretched from Seventy-fourth Street, circled Broadway, and continued down Seventy-third Street to Amsterdam Avenue. I kept patrolling the line that afternoon, overcome by its enormity, and finally summoned my kitchen staff to order coffee and doughnuts for all who waited. The sight of all those men lined up on Broadway, eating doughnuts and drinking coffee, caused passersby to stop and stare and cars on the street to slow down.

We had expected perhaps fifty to a hundred people on opening day, but never such a throng. Frantically I got on the telephone with our towel supply man telling him to rush me fifty dozen more towels. "You're crazy," he said, "I don't even have that many in stock myself."

"Well, get off the fucking phone and find them and get them here like now!" I barked.

Finally it was six o'clock, and I worked feverishly alongside the cashiers, checking people in.

We had opened with fifty rooms and two hundred lockers. Admission was for eight hours at $5 a room and $2 for a locker. Every locker and every room was quickly snapped up, so we had to issue numbered slips to customers who would wait downstairs at the coffee shop until an accommodation opened up.

By midnight, we had checked in over four hundred people, and still the rush showed no sign of slowing down. Taking all the receipts—close to $2,000 in cash—and stuffing it into two large brown paper sacks, I told the staff that I would be gone for about an hour.

In the months prior to the opening, while we were getting the bathhouse together, I had moved my family from Greenwich Village to a wonderful six-room apartment on the second floor of a New York townhouse on Seventy-first Street, only two blocks from the Baths. Our next-door neighbor was Patrick O'Neal, the actor, who later opened O'Neal's Balloon, the trendiest café-restaurant on the West Side at the time. Down the street from us at the end of the cul-de-sac were the Pointer Sisters, so we were in pretty good company.

I must have been crazy carrying those brown bags filled with cash through the streets of New York at midnight, but no one paid me any attention. Soon I was ringing the buzzer and yelling through the intercom to Joanne, "Hey, babe, open the door!"

Joanne met me at the top of the stairs in her nightgown and robe. "What the hell are you doing, Steve? You'll wake up the kids."

Pushing past her into our newly decorated Victorian living room, I then proceeded to dump over $2,000 in greenbacks onto our radiant red carpet. We were like two little kids, hooting and laughing as we waded through the piles of money. It was my Thirty-sixth birthday, and the Baths had opened. We had done it! What a cause for a celebration!

We didn't know it then, of course, but the Baths would herald a new era in modern times, when sexual freedom, liberation, and exploration were nurtured. Like *Hair*, it was the dawning of a new sexual revolution.

Twenty-four hours a day, seven days a week, the customers came—literally and figuratively. They would check into the Baths on a Friday night and not leave till Monday morning. As there was no outside light in the underground levels of the Baths, customers would come up to me and ask what time it was. When I replied, they would ask, "Day or night?" Once in the Baths, people experienced a freedom to become the sexual and sensual self that they had been suppressing.

There soon developed a Baths language, our own code of behavioral ethics, so to speak. When you were open to a sexual encounter, you left your door open. This was a signal that anyone could enter. If you wanted anal sex, you lay on your stomach with a can of Crisco by your side—this was before the KY and Wet Stuff era. If not, you reclined in a provocative manner to indicate that you were receptive to other advances.

If you were not turned on by the visitor, you politely said, "Thank you, I'm resting." If you were into S and M, you lay facedown, with a belt over your back. If you were into orgies, you told your visitor to leave the door open, thus allowing as many as could fit into the room to come in. If you had enough for a while and wanted truly to rest, you then shut the door. I'm surprised no anthropologist wrote a thesis on this new means of mammalian interaction. If they had, they might have called it *Primate Privates: An Examination of Fornicative Communication as Practiced by a Newly Evolving Specimen of Homosexual Sapien.*

As it was, nobody broke the rules, and anyone who did was given warning. Those who continued to annoy or try to force themselves on others were barred from the club. Being banned from the Continental was soon to become the worse possible penalty that could be inflicted on a gay man, even worse than being busted, so everyone toed the line.

As the phenomenon grew and the money poured in, I continued to upgrade the facilities, putting in a real restaurant and a full gymnasium to begin with.

It was obvious from day one that we needed many more lockers and rooms. With the waiting list growing out of hand each night, I came up with the idea of using duffel bags with locks. I built a room just for that, with two hundred duffel bags hanging from hooks on all four walls. No one objected, and this took some of the pressure off until I was able to build one hundred more rooms and add two hundred more lockers. At its peak, the Continental would boast two thousand lockers, five hundred minilockers (we were the first to commission them for a bathhouse), and four hundred private rooms.

The Friday-night chicken buffet was extended to Saturday night and Sunday brunch, with us sometimes feeding one thousand people at a time. Soon the attendance grew to about one thousand customers per weekday, and by the weekend, the seven-day total would have reached over ten thousand. The towel and sheet demand grew to over one thousand dozen a week, so we installed our own laundry taking a lot of the pressure off. Everything was glowing, and growing.

And then it happened.

It was 10:00 PM in the evening on a Tuesday night, almost exactly six months after the Baths had opened. I remember that I was home finishing dinner with the family: my mother, who was now living with us; Joanne; our little son, Scott; and Maria, our daughter, who was now close to six years old.

I was relaxing over coffee and dessert before going back to check in on the midnight shift. The Baths roster was 8:00 AM to 4:00 PM, 4:00 PM to midnight, and midnight to 8:00 AM. I always made sure I was there for every change of shift, ensuring that all employees got to see me, and I them.

The phone rang, and Joanne answered then, turning it over to me, said, "Steve, it's Manny. Trouble." Manny was our elevator and towel boy, and I couldn't imagine why he would be calling us.

"S-S-S-Steve," Manny stammered, "there's been a raid, and they took everyone in the place."

I said, "What do you mean everyone?"

Manny was not known for his intellectual capabilities. He was about nineteen years old and an Adonis of a boy, with bulging biceps, pecs, and shoulders, all neatly stacked on a twenty-eight-inch waist, with a flawless, angelic face under shiny black hair. He knew everyone ogled him, but in his L'il Abner way, he maintained an air of childish innocence. In his singsong manner, he said that the police had come and locked everyone up, customers and employees.

"Who's running the desk?" was my typical businessman's reply.

"No one," he said. "People are lined up, but there's no one to check them in. I was in the laundry, so they didn't see me."

"Hang up the telephone, go to the desk, and tell everyone that someone will be there in ten minutes," I ordered, then grabbing Joanne and racing up to the bedroom with her, I threw on a jacket as I related what I knew.

Joanne didn't hesitate a minute. "Wait, I'm coming to help you."

As we lived only two blocks away from the Baths, it was less than ten minutes after Manny's call when we arrived on the scene. Just as he had said, there was a line of customers waiting to get in. I rushed to the cashier's desk. People were gawking at Joanne. What was a woman doing here?

I started checking people in, while Joanne went inside with Manny. The two of them made up new rooms, brought up the towels from the laundry, and got the place going again. At midnight, when the night shift arrived to relieve us, I grabbed a cab and proceeded on to the police precinct on Columbus Circle.

The dour uniformed officer at the sergeant's desk barely stirred when I presented myself as the owner of the Continental Baths. Prodded for information about the raid, he growlingly referred me to the vice squad, stationed at the West Side Detention Center. He said the officer to see there was Inspector Bonicom. Turning on my heels, I was just about to leave when Joanne rushed through the door.

"What the hell are you doing here?" I yelled.

Just as loud, she yelled back, "I'm coming with you!"

There was no keeping Joanne from a fracas. *She'll always be your best friend,* her mother had said.

Inspector Bonicom proved to be a distinguished-looking gentleman, tall and well proportioned, with graying hair and silver glasses. He was very polite, which threw me off guard at first.

I asked where the people from the Baths were, and he casually directed a uniformed officer to show me.

Well, I wasn't ready for what I then saw: dozens of our customers and employees—still only towel clad—all crowded together in the confines of narrow cells, sitting on bare wooden planks that lined the walls and some just crouching on the floor for lack of room. The detention facility was not designed for such a mass arrest. Making myself known to all the guys behind the bars, I told them I would have them out ASAP, no matter what I had to do.

I then used the public telephone to call my attorney, Fred Zimmerman, who arrived in less than twenty minutes. Disheveled as he was—in what appeared to be his bedclothes, except that he had a tie on—he stormed up to the desk and demanded to know what the charges were.

We later learned that the vice squad had sent four plainclothes detectives, all really good-looking guys, into the Baths as customers. Once they registered, they got into towels and went directly to the steam room. They had obviously cased the joint before—probably having a better time.

The minute one of our customers touched a detective, out from under the towels came the handcuffs, and a radio signal alerted a score of policemen with paddy wagons that had been lying in wait. Dozens of uniformed police then raced in, arresting everyone in sight, handcuffing them and hustling them off, undressed, to the detention center.

There they were charged with "being on the premises of a bawdy house" under an archaic law dating back to the 1800s. Fred arranged for bail to be posted for all concerned, with the Continental paying the tab.

It was ten in the morning before, one by one, the prisoners were released from their dank cells into the brightness of the day. It was very reminiscent of the great freedom scene from Beethoven's *Fidelio*. It would have been too much to ask, I guess, for the New York Police Band to have played Beethoven's joyous *Freiheit* chorus; I'm sure our aesthetic entourage would have known the vocal line. No such niceties prevailed, however, and this was to be just the beginning of a brutal tug-of-war between the police and the gay population of New York City.

During the ensuing months, the Baths was raided at least twice a week. Inspector Bonicom became a familiar figure to us. The police always used the same scheme, "enticement and entrapment," to justify the raids. People were carted out *en deshabillé* in the middle of winter; dragged through the dirty, slush-covered streets of New York; loaded into paddy wagons; and then held overnight. Huddled together in cells were queens, faggots, macho men, transvestites, businessmen, show people, clergy—you name it, they were all there. The gay press screamed with headlines: POLICE BRUTALITY, BATHS RAIDED.

But even as those arrested were being herded out, stalwart new customers defiantly jeered the outgoing police. They kept lining up to check in. Not even the threat of arrest could keep them away.

After the first raid, I had two red telephones installed on either side of our bed at home with a direct line to the Baths. As soon as there was an arrest, the cashier would press a toe button on the floor. This would activate an electric circuit that would illuminate the entire bathhouse in blinding bright lights to warn the customers to cease any activity; at the same time, my hotline would ring, and I would know that there was a raid. This line was to be used for no other purpose, and I went to sleep every night knowing what the president must feel like. Without even answering when it rang, I would then go straight to the detention center and repeat the process of bailing everyone out. To the credit of the judicial system, when the "accused" came up for hearings, the charges were always dismissed. The raids were nothing but a degrading and punishing harassment tactic.

To play it safe, I maintained an office on the ground floor of the hotel, adjacent to the Baths but not part of its premises. It was called the Purple Office for its purple rugs, purple walls, and purple furniture. I had an aspiring artist/customer paint one wall to simulate the great Chagall murals that framed the entrance to the opera house in Lincoln Center. In the Purple Office, I was effectively shielded from the police, who could grab me only if I was ever caught in the Baths proper. In two hundred raids, I was never apprehended.

Letting myself be arrested would have served no useful purpose, for who would there have been to bail everyone else out? To reward my customers for their loyalty, I served buffet dinners every night. More than one hundred thousand chickens sacrificed their lives to the cause during the raid plague.

Finally I found a way to stop the raids altogether. One day I was visited by a plumpish, greying man who could have been anyone's uncle, but perhaps not your favorite. He gave me the name of Richard but said I could call him Dick.

He said that he understood we were having police difficulties. I feigned ignorance and kept my mouth shut. "Dick" proceeded to say that he had connections with the police department and that they had estimated we were grossing about $40,000 a week in revenue.

I neither affirmed nor denied this; but he continued, saying, "Look, I'm sure that something could be worked out. How would you feel about buying tickets to the Policemen's Ball?"

"Well," I replied, "how many?"

"I think forty would do it."

It turned out that "tickets" were a hundred dollars each—and that there was a "Policemen's Ball" *every* week.

"And what would Inspector Bonicom think of that?" I asked.

"Oh, don't you know?" Dick said. "Inspector Bonicom has been promoted out of the precinct."

Bonicom was tough, but it was known that no one could touch him. By now we knew that all the other baths, which were in different police precincts, escaped raids because they had been paying police protection for years. In fact, I always thought that they might have triggered our raids to get our business—and to punish us for not paying graft. Apparently you just didn't decide to open a bathhouse in the city of New York without first making the "proper" arrangements with the police department.

Now Dick explained how the payoff was to be made: every Monday night at 6:30 PM, I was to bring $4,000 in a brown paper bag to the corner of Seventy-sixth Street and Riverside Drive, where he'd be waiting.

The visit from Dick had taken place on a Wednesday afternoon. I agonized over the decision for the rest of that week. I visualized how really great it would be to have a free hand to operate without the pall of impending raids over our heads and how it would benefit our loyal following.

Monday morning I sat down with our accountants. "Guess what?" I said. "We're going to buy forty tickets to the Policemen's Ball this week."

Helen and Ernie, who both looked after the financial affairs of the Continental, gazed at me and said, "That's nice."

"They're a hundred dollars each," I said, "so count out $4,000 dollars and put it in a brown paper sack." It seemed that most of the important cash transactions in my life were to be made in brown paper sacks. I was the original greenie.

For a moment they were stunned, and then they laughed. "You must be joking," Helen said.

"No joke, and I think we'll do it every week for a while," I replied matter-of-factly.

"But the policemen don't run a ball every week," Helen pointed out.

"Well, they will now, so I guess we'll all have to learn how to dance too."

That night, when I showed up at six thirty at the designated corner, Dick was indeed waiting; and when I handed over the large brown paper sack with the money, he actually gave me a booklet with forty $100 tickets to the Policemen's Ball. It turned out that every Friday night, the police would rent a cheap hall and run a mock dance, just to cover themselves. Of course no one ever showed up at the "ball" but the cops. Every cop in the precinct shared in the take according to his place in the hierarchy: the higher the position, the more dollars, until the lowly cop on the street pocketed his $50 pittance. All of this was happening under the administration of the then mayor of New York City, William O'Dwyer. How much was known at top governmental levels, I don't know. But the practice was obviously rampant and had probably been going on for years.

Now that the police were busy dancing at the "ball," the raids on the Baths stopped—for the most part. Every now and again though, Dick would tell me that a token raid would have to be made to keep up appearances, but he would always tip me in advance. I would then empty the club except for one or two of our own employees, who volunteered for "combat duty," which was rewarded by a $100 cash bonus. As they were only kept overnight and then released, we soon had a waiting list of employees waiting to sign up for "duty."

Chapter 7

The Entertainer

It was during the raids that I made the decision to put on entertainment in the bathhouse. I wanted to see if I could take some of the tension out of the air, and as long as I was stuck there most of the time, why not make it more fun. Joanne, who was studying acting at the Herbert Berghoff Studios in Greenwich Village, had told me of a fellow student named Rosalie Marks, who was just starting out as a singer. She performed with her guitarist husband, Eddie, who also wrote their songs.

I called Rosalie and invited her to audition; she never asked me what kind of place it was, and I didn't explain. I was surprised to discover that she was a short, dumpy middle-aged woman with an equally short, dumpy, balding middle-aged husband—not much glamour but worth listening to, I thought. As we had no stage or dance floor at this point, I planted Rosalie on a barstool and announced to the scant clientele—it was a slow weeknight—that they were about to be entertained with a few songs.

Eddie then started his patter about the songs he was going to play and began to strum his guitar. When Rosalie joined in, she sang with a deep intensity of feeling and an instinctive way of interpreting a song that brought it to life. The way she sang just grabbed you.

The patrons were very hesitant at first, but after a while, a few dared to come into the lit area sitting on the floor in their towels, with a few dozen more hidden in the background. During those times, if you were gay, you didn't want to risk being recognized by anyone. There was no telling whom you might be seen by: your neighbor, relative, co-worker, boss—it was a lot to overcome, and it would take years to break down the barriers. But after Rosalie had finished her set, there was a sprinkling of applause, which then grew and grew until it was obvious we had found our first act.

The informal shows that we put on with Rosalie and Eddie Marks became more and more popular. In time, we even built a proper stage, with a gold velvet curtain that we could actually draw open and close; and I found a new role for myself as the emcee. We then moved the show to Saturday nights, and the boys looked forward to "their Rosalie" to entertain them. For some reason, we never had a raid during the show, not even a *token* one. Maybe it was that nobody was in the steam room while Rosalie was singing. But gazing out at the guys enjoying themselves while Rosalie entertained, I knew I had made the only decision I could have in making the "Dick" deal.

Now with things going well, I approached Mr. Starr to see if we could expand our space, taking on the entire second floor, to which he happily agreed. We were fast becoming his Starr tenant, and I don't think he gave a damn what we were doing as long as we paid the rent. I also leased the entire usable space on the roof of the Ansonia, twenty stories above street level, to use as a sundeck.

Starr had given us the use of a private internal elevator that would take you, in your towel, from our lower level straight up to the roof. Trucking in tons of real beach sand, filched at night from Reiss Park, we set up cabanas and chairs with sun umbrellas; and soon the roof deck took on a real resort feeling. Beautiful bronzed boys who would massage and rub suntan lotion into your body patrolled the area, and we even had a Good Humor cart that dispensed soda and ice cream. The Baths soon became even more a place that people checked into for the weekend, if not longer and gay tourists from all over the world started to make the Continental their number one destination.

I didn't stint on revamping the downstairs either, adding a full restaurant, small clothing boutique, travel desk, solarium, fully equipped gymnasium, and even a lavish massage room, with a full-time professional masseur lured away from the New York City Athletic Club. The Baths now rivalled any health club in the city.

In those pre-AIDS days, the things you worried most about catching were crabs, gonorrhea, and syphilis, all curable with a dose or a douse. To combat this, we invited the New York City Department of Health to open a venereal disease clinic at the Baths in a special room downstairs that was open on Monday and Thursday evenings. They agreed and staffed it with two health department doctors who could not only test you and administer medication but, even more importantly, could provide counselling. This was the first service of its kind in the United States—probably the world—and it's a credit to the New York City Department of Health that they too had such a realistic attitude toward education, prevention, and control of disease.

Two men dancing together was still illegal, but still on a roll, we built a dance floor, the first ever to have lights underneath a transparent surface that flashed on and off. We then installed the best light show system in New York City, complete with a revolving disco ball to transform the downstairs into a disco palace.

At the time, all dance operations only used jukeboxes for their music. The jukeboxes got more and more sophisticated, but still the best you could do was to load them up with quarters and select songs in some kind of dance sequence, with no continuity between them. At the Continental disco, we set up a disc jockey in a glass booth to spin records without breaks—a major innovation which we introduced in New York City. DJs in those days were judged more on their dexterity than on their musicality, but the Continental established the first music system utilizing two turntables, so the disc jockey could cue up each new song while the former one was playing, thus eliminating pauses in between selections.

Well, the glass DJ booth, the flashing plastic dance floor, and the incredible Bose sound system were too much to resist. Twenty-four hours a day, towel-clad boys danced their asses off. The sensual vibration and the excitement this added to the Baths created a whole new dimension in the now-changing gay scene. The Baths was the place to go, not just for sex but to party, dine, exercise, sunbathe, and be seen.

New York City in those days was a pretty depressing place to be in terms of natural beauty. The skyscrapers are awesome, and the energy of thousands of people bustling on the streets is exciting, but from a physical point of view, the concrete and steel city can be forbidding and cold. That's why I tried to make the Baths a beautiful protected cocoon, where you could bathe in sunlight, fill your ears with music, and feel that you belonged. Perhaps in places like San Francisco, which are naturally beautiful, such a controlled, enclosed environment would not have been as appealing; but in New York City, people seemed to be yearning for a beautiful world of their own, where all their senses were catered to.

To further enhance this idyllic world, I sought out the services of the top New York interior designer of the day, Richard Ohrbach of the Ohrbach family department store. Richard was young, talented, and brilliant; and his work was constantly featured in *Architectural Digest* and all the other leading style magazines. I gave Richard a free hand and an open budget—with incredible results. The Baths, which had always been clean and efficient—if perhaps a tad on the spartan side—was transformed into a fairyland.

The interior stairs for the downstairs area were plated with mirror and chrome. The walls were done in psychedelic colors, as if you were perpetually high on LSD—as indeed a lot of people were in those Timothy Leary days. The columns surrounding the dance floor were covered in mirrored glass to reflect the gyrating bodies. Dancers could not only narcissistically view themselves from every angle, but people could also cruise the towelled bodies all around them without being obvious.

Knocking down the existing steam room, we created a gargantuan labyrinth made of black marble that seemed constantly to change direction so that you lost all sense of orientation. At various turns in the eerily lit black tunnel were rounded perches where you could loll, stalk, or just be private. Background sounds of birds singing and water falling were piped in through ceiling speakers.

The new steam room ran circuitously like the coils of a serpent, close to a city block long if you untangled it. The bathrooms were equipped with mirrored vanities and blow-dryers, and positioned throughout the Baths were large watercoolers filled with crimson Lavoris mouthwash. After all, you did want to be kissing sweet.

On the second floor, we built our so-called Orgy Room, a huge space resembling a Roman amphitheater, with carpeted wooden risers like bleachers running along the four walls. In the center of this room was a foam-covered hexagonal platform the size of ten king-sized beds. All lights in the Baths were diffused amber in color to enhance flesh tones and to give the rooms a soft red glow. Even the private rooms had dimmer controls so that you could bathe your body in the most flattering light.

At one end over the pool was a waterfall cascading downward in an illuminated rainbow of water and color. Not only did it look dramatic, but the sound of falling water was soothing and stimulating. Your every sense was aroused, born to give you pleasure and to drown out the reality of the outside world.

I got so that I only had to walk down the mirrored stairs, and I would be able in a moment to know if the club was functioning properly. I became so attuned that I could pick up the slightest variation in the ambiance of the club, whether it be temperature, lighting, sound, or just the inexplicable heartbeat that determines whether a club is successful. Nothing escaped my control, and my employees knew that. The patrons liked seeing me there, as it made them feel protected. They looked to me almost as a father figure knowing that they could play in safety while I was watching over them.

Once again, I had become the *man* in the family, a role that destiny had typecast me in.

* * *

Meanwhile, Rosalie had started to develop problems. Always a bit neurotic, she and her husband Eddie were having big-time battles, and it was showing in their performances. Gone was the magic that had existed between the two—he creating the songs and she bringing them to life. It wasn't very long before they reached the end of their relationship, and Eddie disappeared.

When that happened, Rosalie went into a terrible depression. She could no longer sing the songs that they had performed together without falling apart. I had to look for another singer; and Robert Elston, Joanne's drama teacher at the Herbert Berghoff Studios, where she had met Rosalie, told me about a girl named Bette who was working at the Improv.

Richard Orbach decorator and me

Chapter 8

A Star Is Born

The Improv on Forty-fourth and Broadway was, and still is, a New York City icon. It's a combination of a Greenwich Village coffeehouse and East Side supper club, with sawdust on the floors and bare wooden tables overlooking a simple stage where countless young entertainers have tried out their dreams. Even the "waiters," guys and girls, were, for the most part, students, aspiring actors, comics, and singers. They would wait on tables and then take turns throughout the night laying down their trays to workshop new comedy routines or belt out songs. The club soon became a hangout for agents in search of new talent to sign or keep an eye on for the future.

I dressed to the nines for the occasion, both to impress any new talent I discovered with the fact that while a bathhouse might sound seedy, it was one of the most glamorous scenes in New York—and because I could. In the 1960s and 1970s, for the first time in decades, men were able to dress as luxuriously and as flamboyantly as women. Not to be outdone, I had commissioned Ben Kahn, the best furrier in New York City, to custom-make me an Alaskan hair seal coat, which I helped design. Fashioned to resemble a Cossack's coat (my ancestry being Russian), it was midcalf length and double-breasted, with a massive folding collar and great masculine dark bone buttons. The pièce de résistance was its magnificent wide wraparound fur belt that could be replaced by a more informal leather version for more casual occasions. Now at a trim six feet tall and dressed in my Ben Kahn creation, long frosted blond hair flowing over my furred shoulders, and moleskin trousers tucked into knee-high Bally boots, I stormed into the Improv, feeling that I was cutting quite the figure!

When I entered, the room was abuzz with the sounds of noisy conversation, punctuated by the clatter of cups, dishes, and saucers and the clanging of cutlery. Through the smoke-filled atmosphere, I could barely make out the stage. Without introduction, a black comedian telling really off-color jokes appeared, followed by two waiters singing a medley of show tunes, succeeded by a stand-up performer whose monologues I couldn't judge to be serious or funny, so straight-faced was he. Through it all, the chatter and bustle never stopped.

Then one of the waitresses, squat and not a raging beauty by any means, walked over to the tiny stage. She took the microphone and, her face lit only by a solo spot and the rest of her in darkness, began to sing in a soft, plaintive voice, "My sweetheart's the man in the moon, I think I will marry him soon . . ."

This demure little girl, singing this old-fashioned tune, slowly transformed the room. Little by little, the chatter and clatter subsided; the movement of people ceased; and it seemed as though even the smoke dissipated. The girl finished on the lyrics, "Then behind some dark cloud, where no one's allowed, I'll make love to the man in the moon," and the silence afterward was more of a testimony to her artistry than the thunder of applause that followed.

I knew then I had found our next act.

Signaling the nearest waiter, I asked, "Who was that?"

"Oh, that's Bette."

"Bette who?"

"Bette Midler."

So this was the girl Bob Elston wanted me to see, I thought. "Could you please ask Ms. Midler to come to my table?"

The waiter took off and, grabbing the girl by the arm, escorted her to me.

"Yeah, what's up?" she said in gritty tones.

Up close, she looked even shorter and her red hair more frazzled, but her complexion was flawless. Above all, it was her eyes that grabbed you, lit by her inner energy and verve.

Introducing myself, I explained that I owned the Continental Baths and was looking for a new act.

She seemed shocked. "You want I should sing in a steam room?"

I assured her it was all very aboveboard and that we even had a little stage.

That seemed to relax her, and then she asked, a bit fiercely, "How much?"

I said, "One hundred and fifty dollars a week for three shows, one on Friday and two on Saturday."

That got her attention. It was real money in those days. She then told me of her friend who was a stand-up comedienne named Liz Torres, whom she could bring along as her opening act for an additional $25.

"Where is she?" I asked. Bette then ran over to a tall skinny dark-haired girl, obviously of Spanish background, and grabbing her by the hand, pushed her through the crowd and planted her before me.

What the hell, I figured. A girl comedienne, why not? "Okay, you've both got a deal," I said.

"I need a drummer and a piano player," Bette demanded.

"Okay, be there Monday afternoon, 3:00 PM, for a rehearsal. I'll show you the room, and you'll find a band waiting." I gave Bette my card with the address of the Baths, and off the two of them went, giggling and embracing each other.

Billy Cunningham, who had been freelancing at the Improv as an accompanist, became our first piano player. He was a tremendous musician—the music just rolled out of his supercorpulent black body. It was all Billy could do though to make it down the stairs, and once seated at the piano, he didn't move until the show was over. Billy had asthma and emphysema, combined with a weak and overtaxed heart; and his breathing was so bad that we kept an oxygen tent, complete with mask, underneath the piano. We never really knew if he would make it through a show, but Billy never gave less than a hundred and fifty percent in any performance, and we soon made him our music director.

For a drummer, we didn't have to look any further than one of our own customers. Joey Mitchell looked like a young Eddie Murphy, and boy, could he play those drums! Our Continental Band was ready when Bette showed up for her first rehearsal.

Liz was a gangly but basically beautiful girl, while Bette was more of a character, dressed in a charismatic array of *schmatter* she had picked up in secondhand clothing stores. She and Billy got along famously in the beginning. Billy would improvise around her, and with Joey nailing the beat on the drums, the result was electrifying. It was as if the music had just been written. Liz, for her part, had the guys laughing their towels off at her sexy humor.

The Baths customers were used to afternoon rehearsals by now, but they were not ready for Bette. Rosalie, once parked on a stool, never got off; but Bette was forever moving on stage. She was frenetic, a redheaded ball of energy—that is, until the slow ballads, when she became the plaintive waif whom I had seen at the Improv.

We opened Bette's first official show at the Baths on a Friday night. When I asked her how she wanted to be introduced, she said, "Gee, I don't know, just call me Ms. M."

There were a fair number of guys sitting on the dance floor waiting for the show that night. We usually started the show after midnight. This was to make sure that everyone had time to get their rocks off and be receptive for entertainment. Over the years, I had learned to leave people alone on weeknights: they were into *serious* business. But came the weekend, and they were ready to sit down and be entertained. By Sunday afternoon, you could have given them a church sermon—and we sometimes did.

Sunday afternoons in fact I even introduced a modeling class for the more *artistic* of our clientele. We presented beautiful nude male models in a special room where you could sit and use chalk and canvas to sketch. It was very popular, though hardly anyone ever bothered to draw. Sunday night, even something educational would go over, and we would show documentaries and movies.

The Baths was a tough gig for a performer because there was a lot of action to compete with. People were always drifting in and out, and from the stage, you could see nude guys jumping into the swimming pool or coming out of the steam room. It all added to the bizarre ambiance.

On that first show, Liz Torres opened for Bette with her comic routine. Liz was a very natural performer who used a lot of dialect in her act, commenting on her own upbringing and experiences in Spanish Harlem. She was really very funny in a self-deprecating way, and the guys loved her. Liz also was a talented singer herself; but when she started her rendition of *The Man Who Got Away*, on her lyric, "And all because of the man that got away," the PA system in the Baths blasted out, "The Orgy Room is off limits for the next hour while it is being cleaned."

Of course everyone cracked up including Liz, and that was the end of her serious incursion into ballad singing for the night. It was now time for Bette to make her entrance. I was dressed in a one-piece white jumpsuit open to the navel and taking the mike announced, "Hi, guys, tonight I am privileged to introduce a brand-new talent to the Continental, someone I'm sure you're gonna take right to your heart. Let's have a warm welcome for the one and only, the *Divine Miss M*." And that's how the epoch began. I had beatified Bette long before her time.

The guys didn't know how to take her and were very cool at first. But she won them over—of all the entertainers I have encountered, I never knew anyone to work as hard as Bette. She would rehearse every afternoon from Monday to Saturday and drive everyone crazy. She had to have every nuance of the performance choreographed. She would even enlist the help of friends like Bill Hennessey and Ben Gillespie to write down in a notebook all the clever throwaway lines she would use in the performance. Bette was never one to leave anything to chance. And then when showtime came, she would strut out on the stage and improvise madly, such was her talent. Her creativity, like all great performers, came from the security of having done the work at all those rehearsals.

When Bette first came on, however, she was not as mobile as she later became, and her act was pretty straightforward. But the sincerity of her singing, and her outlandish getup, kept the guys watching. But by the next weekend, she pulled out all the stops. Wearing a black lace corset and gold lame pedal pushers, she trounced out with a fast patter of slightly off-color Jewish—and gay-flavored jokes. Then she sang a medley of songs, starting off with "Empty Bed Blues," "Super Star," and "Chattanooga Choo Choo."

In between numbers, she talked about her childhood in Hawaii and camped it up with the audience. She then banged out her own inimitable renditions of "Honky Tonk," "Boogie Woogie Bugle Boy," "Great Balls of Fire," and "Sh-Boom" closing with Billy Cunningham's fabulous arrangement of "The Continental."

Talk about giving head, she blew everyone's mind.

As the weeks progressed, Bette started to draw even more of her energy from the audience. She would break out of her stage persona and talk to the guys as if she knew them all. No one escaped her gaze and her barbs, and you never knew when you would be the target. The guys loved it. Even after a few short weeks, she seemed to have the makings of an icon, a Judy Garland, or a Streisand, but a more down-to-earth one, one who could step off the stage and dish with them, an idol they could touch and camp with.

"I was an ugly fat little Jewish girl who had problems," she said in an interview much later. "I was miserable. I kept trying to be like everyone else, but on me nothing worked. One day I just decided to be myself. So I became this freak who sings in the Tubs. It was then that my career took off. Those "Tubs," the Continental Baths, became the showplace of the nation."

The word got out, and it wasn't long before the show area was packed with hundreds of guys in nothing but towels sitting on the floor, propped up against one another and having the time of their lives.

As *New York Daily News* critic Rex Reed talking about what was happening at the Continental during a Bette performance wrote, "Magic is in the air. Magic that removes the violence of the cold dark streets. The insecurities, the hates, the fear, the prejudices outside vanish in a haze of camp."

A phenomenon was taking place. The Baths and Bette were becoming synonymous. The timing was right; everyone was in the right place at the right time. Gay people needed Bette, and Bette needed them. I don't think it could ever happen again.

* * *

In time, Bette completely took over the little room behind the stage that I called my downstairs office, I used it as a kind of place to shave and frump up my hair when I was in the Baths. I was also not above using it for an afternoon quickie on occasion, though it was really a bathroom. But Bette soon jammed it with her costumes, and she would spend hours before each show sitting on the—you should pardon the expression—throne, surrounded by her considerable entourage. This usually included her hairdresser, publicist, guitar player, and as many other people as would fit in the space.

Even Joanne started coming to the show on Saturday nights, and that was fine by everyone; she fitted in as one of the boys. She and Bette hit it off from the very beginning. They were both "real" people; they shot from the hip no matter who got hit. On Sunday afternoons, Joanne would even bring in Maria and our little son Scott to visit me in my office. Soon everyone got to know my family and accepted them.

My kids kinda grew up in the Bathhouse. It was probably the only place and time when they could see "Daddy," and guys in towels were just part of that world. They also provided a vicarious family for many of our patrons who had been estranged from their own wives and kids. It was a much-appreciated touch of normality in our never-never land.

One Christmas Day in the early '70s, we turned the Baths into a *real* fairyland. All the guys brought in toys and clothing, and it became a charity affair for orphaned children. Helen and Joanne took charge of the day, and the kids had the run of the place. Walter Kent being the most corpulent of us played Santa Claus, and it was good to see everyone mingling together with no thought of gender. Kids just accept you for how you are with them.

On this festive occasion, all patrons who wished to use the downstairs area had to be clothed. Notices had been posted for weeks before, and huge bundles of toys had been donated. Much of the local gentry—shopkeepers, street cleaners, firemen, yes, and even policemen—were invited and came bearing gifts. Carols poured out of the DJ's booth, and I even had a cover built for the pool and an artificial plastic skating rink constructed so that the kids could ice-skate.

We had all the help dressed as angels with silver wings, probably the closest that they would ever get to such an incarnation. The stage was set with a huge Christmas tree, and all the presents piled around it. The look on the faces of hundreds of orphan and underprivileged children who passed through the Continental that day did more to bless the place than would have a papal edict—not that one had ever been forthcoming.

Christmas Day at the Baths became a regular annual festival for the kids—and for us.

Bette at the Baths in 1971

Chapter 9

The Count

Shortly after we had opened, two Peruvian boys came to the Baths and asked if we had any job vacancies: a rather sweet-looking lad by the name of Jose, who spoke quite passable English, and his friend Jorge, who could just about manage at the time to make himself understood.

We hired them both as towel boys and cleaners; but it wasn't long before Jorge, by virtue of his own driving intensity, was able to carry on a conversation at quite a respectable level.

Jorge, we later found out, was from a noble family and was really Jorge de La Torre and in line to be a count, although his father disowned him when Jorge told him he was gay. It was then that he left Peru to come to the land of the free.

Jorge was the most exotic boy I had ever seen. He had an incredibly lithe physique with a waist so narrow that you could almost encompass it in two hands. His hair flowed down his back in a glistening cascade of black, like the mane of some young stallion. His eyes were the deepest shade of brown and could at once burn with searing intensity or soften to a warm and passionate glow like melted chocolate.

Even with the meager funds he had from his cleaner's pay, there was no one in the Baths who outshone Jorge in the style in which he could carry any garment that he chose to wear. Jorge had the kind of grace that soon was to make the leading avant-garde designers of the time seek him out to wear their clothes, knowing that whatever Jorge would wear, everyone else would clamor to have.

It wasn't long before Jorge became our head cashier. From that position, he came to know some of the most influential gay men in New York City. He had a way of talking to them that would get their juices flowing before they even entered the bathhouse proper.

My relationship with Jorge was very businesslike; after all, I was the boss, and we maintained a very cordial demeanor. But although we were quite formal with each other, there existed between us an electricity that was almost visible. No matter where we were in the Baths, we were always aware of the other's presence. We never touched or indeed had anything other than polite conversations, but the spark that was ignited from our first glances was to grow into an all-consuming inferno.

It was Jorge's flair for fashion that inspired me to open a smart, well-appointed boutique near the Baths in the upper seventies. One that would cater to the new breed of "out" gays that the Continental was nurturing. Men's clothing at that time was dull. Suits were traditionally cut, and jackets were loose and unflattering. Pants were straight legged and baggy—bell-bottoms had not yet been picked up in the United States. The trend overseas was to a more closely fitted tailored jacket, with armpits snug to the skin and the skirt of the jacket flaring out, all of which seemed certain to appeal to my sophisticated clientele.

I wanted the boutique to feature highly styled clothes from European designers such as Pierre Cardin, Yves Saint Laurent, Schliesser, and the magnificent Jacques Esterel, who died too young—*but* with a price break. To do that, I planned to have the designers create the styles in Europe but obtain the fabric and labor in Canada where labor and textiles were much cheaper. The dollar conversion rate being also in our favor, we would then be able to sell high-fashion quality apparel at a lower price than imported European goods.

Montreal was a fashionable cosmopolitan city and also a home base for the then very popular Pierre Cardin in North America. It seemed a natural place to start. Still under the threat of the federal indictment, I checked with my attorney, who said that there was no reason why I couldn't go because as a US citizen, I didn't need a passport or a visa to go to Canada. Just to make sure, however, I had him get an okay from the federal department for me to take such a trip. They granted approval conditional on my not leaving continental North America.

Since Jorge had an eye for fabrics and colors, I invited him to come along on what was to be a whirlwind three-day exploratory mission. Jorge flashed a brilliant smile and without hesitation said, "Let's go. I'm ready."

With all systems go, I booked us on Canadian Airlines and reserved a suite for us at the newly built Bonaventure Hotel on rue La Gauchetière, which at the time was considered to be an architectural wonder. The first seventeen floors of the hotel were shops and convention centers, ballrooms, and offices. The hotel rooms sat on top of all this featuring luxuriously appointed magnificent suites, each having a large balcony overlooking the city. In addition, it boasted one of the finest restaurants in North America, the Salon Le Castillon.

As if that wasn't enough, the roof of the hotel housed a fabulous health club with both an indoor and outdoor swimming pool. The indoor pool was enclosed in glass, but you could swim under a concrete slab, and you would then be out in the cold Canadian air. The outdoor pool was heated and sent great clouds of steam rising from its surface, as did you. It was an exhilarating experience to swim in it, especially when it snowed, as it often did.

But we had a bit of a shock when we checked into our suite and found, in the center of the bedroom, a four-poster, king-sized bed with a pink and white lace canopy adorning it. Somehow we had been assigned the Bridal Suite! I flushed a deep shade of pink before stammering, "I . . . I didn't order this, Jorge, they must have made a mistake. I ordered a twin-bedded room. I'll call right now and change it."

But before I could dial out, Jorge came over to me and, putting a hand on my arm, gently pushed the receiver down, saying, "It's okay, Steve, this will do fine."

That afternoon, we visited the Pierre Cardin head office in Montreal as well as several clothing manufacturers who specialized in assembling goods on order and found out that we had a lot to learn about what sizes to order, what colors would sell, how to manage getting the right line in for the right season, and what quantities to order in each size. As we were going to be a small boutique, we were told it was crucial to stay in advance of the fashion trends and not overstock. So we ordered heavily in medium and small sizes and tapered off as the sizes got larger, figuring that our customers would tend to be of slim to medium build.

By early evening we were exhausted, so back to the hotel we went for a swim and some well-earned exercise. Feeling refreshed and hungry, and donning our best evening attire, we descended on Le Castillon for dinner.

This culinary masterpiece outdid even the Forum of the Twelve Caesars, one of my favorite restaurants in New York City. Formally dressed waiters wearing white gloves handed us menus that were almost the size of the tablets that Moses had brought down from Mount Sinai, only these were bound in rich dark leather. The tables were of solid mahogany with the finest damask linen adorning them. The crystal was of course Baccarat. Our places were set with enormous solid brass engraved serving plates with fresh flowers and silver candelabra completing the setting. The food was impeccable—even inspired! But the pièce de résistance—which I still admire, even today—were the gold-embossed matchbooks bearing our individual names that greeted us on the table. After a princely repast, we made it back to our suite, where I collapsed, exhausted, on one of the great armchairs and lit up my favorite meerschaum pipe.

Jorge was putting some music on the stereo. I was too tired to get out of the chair to undress and said I could probably fall asleep right there. Closing my eyes, enjoying the pipe and the music, I soon became subliminally aware of a presence near me.

Through half-opened eyes, I could see Jorge on his knees before me, gently undoing my cuff links. That done, he proceeded to remove my tie. I could sense the buttons of my shirt being released, one by one. Totally under the heady influence of the dinner and the alcohol, I could only just let it all happen.

I had by now experienced many sexual encounters, both male and female, but I don't think I was ever much of a lover until I met Jorge. Jorge took such pleasure in raising the erotic to the exotic that you couldn't help but learn from him. It was as if he was totally aware of how you felt: your every sensation; how your skin responded to his touches, caresses, kisses, mouth, and body. Having brought you to a heightened ecstasy, he would play on every quivering nerve fiber as would a master musician, which in a sense he truly was. I have always enjoyed sex with a woman; it makes me feel whole, integrated, a kind of pushed-together feeling, where everything feels good. Sex with a male, for me, was always more erotic, more athletic; and although exciting and pleasurable, it had been rare that I had that same feeling of oneness that I experienced with Joanne in our best moments.

But the count opened up a whole new world of passion for me that I could not ignore. The eroticism of sex beyond the marital bed was too much for me to resist. And I wasn't alone. Sexual experimentation and awareness were the coda of the decade. The puritanism of the '50s and '60s was passé.

On our return, Jorge and I built the boutique from the ground up with the smartest of accessories and fittings. On the street level, the floor was carpeted in thick beige pure wool. Copper, chrome, and brass display counters housed ties, shirts, hats, jewelry, accessories, shoes, and sweaters. Mirrored walls served both to lend an air of space, light, and modernity as well as being practical. And all of it crafted in a contemporary but artistic way by Earl Combs, one of the leading architects of the day.

A steel spiral staircase in the center of the shop took you to the second floor, where an array of high-fashion suits, jackets, and shoes were displayed as works of art. The shop was truly a miracle on Seventy-second Street, and I called it Uptight Boutique, named after the form-fitting cut of our jackets.

It wasn't long before *Vogue, Cosmopolitan,* and *GQ* discovered the shop and did full-page layouts featuring "Count Jorge de La Torre" himself in the photos. We soon attracted a society-page clientele: Helen Gurley Brown, editor of *Cosmo*; the Annenbergs; Prince Egon von Furstenberg; and Andy Warhol, plus a whole glitterati of show people who embraced our new "Continental" look. And it was only around the corner from the mother lode itself.

Chapter 10

Decriminalized

Shortly before the Gay Liberation Rally in Washington Square Park, Billy Cunningham, our pianist, had become too fragile to make the trip up and down the Baths stairs for the show; and so I had sent out feelers for a replacement. The name Barry Manilow had come up.

Barry at that time was a struggling young musician whose claim to fame was writing jingles for radio commercials. When I interviewed him, he seemed a really nice conservative sort of a guy, and I wondered how he would fit in with the Baths' frenzied scene. Barry was Jewish middle class, and while I wasn't sure of his sexual identity, he seemed very uncomfortable as the parade of half-nude customers passed by.

I offered Barry $125 a week to play for Bette and then turned him over to Joey Mitchell, our drummer, for an indoctrination. Barry and Bette got together for rehearsals; and it was soon evident that although they were really impressed with each other's professional talent, their personas were as different as black and white, Barry being almost semiclassical in style, and Bette, well, Bette was Bette.

When they joined with Joey Mitchell for the first full rehearsal, Bette insisted on doing one song over and over again, each time changing the lyrics, the melody line, and the tempo. I could see Barry staring at her as if she was from another planet. He would politely offer suggestions. She would just nod and then continue to do her own thing, incorporating Barry's comments in her own time and manner.

I didn't think that Barry was too optimistic as to how the actual performance would go. But on their first night together, when she came whirling out, launching into "Friends," it was all there. As Barry puts it in his own lovely autobiography *Sweet Life*:

She shouted, she screamed, she kicked, she flailed her arms and legs. It was the same song and the same musical arrangement we had rehearsed, but she was finally *performing* it. And she was filling it with such energy and personality I could hardly recognize it. The audience, who had never heard this song before, went crazy at the end of it. And I was in shock.

I'd never experienced anything like it. I sat ten inches away from this explosive energy source and I felt as if I had struck my hand into an electric socket. As the show went on, I found myself laughing hysterically at her outrageous jokes, during "Am I Blue," I welled up with emotion as she poured out her breaking heart, and I played as delicately as I'd ever played before. I played with as much crazy energy as she performed with during "Chattanooga Choo Choo," and at the end, when she sang "I Shall Be Released," I broke three piano strings pounding out the accompaniment to her fury.

The audience wouldn't let her go. They stood, they hollered, they waved their towels in the air until she came back. When she came back on to the stage, I was standing and cheering too. We closed with an encore of "Friends" and when it was done I just sat there stunned.

Bette would often throw a fit wanting more freedom, and Barry would rein her in. But somehow it worked. He gave her class, and she gave him crass, and the end result justified the means. It wasn't long before the combination of Bette and Barry was to take off into a whole new world of musical expression that was to elevate the already-popular shows into something approaching world class. Indeed, it was the beginning of a relationship that was to see both reach the heights of their profession, and it all happened in a steam bath.

* * *

The Baths were going strong. The raids had stopped for the most part, and the Bette shows with Barry were a smash. Each week she and the patrons bonded more. Bette had an incredible knack for getting into people's deepest, most taboo thoughts and then skewing them open for all the world to see.
She would stomp around the stage and then staring at the guys in the first row say, "Gee, thanks, guys, for coming down to see me. I know you've left your friends behind . . . upstairs." Lots of giggles and hoots. "And don't think I don't know what's under those towels. I mean I may be Jewish, but I know a sausage when I see one."

At this point, off came the towels as the guys threw them onstage. Needless to say, nobody minded, least of all Bette.

She thrived on the gay persona and became more outrageous every week. Her impressions of Carmen Miranda and Judy Garland were to die for. She took on Marlena Dietrich, Mae West, and Sophie Tucker, to name just a few. Even the sacred Billie Holliday and Janis Joplin were reincarnated in her act.

But there was another side to Bette other than the raucous redhead she personified, and that was her inimitable ability to embrace pathos and make an audience empathize not only with her but with the poignant subjects of some of her songs. And nowhere was that more in evidence than when she would close her act with the great Bob Dylan song "I Shall Be Released." In this one song, she encompassed all the years of frustration and discrimination that gays everywhere were living with.

Rather than her vulgarity, it was her empathy that made her "the Divine Miss M"

* * *

With all that going, I decided to direct my energy into seeing what the Continental could do to change the archaic laws that still threatened the gay community. I must admit it wasn't all altruistic on my part as I wanted to put an end to the $4,000 a week we were still paying to allow the police to dance each weekend. The Wagner administration had just been voted out of office; and a new, young, and vibrant mayor elected.

John Lindsay was in the Kennedy mold: tall, handsome, and liberal thinking. With Joanne helping, we set up stalls all over Broadway and Greenwich Village, staffed with volunteers getting petitions signed by passersby. The petitions demanded the rescission of the laws of enticement and entrapment and also lobbied for homosexuality to be legalized.

At the height of our push to petition the government to repeal antihomosexual laws on the books, I called upon the assemblyman who was representing the Harlem community. Surely he, if anyone, would be sympathetic to our plight as a vilified minority. And so he was.

Carl McCall was movie-star handsome, even outdoing the then-young Sidney Poitier. At my request, he was happy to give me an appointment, and I met with him at his spartan office on 145th Street and Broadway.

"Okay, Steve, what can I do for you?"

The outstretched hand of this affable gentleman was the start of a friendship that would last for many years. Carl was unflinching in assisting us in our battle for equality and the right to be, calling upon his fellow lawmakers to pressure the city magistrates.

When the laws were finally rescinded and homosexuality was legalized, Carl was one of the dignitaries at the Continental victory celebration at the bathhouse. Thereafter, he was a regular visitor—to the shows only, accompanied by his gorgeous wife—and there came a time when he was running for senator that he called on *us* for support.

I got him up onstage and asked for all gays to get off their asses, or anyone else's, and pull the lever for Carl McCall as senator on election day.

Carl won hands down. Senator McCall had his victory celebration—guess when and where? You're right: Saturday night at the Baths.

Over a period of six months, we collected over two hundred fifty thousand signatures, from both the streets and the Baths. Then on June 28, 1970, exactly one year after the Stonewall riots, we cosponsored a gay liberation rally that started in Washington Square Park in the Village. On the podium with Bette, me, Michael Greer, the great comic, and countless other stars of the bath circuit was the feisty and indefatigable Bella Abzug, then running for the Nineteenth District Congressional seat in New York City and one of the first major US politicians to openly court the gay vote.

Bella was met with a standing ovation and opened the ceremonies. Later Bette and I both sang—no, not in a duet—and then after Michael had everyone in hysterics, Barry struck up the Continental Band in "You Gotta Have Friends," and an estimated ten thousand gays and lesbians joined us in a march up Sixth Avenue, culminating in a "gay-in" at Central Park.

The marchers were chanting slogans. "Two, four, six, eight. Gay is just as good as straight." "Out of the closet and into the street." "Homosexuality is not a four-letter word." But nothing outdid a little dachshund tagging along with its owner with a sign tied to its back: Me Too.

Once we hit the park, everybody held hands and kissed in a cloud of pot. After a regrouping, we then marched en masse to city hall, where we presented the petition to the mayor's office.

Through our perseverance, the Stonewall affair, and the efforts of hundreds of others, Mayor Lindsay passed an edict to the effect that all laws relating to enticement and entrapment be rescinded; and a bill legalizing homosexuality in the city of New York was finally passed.

The day it was announced, we had a party at the Continental, throwing the doors open to the public, with twenty-four hours of free nonstop entertainment feasting and dancing. A new era had been born. We were legal. A governmental agency had given us legitimacy by decree. Never mind that the original declaration of human rights—albeit chauvinistic—had stated that all men are created equal and guaranteed the rights to life, liberty, and the pursuit of happiness. It had taken over two hundred years for the city of New York to proclaim that consensual sex between adult homosexuals, conducted in private, was legal and that the practices of entrapment and enticement were to be struck.

One of the last God-given rights had been won. Can you imagine how we felt, looking at each other and knowing that we were no longer criminals?

Yes, we partied as never before. The disco floor was all but hidden by the mass of humanity that was gyrating on its flashing surface, the disco ball itself not unlike the torch of the Statue of Liberty. People who had never danced before frolicked with each other. Bette's song "I Shall Be Released" took on a new poignancy in between the pop-chart tunes. The pungent odors of pot and amyl clouded the entire subterranean cavern that was the Continental's public area.

And then, one by one, and two by two, and three by three, and so on, the triumphant gladiators disappeared into the upper reaches of the Baths to practice what they had been preaching. It was like everyone was a virgin all over again. Little did we know how short lived this newfound joy would be before a microbial monster, just one hundred manometers across, the greatest biological scourge ever to plague a minority, would decimate us.

Chapter 11

A Kiss Is Still a Kiss

Not only were the '70s a time for sexual liberation, but even more so, a time of sexual exploration. It was as if every forbidden fetish was now the "in" thing. After all, once procreation was no longer the raison d'être for cohabitation, there were in fact no holds—or should I say, no holes—barred. If there was an orifice, it was put to use. Nothing was sacred anymore. The sanctity of the body was defrocked, and no version of sexuality was considered a perversion.

If we were going to be called queer, then *being* queer would be the norm. It seemed like mere skin was not enough, and all kinds of toys and accoutrements were employed to heighten the sexual pleasure. Cockrings, nipple rings, dildos, rectal beads, whips, chains—it wasn't long before you had to go to a hardware store before contemplating sex. Sadomasochism, bondage, flagellation, water sports, rimming, docking (placing the head of a penis under the foreskin of a partner's penis), finger-fucking, fisting, scat (sexual contact with feces), felching—now there's an exotic one! Felching, for the uninitiated, is the practice of ejaculating into the anus of a sexual partner and then sucking the ejaculate out of the anal canal.

Walking through the hallowed corridors of the Baths, one could hear all kinds of primordial squeals, grunts, and gasps, not unlike what one would hear in the primate section of a zoo. Combine the above with the aphrodisiac virtues of amyl nitrate, LSD, angel dust, and marijuana and you get an idea of what was transpiring twenty-four hours a day in four hundred eight-by-ten cubicles in the bowels of the staid Ansonia Hotel.

But don't think that these practices were limited to the Baths. The sexual revolution was going on in every gay bedroom in New York City. It's just that at the Baths, your choice was unlimited. And for those that didn't like the pseudo formality of the Baths or the privacy of the bedroom, there were the beats and the backroom bars. If you fancied a bit of danger with your orgasm, you could opt for the midnight mystique of the Manhattan waterfront via "the Truck" scene, as it was called. And like every major fashion trend, the heteros picked up on it right after the gays showed the way. The hippie generation, the flower generation—all of it was a rebellion against prudery, monogamy, and chastity. Private swingers' clubs were sprouting up all over town. The only difference between gays and straights was that gays were more anal about it. But I can personally assure you that it didn't take very long for straights to take it up too. Not only was sexual proclivity the "in" thing, but anonymity was the key word.

Guys at the Baths would have five to ten partners or more a night, depending on their persuasion. And come the next morning, no one had any idea of whom they had been with or in. This was the last golden era we humanoids would experience before the AIDS plague would push everyone back into the closet. Those who lived it would never forget it. And those who didn't can only regret it.

Being a straitlaced, nice Jewish boy, I never got into sex for the sport of it. For me, sex was like the song from the movie *Casablanca*:

> And when two lovers woo
> They still say "I love you"
> On that you can rely
> The fundamental things apply . . . as time goes by

Chapter 12

Stardust

One night after the show, a young man approached me saying that he managed a group comprising several musicians and a lead male singer and asking if I had any rehearsal space to rent out. As it happened, I had taken an area on the second floor that I was using as a rehearsal room for the band and also for my own singing. It was only bare walls and floors, but I had put my beautiful Bösendorfer piano in it. Notwithstanding, I made a deal to rent it to them from eight to twelve in the evenings.

On the first night, the manager came to my office to get the key; and I escorted him and his friend to the area and, showing them the piano, said, "Now, please look after it." The other musicians were getting set up; but the lead singer and pianist, who couldn't have been more than twenty, sat down at the piano and started to play in a most magical fashion, his black fingers literally dancing on the keys, alternately stomping and caressing and eliciting fabulous rhythms and harmonies. He was playing by ear, his head bobbing from side to side with the cadence of the music; and then he began singing in a sweet, youthful but energetic voice. He was obviously a professional, but not being an opera singer or a bath entertainer, he was an unknown to me. I was quite impressed but had to get back to the Baths for the next shift.

The next morning I went to the space, opened the door, and turned on the lights. The smell that greeted me stopped me in my tracks. The room was scattered with empty soda bottles and half-eaten pizzas. The piano had been used as a bar and picnic table, and beer cans and coffee cups had been strewn all over it. Dozens of cigarette butts and stale doughnuts added to the litter. Incensed, I called downstairs and organized a cleanup crew to do the whole room.

That night, still seething, I waited for the manager to come for the key. When he showed up at eight with his lead singer, I vented my anger, calling them vandals and pigs. The manager seemed indifferent, but the lead singer said, "Gee, I'm very sorry. I didn't know the group had done that."

I yelled back, "How the hell could you not know? You'd have to be blind or stupid or both."

To which the young black man quietly replied, "Well, I'd hate to think that I'm stupid, but I am blind, and I apologize for my band. It will never happen again."

His simple dignity rang true, and all the anger dissipated from me. He used the room for the next four months, always making sure it was spotless, during which time I got to know him pretty well. Shortly afterward, he went on to make his hit record "My Cherie Amour."

His name was Stevie Wonder.

* * *

* * *

Bette's career was starting to explode. Our original contract called for her to give us twenty-six weekend shows a year with options over a three-year period. Her starting fee of $50 a show was to increase by 100 percent each year, finally reaching the grand sum of $150 in the last year. In between Continental shows, Bette was of course free to work anywhere she could get a gig, and work she did.

Following on the success of the Continental shows, there were a few small intimate and mostly gay supper clubs that were starting to emerge. Reno Sweeney's and the Upstairs at the Downstairs were the two most successful at the time. Wherever Bette would appear now, her loyal bath crowd would follow to cheer her on.

There was so much media coverage, gay and straight, about was happening at the Baths that it was obvious to me that a phenomenon bigger than all of us had foreseen was taking place. So, I figured, why discriminate against the straight population?

I then took a giant step and placed our first ad in the straight press, announcing that the Continental Baths would open its doors to *everyone* on Friday and Saturday nights.

We set a price of $15 for a show ticket, $25 for a couple. This would allow anyone to come in just for the show. The clothed people would be restricted to the downstairs area, where we set up real chairs for the first time. The show tickets would go on sale at 11:00 PM for the midnight show. Everyone would be permitted to stay after the show and join in the dancing on the disco floor. Promptly at 2:00 AM, the bright lights would go on, and everyone who was dressed would have to leave or else check in at the desk and get into a towel. All the ladies of course would be required to leave. Our own patrons, however, would get the show for the price of their bath admission, which would remain the same.

On the first Friday night, the line outside the Baths once again stretched all the way down Broadway. But this time it was made up of the most stylish and glamorous people in New York, male and female and in between. Fortunately I had hired special security officers so that some semblance of order could be maintained. We also set up a separate queue for the show tickets so that our own customers would not be inconvenienced.

To say that there was electricity in the air would be a gross understatement. Once the crowd was in their seats, the lights came down, and Barry gave the downbeat to the Continental Band to strike up the overture. It was like being at Radio City Music Hall, except that instead of the Rockettes, we had the "Rocks Off," guys in drag doing a cancan.

Then suddenly, from behind the tacky gold curtain, a burst of energy in the form of a short, rather busty redhead converged on the bizarre audience, igniting the damp surroundings. Bette was at her most outrageous, stomping the stage as she belted out, "Well, you've got to have friends," a song that was to become her signature opening for years to come. But this night it had a special meaning. The vibrations of straight and gay people openly mixing and sitting down together did more to break down the barriers of discrimination than any edict, law, or proclamation.

Two hours later, having devoured, consumed, and otherwise ingested the mass of New York's most blasé and sophisticated genitalia, having led them from one frenzied climax to another and then spat them out, the curtain came down. But a new era in the gay life of New York—and perhaps the world—had been ushered in.

From that moment on, the success of the shows propelled the Baths into national and international prominence. Limousines would pull up Saturday night at the Baths, and the most famous luminaries of the era would join the queue trying to get a seat for the show. Valentino, Rudolf Nureyev, Andy Warhol, Peter Dallas, Prince Egon von Furstenberg, Bob Fosse, Donald Pleasance, Bobby Van, Valerie Harper, Helen Gurley Brown, Francesco Scavullo, Monique van Vooren, Diane Judge, and Liz Smith were just some of the glitzarratti that would be seen regularly.

I would always open the show by welcoming the audience and spotlighting as many of the famous people as I could, giving Bette a chance to pick on them later. One night, rumor had it that Mick Jagger had entered. So after my customary salutations, I said, "Ladies and gentlemen, there is a rumor that Mick Jagger of the famed Rolling Stones is with us tonight. If that's so, will the real Mick Jagger please stand up and take a bow."

There was a hush in the usually noisy audience, and then a continuing silence, as slowly, a slim tall figure arose from his seat in the audience . . . and yes, it *was* the "real" Mick Jagger.

The applause was thunderous. All eyes were on Mick—and then Bette got into her act. In minutes, she had the audience in the palm of her hands, and even Mick Jagger had to take a backseat to her talent.

* * *

Now that the Baths were open to the public on Friday and Saturday nights, the beautiful people, the glamorous people—those into fashion, theater, the arts, partying, and dancing—were coming to the Baths as *their* resort, so much so that the demand for rooms over the weekends was so great that you might have to take a locker and wait hours for a room to free up, if it ever did. People tended to check in Friday night and stay till Monday morning, paying a new admission every twenty-four hours. It was so popular that we went from twenty-four hours down to twelve hours, then eight hours, and finally to six hours—and it still didn't stop people from staying.

To satisfy some of our most faithful clients who actually preferred to live in the Baths and commute to work, we developed a three-month "condominium" rate. This would entitle a customer to keep a room for ninety consecutive days. I think I could have sold out the whole bathhouse this way, but I limited it to twenty-four rooms so that we would not shut out the rest of our clientele. Richard Ohrbach not only decorated his "condo" at the Baths in high tech but installed a television, carpeting, water bed, and then went on to hang paintings on the wall. But then Richard was always well hung.

Still, there was a segment of the Baths clientele that had little interest in the shows—who, in fact, resented the shows from the beginning as they tended to take people out of action, so to speak. Those who were into serious business avoided the weekends and came only on weeknights.

With an entire bathhouse to play in, my now-awakened sexuality was turned on from morning to night. After all, I had created this pleasure palace to do just that to people. The vibrations in the bathhouse, the eroticism of the beautiful bodies, and the knowledge of what was going on twenty-four hours a day downstairs were too much for me to resist. With several thousand bodies ornamenting every corner of the Baths, it was like having my own candy store. And I was always partial to chocolate and butterscotch.

I of course had my favorites, and they would be waiting for me as I made my rounds, in rooms that I'd given them. There seemed to be no limit to my sexual appetite; and I felt that I derived energy from the bodily contacts that I made, enabling me to handle the stresses of the business and my life.

All of this was just a sexual exploration and fantasy trip for me, as it was for most of us nouveau out of the closet-ers, and in my mind had nothing to do with the emotional bond that I felt with Jorge. In those days, you just didn't think of living together—two guys, that is. I had toyed with the idea of getting an apartment outside the hotel for Jorge and me to share, but after a few negative responses from landlords, I gave the idea up for the present. It was inevitable, however, for Jorge to be aware of my playing around; the gossip around the Baths traveled faster than the speed of light, and I could see that his Peruvian pride was hurt.

Chapter 13

Fire Island

In the middle of all this, my lawyer Fred Zimmerman called and jubilantly announced to me that the US government had decided to drop all charges against me under a nolle prosequi, failure to prosecute. The Baths had been born out of the trauma of the federal case, but now, the very thing that the federal case had been built on—loan companies making loans in different states by mail—was now common practice in the industry. Every loan company was now doing *exactly* what I had been arrested for at Freedom Finance Company. Finally, the cloud that had hung over me all those years had lifted. I was free to go anywhere.

Perhaps now I could even have the singing career I had always wanted. I contacted one of the leading classical agents in New York City, Joseph Scuro, who, after listening to me, told me that I should take myself to some little town in Germany and spend a year immersing myself in music and training and just building repertory. It certainly was tempting but not too realistic. Not only did I have the Baths, but there were Joanne and the kids to be considered. Thinking there had to be some happy medium, I contacted a European agent, who, after listening to a tape I sent him, offered to arrange a European audition tour for me of most of the major German and Austrian opera houses, spending at least one month overseas.

With three months to prepare myself for the tour, I decided that I needed a place to get away to during the week that was still close enough to the Baths in case of any emergency. Fire Island seemed perfect. It had long been known as an artists' and writers' hideaway. There had always been a large gay population there, which for the most part was rather conservative and old-line gay.

My first experience with Fire Island had been through my decorator Richard Ohrbach, who had invited Jorge and me to stay with him. I, of course, could never leave on weekends because of the show, so we all flew down on a Wednesday night. The island was serviced by a chartered seaplane, and the three of us clambered on board the small but sturdy aircraft, and for ninety minutes we had the airborne equivalent of a ride on the Coney Island Ferris wheel. It was exhilarating, it was fun, and it was liberating. There was of course a ferry that went also, but after all, we were the new jetsetters.

Arriving on Fire Island, I experienced a whole plethora of emotions that was new and exciting. What I saw was a revelation: the beach was white and sandy, with the blue Atlantic Ocean sending white-capped surf pounding on one side, while on the other, the gentle waters of Long Island Sound caressed the more vegetated terrain. The houses on the beach were rustic and, for the most part, made from natural pine and timber. Weather-beaten wooden walkways traversed the entire length of the island, connecting the houses. The effect was charming, but what struck me most was seeing so many beautiful and not so beautiful people—all of the same sex—walking on the boardwalk actually holding hands and kissing in public. This was not something you saw back then, even in New York City. But here was a whole community, living freely and openly, au naturel.

The island was divided into two main areas: the Pines, which was a more upmarket and sedate community, and the popular and more boisterous Cherry Groves, where the younger crowd tended to go and party. In the coming years, this secluded haven would be transformed into a gyrating, seething, sensual gay paradise—more like an outdoor bathhouse, beckoning the whole happening gay set to come and party in an unrivalled naturalistic playground.

It was hard to define the feelings one had on being set down in this totally different environment. It was as if all of society's inhibitions that had been inculcated into your psyche since birth were now stripped away and you were free to become the person you really were, a romantic and sexual being open to all kinds of feelings and emotions that had hitherto been suppressed.

The very air of the island, once you set foot on it, seemed to transform everyone. People whom you experienced on the mainland as prosaic and conventional would become totally different and almost unrecognizable, letting themselves just be, and then, once back in town would revert to their structured persona.

Richard was a warm and wonderful host, and we enjoyed three magical days in his house, with him cooing over us and seeing to our every need. Days were spent on the beach basking in the sun and swimming in the surf. Evenings we would have dinner in the Sandpiper, a combination restaurant and disco. After a leisurely seafood extravaganza, Jorge and I would take a walk on the beach and witness the sunset turning the sand all colors of the rainbow. After dusk had descended, it was back to the Sandpiper for hours of dancing under the stars.

That sojourn to Fire Island had convinced me that it was the perfect place for me to get myself together for the audition tour. I would have the whole summer to prepare, as the tour started in late September just after my birthday, when all the German opera houses were starting their new season.

Architectural Digest had just done a feature layout of a spectacularly new modern house built in the Pines by Earl Combs for his own use. Earl was the architect who had designed Uptight Boutique for me. He had built two other houses on the island, the most famous being the Octagon House.

I called Earl and asked if he would consider renting his house to me for the season. Expecting him to laugh at me, I was shocked when he said, "Hey, Steve, it just so happens that I'm going to Europe for a year, and I'm thinking of selling the house to finance the trip."

I seized the opportunity, saying, "It's mine. Don't even show it to anyone else. I'll meet you at Fire Island any day you say, and we'll talk."

That very week I flew down for the day to meet Earl. The house was situated about a hundred feet from the beach, with nothing in front of it but glistening white sand. It was a compact modern masterpiece constructed of grey weather-beaten pine.

The front deck resembled the bow of a ship with the house raised behind it on a semicircle of steel and vast expanses of glass facing the ocean. Inside was all light and space, with one long built-in window seat of gleaming white leather under the windows stretching the length of the house. The open plan living area included a galley kitchen that was equipped with every modern culinary device.

In the center of the house rose a steel spiral staircase, as if you were going to the top of a lighthouse. Earl was big on spiral staircases. The stairs took you to a loft area, which housed an immense water bed that sort of floated in the air, suspended from steel cables secured from the skylighted roof. At night, you could draw the stainless steel floor-to-ceiling blinds shut to seclude you or gaze directly out to sea through the panoramic glass area that fronted the house. It was fabulous, and I knew I had to have it.

I closed the deal on the spot for $25,000 (remember, this was 1969) and flew back to the city with the keys.

As soon as I got home, I grabbed Jorge and told him. He was ecstatic. It would be our chance to live for the first time as a couple, at least during the week. On weekends, Jorge would leave; and Joanne and the kids, who came to love Fire Island, would come out.

By this time, Joanne was fully aware of what was happening between Jorge and me and sensed that this was something stronger than some of the casual relationships I had had.

Bette would very often join us in Fire Island on weekends, between shows, and we got to know the side of her that didn't live on the stage. Although on the stage she was ribald and vituperative—I can remember her berating one of our towelled patrons who wasn't responding to her jokes quick enough, screaming, "Laugh, you motherfucka, you're sitting in the first row"—in real life Bette abhorred anything off-color or crude. We also discovered that she was one of the first "greenies," always concerned about the environment. She would lecture us on waste and even chastise us when our dog Taj crapped on the sand. Bette was also quite domesticated, insisting on doing her share of the cooking, and always the first to clean up and wash the dishes.

As brazen as she was a performer, I believe she suffered from a very low self-esteem back then. She would take up with the most undesirable people: drugged-out guitar players, social dropouts. She would even have one-night stands with the Brazilian boys who were cleaners at the Baths—not that I wouldn't either, but I wasn't looking for a relationship. I believe she was personally unhappy for many years, even with all the fame and stardom. Certainly not the happy family Bette we now know. I think *The Rose* depicted Bette's own life then, as much as Janis Joplin's, except that Bette was never attracted to drugs and alcohol.

That is, except for one weekend on Fire Island. It had been a tough week, and on Saturday morning, Bette had flown up with me from the city. The family was already there. With me being such a steady customer, the pilot of the chartered airline that flew us to the island always let me fly the plane once we had taken off from the mainland. It was an exhilarating and fabulous feeling to be far above the horizon and free from the pull of the earth—the small seaplane, pleasantly humming its way south, following the eastern seaboard of Long Island.

The sky that morning had been a pale blue laced with feathery whispers of white cloud. Seagulls accompanied us on our flight, and in the distance, the long thin line of Fire Island Beach reflected the early morning sun like liquid gold. Once we made our approach, I turned the stick over to the pilot, who brought us down into the surf with nary a splash. Barefoot, we stepped off the pontoons into the water and sloshed our way to the beach house.

On our arrival, Joanne, the kids, and our dogs Taj and Snoopy greeted us with hugs, yells, and yelps respectively. Once everyone was inside, I decided to go for an early morning swim to wash the city away.

On my way to the beach, I saw an object that looked like a man, but more like a sandman. I almost paid it no mind, except that I would have tripped over it. To my surprise, I found that, yes, it was a man, fully dressed—and totally covered with sand.

My first fear was that he was dead, but as I got closer, I could hear drunken snores emanating from the figure. I yelled up to the house; and Joanne and Scotti, my assistant manager, who was up for the day, came running. It took all three of us to get him up and inside. I mean, he was pissed. Once inside and with the sand shaken off, we could see that the figure we had recovered from the surf was a quite nice-looking young man in his early thirties. Then Bette let out a scream that I'm sure was heard back on the mainland, exclaiming, "My god, that's Peter Allen!"

To which I replied, "Who the hell is Peter Allen?"

"Liza Minnelli's husband, stupid!" snapped Bette. "Judy Garland's son-in-law! Hello in there, do you get it now?"

Although Judy was the gay icon of all time, and I personally had always adored her, I hadn't paid too much attention to the tabloids. But now I recalled that even the *New York Times* had recently carried an article about Liza splitting with her new husband.

"Yeah, I got it now," I said. "Let's put some coffee into him." And with that, Bette went into the kitchen to get the coffeepot.

Peter came out of it slowly; in fact, it took all afternoon for him to make any sense at all, and then the whole drama spilled out of him.

He was devastated. He really loved Liza, but his ambivalence about his own sexuality was the breaking point between them. Peter was a late comer-outer, and he was just starting to emerge from the closet. Not until much later did Peter really accept himself, and once he did, he became outrageous. But that's what freed him *and* his art up, and it was then that his career took off. For now, though, all we had was a shell of a man.

By evening, he was calmer. That night, Richie Ohrbach joined us for dinner, and afterward Richie, Scottie, Joanne, Bette, Peter, and I lazed on the great white leather window seat, and with night falling stars just starting to decorate the sky and Nat King Cole on the stereo, we were all in a wonderfully relaxed mood.

As the mood lingered on, Peter took out a metal case and, using a dish on the coffee table, began rolling a cigarette. It took me a while to realize that these weren't just your everyday smokes but were instead marijuana joints. I'd never experienced grass; in fact, to that day, I'd never taken an upper, downer, or sideways in my life. I never really had the urge even to experiment because I enjoyed getting high on life without any chemicals. People, music, and creativity turned me on; and I'd always felt a natural buzz.

That evening, however, was a unique opportunity. I was away from the Baths, among friends, with no obligations or responsibilities for the moment, so why not? I wanted to see what everyone else was getting off on.

Slowly but expertly, Peter rolled joint after joint. Everyone would take a few drags and then pass them around. When it came to my turn, I took a few puffs, but nothing happened. Everyone else, meanwhile, was having a great time. Peter finally looked at me and said, "Steve, you have to inhale and swallow the smoke." I took several huge puffs and swallowed the acrid smoke. Still feeling nothing, I passed the butt over to Scotti, who seemed to be floating somewhere, like everyone else in the room.

Then it hit me. I broke out in a stupid, uncontrollable grin and started to laugh and laugh and laugh, having a merry old time but not knowing what I was laughing about. I saw wonderful colors—blues, purples, reds—and after about thirty minutes of silly laughter, with everyone enjoying my ridiculousness, as suddenly as it had come upon me, it left.

But what followed was the worst headache I'd ever experienced. It was my first, and to this day, my last venture into space.

* * *

Peter stayed at the beach house for the next two weeks. Gradually he pulled himself together, and before long he was writing songs on the white upright piano I'd brought in from the mainland for my own practice. There were only two pianos on Fire Island at that time: mine and Jerry Herman's. Many an afternoon we spent at Jerry's house, where he would regale us with songs from his hit shows: *Mame, Hello Dolly, La Cage aux Folles,* and others.

One afternoon I said to Peter, "What would you think about performing at the Baths?"

Peter looked at me quizzically, with that mischievous twinkle in his eye, saying, "What kind of performance did you have in mind, Steve?"

"A musical one, dummy," I replied.

Bette was going to be in Chicago for a month, doing Mr. Kelly's, a musical showplace, and it seemed like a good opportunity. We had never had a male performer at the Baths before. Barry had taken to doing a few songs with the band as an opener to Bette and also when she changed costumes, but the audience never really went wild, just kind of accepting him. But a full-on male act? Well, we'd see.

Peter agreed and spent another week at the house preparing the act.

The night he went on, there was a kind of silence as I introduced him. Most of the crowd knew about his troubles with Liza, and I think they were sympathetic to him. Peter did a very straightforward musical show. He sang and played the piano and was pleasantly received.

I had booked Peter for a month, and with each show, he would gradually become more and more mobile. By the end of the run, he was tap-dancing on top of the piano, interacting with the audience, throwing out outrageous double entendres; and the frenetic slap dance singer/hoofer Peter Allen had been born. His act became so over the top that those moments when he would just sit quietly at the piano and sing, letting his emotions infuse the words, were wonderfully intimate and all the more magical. Peter went on to become a steady at Reno Sweeney's and started to play the "Baths circuit," as it was to be called.

Cabaret, which by the late '60s had been dead in the city of New York, was reborn with the advent of shows at the Baths. People had grown tired of formal venues, where a suit and tie were de rigueur. It took the Baths to undress them, and they loved it.

The entertainers that the Baths spawned became so popular that other clubs began opening in and around the city, grabbing our acts as soon as they had finished and drawing on the audience we had built. But no club, no matter how sophisticated, had the pulling power, stature, and ambience of the Continental. And no showplace had the prestige the "Tubs," as Bette nicknamed the Baths, had in the city of New York in those golden days.

CONTINENTAL BATHS, INC.

A new total concept for
the sophisticated New York male.
The glory of Ancient Rome
Recreated with you in mind
Russian and Finnish Sauna
and steam rooms, Olympia blue
swimming pool, Scientific Swedish
massage, Ultra clean private
state rooms, checkers, chess etc.
Continental cuisine and canteen
And now introducing another
new feature — the CONTINENTAL
"SUN AND SKY CLUB."
20 stories high overlooking the
Hudson, private elevator from the
baths, showers, massage,
juice bar, music, sun and fun

Open twenty four hours a day,
seven days a week

American Express, Diners Club and
Bankamericard Accepted

230 West 74th Street

Chapter 14

Dreams

My sojourn in Fire Island had prepared me well, and it was now time for me to go off to Germany. While I was gone, I would need a good MC for the shows in the Baths and also someone I could trust to look after the back-office operations.

At the time, John Reed King, my father-in-law, was having difficulties in his own career. He had been a fixture on radio and TV for so long that he was being passed up now as host on the game shows *Queen for a Day*, *The Price Is Right*, and his long-running stint on *The Sky King Show*, which had come to an end.

Although the Baths was a bit outlandish for the quite proper John Reed King, it *was* now an institution. Politicians regularly sought to get a spot on our shows to solicit the gay vote. Gays in New York City were in the upper-income bracket; they were influential; they were outspoken, now that they were out—*and* they voted. You could hardly be successful in New York City politics in the seventies without the gay and Jewish vote behind you. So we were becoming almost respectable!

Gathering up my nerves, I offered my father-in-law the position of MC and general manager; and much to my surprise, he accepted.

I left for Germany, feeling that the Baths was in good—if unlikely—hands. There were six other singers in the audition tour, and every other day we would be in a different city or town: Bremerhaven, Düsseldorf, Frankfurt, Hamburg, Hanover, Dortmund, and so on.

The last stop on the tour was Kaiserslautern, a small cow-town kind of city whose saving grace was a decent opera house. Germany tends to have opera houses in each city, much as we have movie theaters.

It was the end of the tour, and I figured, what the hell, I'd give it all I had, so I sang the "Esultate" from *Otello*, the Prize Song from *Die Meistersinger* and *Vesti La Giubba* from *Il Pagliacci*, all the "heavies," as Bette would have called them.

Well, they *were* impressed. A hurried meeting was held between the Interdant—that's the general manager in Germany—and my agent, and before long I was summoned to the back office where everyone was speaking in German. My agent, Wilhelm Schmidt, a wizened little man of Austrian descent with a mischievous sense of humor, said, "Herr Ostrow, the management of the Kaiserslautern Opern Hauser wish to offer you a three-year contract requiring you to cover all the Hochdramatische roles that the company will put on during that time"—and then, with a wink of an eye, as he turned away from the Interdant—"for a substantial fee."

I of course was shocked and flushed with joy and excitement and said, "Wunderbar! What's next, Herr Schmidt?"

"Vat's next is we go to lunch and discuss it over *eine platte* of *kartoffel salat mit ein stein* of *bier*."

* * *

At the local Hoffbrau, Herr Schmidt moistened his lips with the German brew, which, unlike at home, is served warm with a full creamy froth that, together with the lager, reminded me of egg creams in Brooklyn, but with rather more of a kick. He then went on to explain the finer points of the arrangement to me, including what I would be paid—500 DM monthly, with an additional 50 DM per month for my children's expenses. The German deutschmark at that time was 3.3 DM to the US dollar, and so it meant that I would receive about $150 a month, with another $17 a month for the children.

"But my kids' nanny makes that in one week at home," I protested.

"*Ja*, but this is Germany, and you are as yet an unknown," Herr Schmidt pointed out. "Besides, your expenses in Kaiserslautern would be very small compared to New York City."

As I listened to Herr Schmidt and gazed out the window of the tavern, past the cows that were grazing, I could see practically the whole town; and there was no doubt that this was not New York City. After a long pause and more beer, I said, "Herr Schmidt, thank you for all of your help. What I must now do is go home and consult with my wife and children and then give you an answer."

"As you wish, Herr Ostrow. I understand," he said as he lit up a fat cigar.

I can still remember the bemused look in his eyes as he watched the rising smoke rings wafting upward.

* * *

The silver DC-3 made its way silently through the night, crossing the black Atlantic. The Lufthansa crew had long since tidied up after serving a sumptuous meal, and now the lights were dimmed, and most of the passengers were dozing under woolen blankets, but I knew there was to be no sleep for me. I sat awake, pondering my choices. Now there was no government case to make the decision for me. I had attained a lifestyle that I could only have dreamed of as a kid.

But a singing career! Well, wasn't that what I always wanted? The thought of giving everything else up to pursue it was really scary. Maybe I could get a good manager for the Baths and just let them send money to me in Germany. Maybe John Reed would stay on. I could certainly trust him. Three years in Kaiserslautern! I really didn't know what I would do.

The first thing I did do upon landing at what was Idlewild Airport—now JFK—was to taxi to the Baths, baggage and all. Somehow it was my security blanket, and I needed to feel its warmth.

It was early morning, yet I still had to push my way through the crowd in the entrance foyer. Throwing my bags in the back office, I was greeted by Helen and Ernie, my accountants, and John Reed. They quickly assured me that all was well: all accounts balanced, bills paid, and payroll made. They'd all done a great job in keeping the back office going.

Somewhat relieved, I next went down the mirrored stairs to the main level of the bathhouse. This was where its heartthrob was. I was not halfway down the stairs though when I sensed that all was not right. That intangible vibration that made it all go was missing.

I got to the bottom and then just closed my eyes. The temperature of the air was too cold. The lights, even with my eyes shut, were too bright. There was no disco music on the PA system. The cascading sound of the waterfall as it beat upon the pool was missing. Opening my eyes, I could see that the area was clean and orderly for sure, but that was not what it was all about.

I opened the steam room door. The vapors that greeted me lacked the fine eucalyptus fragrance that I always insisted be maintained. The sauna was next. You could have sat there all day without raising a sweat. The dance floor. Where was the music that should have been playing? The disco ball that shot pinpoints of light throughout the show area was not turned on.

And so it went. Not enough soap in the showers. No mouthwash in the water bottles. Upstairs . . . too much light in the corridors. Too little light in the toilets. Dirty towels in the rooms. White and blue bulbs had been put in some areas where pink and amber lights had blown. I had seen enough. I ran upstairs and, grabbing my bags, made a hasty exit and took off for home.

I had been away a month, and the Seventy-first Street terrace house greeted me with its elegant but comfortable warmth. Once I had pushed the bell, there was a whirlwind of noise and motion as Maria and Scott competed with Taj's barking to welcome me. Joanne waited at the top of the stairs, and soon we were all seated at the fireplace for a family conference.

After going on a bit about the trip and the German people, I was cut short by Joanne.

"Steve, what happened with the auditions? Did anyone offer you a contract?"

"Well, yes and no," I replied.

"What's yes and no mean, either they did or they didn't," was her logical retort.

I then explained about the major opera houses not being willing to take the risk with a first timer and finally said, "But the Kaiserslautern Opera has offered me a three-year contract."

"The what opera house? It sounds like something you buy in a delicatessen store." Both kids broke up with laughter, but Joanne was anything but amused, especially when I told her the terms of the contract.

"Steven," she said, as she tended to call me when she was upset, "how do they expect us to live on what amounts to $150 a month?"

I then told her that they were also throwing in 50 DM a month for the kids, at which she got hysterical. Our daughter Maria after all was presently attending the Lycée Français, the best private French school in the country, and our little son Scott was in a school that catered to children with learning difficulties, as he had an eye dysfunction that made it hard for him to read.

When she had calmed down, Joanne said, "Look, if you want to go, then perhaps you should go alone. After all, the kids and I don't speak any German; they would have difficulty in school and would have to leave all their friends, and Scott has problems with English, let alone German. Besides, what would you do with the Baths, 'cause my dad has just accepted a job as a real estate officer in a bank in Fresno, California, and he and Mom were leaving as soon as you got back?"

The truth of the matter was that I really didn't believe it was possible either and was probably looking for someone else to make the decision for me. My short visit to the Baths had confirmed what I really had always known: that if you can't run your own business, you should sell it. And the Baths was not the kind of business that you just put on the market and sold.

The obvious solution was for the Metropolitan Opera or the New York City Opera to offer me a contract. Then I would be on home base and could still look after the Baths. One reason that would probably never happen, however, was that most of the top brass at both those establishments were frequent patrons of the bathhouse. They knew me as Steve Ostrow, the owner of the Continental, and never took me seriously as a singer.

Kaiserslautern, much like the Met, was not destined to happen; and so it was back to the bathhouse for me to see how else I could shake up the world.

Little did I know then that I would one day bring the Metropolitan Opera itself into the Baths—and have RCA Victor record it on a Red Seal label!

Steve Ostrow, heldentenor

Chapter 15

Captain Hook

Not only was Kaiserslautern not going to happen, but on my return I found that Jorge, probably tired of my meanderings, had taken up with a nondescript guy called Terry. He had done it all, and now his Peruvian pride demanded exclusivity, while I a late comer was just finding myself. As usual, I immersed myself in business to try to forget my personal losses. Bette's career was now going nonstop. Her spots on the Johnny Carson show had brought her to national recognition. Johnny loved bantering with Bette about "the Tubs," and then she would knock them dead with her singing.

At the time, Bette was preparing a concert at Carnegie Hall, no less. She had come to me with the proposition that I become her manager. Bette was a tough broad, as she would have put it. She would steamroller right over you, and I had seen Bette make mincemeat out of many of her entourage. But I was always strong with her and in an argument could shout as loud as she, and so I had won her respect.

But with the Baths, Uptight, my singing career, and several new projects of my own that I was contemplating, I couldn't see how I could handle it all. Besides, I never wanted to be responsible for someone else's life, personal or otherwise; and I knew that's the way it would be. So I had to say no to Bette, who soon after linked up with Aaron Russo just before she did *The Rose*.

Realizing that Bette's burgeoning career would eventually take her away from us, I held regular auditions on Wednesday afternoons at the Baths. The auditions themselves became quite popular with the clientele, but more importantly, they gave us an opportunity to see how the auditionees would go over in the actual room. I had advertised the auditions in *Show Business*, and it wasn't long before every theatrical agent in town was clamoring to get their performers on the Baths circuit.

Till then, I had done all the advertising and publicity for the Baths myself, but things got so hectic that I decided to put on a full-time PR man.

Ted Hook, who years later went on to build the famous Backstage nightclub, had his own small advertising agency and was emceeing a showroom in the Village in a club owned by none other than Gypsy, the famous drag queen. Ted's very first job had been as personal secretary to the famous actress Tallulah Bankhead, and he had remained starstruck ever since.

I liked Ted's feisty manner and energy and offered him the PR position at the Baths. He jumped at it. Ted would get all the auditionees organized, and then I would saunter in and observe. It never took me more than twenty or thirty seconds, if that, to tell if they were right for the Baths.

I would always first address the group, saying, "Look, guys, if I stop you early, it's no reflection on your talent; it just means that this is not the right setting for you." As a performer myself, I knew how much each audition meant to people and how their egos were on the line. However, with twenty or thirty hopefuls to see each afternoon, I had to be brutally frank. It wasn't long though before we started to uncover new and fabulous talent that we could nurture.

In the meantime, I decided to completely redecorate the downstairs area of the Baths and to air-condition the entire operation, a luxury that to that day no other bathhouse had ever boasted. Richard and I put our heads together and decided to redo the Baths in a jungle theme. Where there had been neon and high tech, there would now be bamboo and greenery. The whole downstairs would become a verdant panorama, complete with tropical birds and vine hammocks swinging between trees.

The first show after the redecoration was an extravaganza choreographed by Bob Fosse and featured Patti LaBelle and her company in an outrageous fantasy production. Patti had just split from her very successful group, Patti LaBelle and the Bluebelles, and was seeking to forge a career on her own. She already had a huge following and was fast becoming a gay icon herself.

At the first rehearsal, Patti showed up with her little baby daughter in her arms. Bette, who was appearing at Carnegie Hall, came down to the rehearsals just to see Patti. Bette was ecstatic and in awe. As Patti was singing, she whispered in my ear, "God, she's great! She's got it all. She's the best!"

And Patti was. The power of her singing and her dramatic intensity were unique and would soon catapult her to ever-greater heights.

Suddenly Bette jumped from her seat and climbed onto the stage, her face purple with rage as she shouted, "STOP!" Then looking at me, she yelled, "Steve, are you crazy? There are no backup speakers on the stage here. Do you know who this is? This is Patti LaBelle, the greatest!" Then turning to Patti, she said, "Patti, don't you sing another note till they get you backup speakers."

Patti looked at her in amazement, saying, "Girl, you are right. I never even noticed!"

Backup or fallback speakers, as they are called, are used for rock and pop artists. They are speakers placed on the stage, facing the performers, so that they can hear their own voices over the din of the electronic band. Without them, there is a risk of oversinging and forcing that could endanger a less professional artist. Patti's voice was of such power and size however that she hadn't noticed; but there was no doubt that, without backup speakers during the run of the show, it would be much more fatiguing even for her. It wasn't until I had the speakers brought onstage and turned on that Bette relaxed back in her seat.

"God, she's great," she repeated with a beatific smile on her face as Patti's trumpeting voice echoed through the Baths.

Along with Patti, Manhattan Transfer, Nell Carter, Laura Kenyon, Phoebe Snow, Linda Hopkins, Esther Phillips, Peter Allen, and others, all got their acts together at the Baths before going on to stardom. Established acts such as Lillian Roth; Sarah Vaughn; Lana Cantrell; Margaret Whiting; Cab Calloway; Morgana King; Melba Moore; Patti LaBelle; Lorna Luft, Judy Garland's other daughter; Julie Wilson; and others would regularly appear and continually raise the prestige of the Baths until it was unquestionably the cabaret showplace of New York City and the place where everyone wanted to be seen.

The newly decorated area was a huge hit, and it became a practice to change the theme of the Baths at least twice a year. Even with the addition of more rooms and lockers, we were still selling out by early evening. So for our next makeover, we took an area of the club that had fifty rooms and erected an open-steel floor over them, building on another level of cubicles in a double-decker fashion.

With steel catwalks and ramps serving as walkways and corridors, the entire area resembled a prison block. In addition to doubling the room capacity of that section, it quickly became one of the most popular areas of the club for cruising, particularly with the S and M crowd.

Now, just in case you haven't figured it out, S and M doesn't stand for Sunday and Monday, but rather sadism and masochism, or sadomasochism. This is a whole subculture of gay and straight life that includes bondage, discipline, flagellation, torture, and a whole glossary of terms peculiar to this persuasion.

In the Continental world, there were those who were masters and those who were slaves. All masters are dominant, and all slaves are submissive. Masters are also called tops, and slaves bottoms—but not necessarily having the same sexual connotation as in the act, where a top is the penetrative partner in anal sex and the bottom is the recipient. In S and M, these are generic rather than specific terms, having to do more with attitude than latitude.

A sadist is, of course, one who inflicts physical pain, and a masochist, one who wants to receive physical pain. In its most altruistic form, this can be a rather beautiful experience. There is also much trust and love involved, so that the sensation of hurt inflicted does not cause lasting or irreparable bodily harm.

There were those at the Baths who merely had to command, with a word or a grimace, to enslave a willing bottom. If that wasn't enough, there were a host of other devices available for implementing pain and control. The dungeon scene at the Baths featured paddles, straps, canes, crops, whips, clamps, candles, and—yes, for the more imaginative—ice cubes, feathers, needles, and even electricity could be employed. Some enjoyed their fancy being tickled while others their fannies being paddled. For some, humiliation was sufficient, while for others, flagellation was implicit.

In S and M, there is no right or wrong; it's whatever turns you on. Often a master and a slave would form a permanent relationship. They could be seen strolling the corridors, the one wearing a welded slave collar and the other a studded leather belt. Today you can see them in daylight on the streets of any cosmopolitan city.

Bondage (any form of physical restraint: handcuffs, ropes, and so on) and discipline (the use of rules and punishment to control behavior) were, and still are, whole subcultures of the gay ethos.

As Noël Coward so aptly summed it up, "Anything goes." And it did.

Chapter 16

The Visit

The '70s continued to be the decade of liberation in New York City. Aside from the sexual revolution, there was also a liberation being expressed in women's and men's clothing. And the Uptight Boutique and Continental Baths were doing their part, one to dress you and the other to undress you.

Particularly for men, the 1970s were a time of adventure in fashion. The everyday suit was being replaced by the jumpsuit, a one-piece affair usually belted and with safari pockets. Cravats had come back into style, as were brocaded vests, bell-bottom trousers, and ruffled shirts. The Edwardian look was very big, and men's accessories were exciting and diverse. Much of this was due to the influence of rock groups like the Beatles and the Rolling Stones and androgynous performers like Mick Jagger, David Bowie, and Michael Jackson.

It was even common back then for gay guys when they went out at night to actually put on makeup. A bit of mascara, a little blush, and some lip gloss and you were ready for the evening. Being a performer myself, at this point in my life I was having my hair streaked. And whenever I was emceeing the shows at the Continental, I would always wear a bit of makeup to kind of dress things up.

It was a Friday night at the Baths when I was doing just that in my little dressing room toilet, getting ready to put the show on. It was going to be a big night.

Linda Hopkins, one of my favorite performers, was appearing. Linda had a voice born out of gospel with a soul to match. Her gutsy voice could bellow with the best, and then when you least expected, she would take off for a stratospheric note that she would hold with an energy force that bored deep inside you till you begged for mercy. When she started rockin', the room started swaying, and the towels would fall off . . . and nobody cared.

Linda had come up the hard way, plugging along for years through all the little clubs and pubs in town, but she had found herself at the Continental, and everybody was there when Linda was gonna stomp. I had booked her for two consecutive weekends, knowing that after tonight, the frenzy would build, and next Saturday would be a sure sellout.

"Steve, there's two guys upstairs who want to see you," said Joe Iannone, my right-hand man and manager. Joe was cool in most situations, but he looked a little perturbed as he delivered the message.

"Who the hell are they? I've got no time to see anyone now, Joe. You should know that."

"Yeah, well, I think maybe you better see them, Steve," Joe said, "'cause I don't think they're gonna go away too easy."

I had learned long ago to trust Joey's intuition. Very little ruffled him, and when it did, there was usually a good reason.

"Okay, Joe, send them down, but tell 'em I only got a few minutes."

I was putting the finishing touches to my hair, which was now a golden blonde reaching down to my shoulders. Lots of spray kept it in place, and I was just dabbing a bit of blush on my cheeks when Joey appeared at the door with two guys who looked totally out of place, as if they were going to a funeral. They were large, squat, powerful, and ugly. Dressed in black suits and fedoras with bulges under their jackets, I could now see what Joey was talking about. These guys weren't looking to check in at the Baths—that was obvious.

"Want me to stick around?" Joe offered.

"No, you watch over things. I'll call you if I need you." And with that, Joe left.

"Okay, guys, what can I do for you?" I said, still blow-drying my hair.

"You got a nice place here, kid," said the only one that did any talking.

"Gee, thanks. Is that what you came to tell me?"

"Is this your joint?"

"Yeah . . . so?"

"So how would you like to sell it?"

"Not interested. It's not for sale. Now look, I'm busy, I've got a show to—"

"We think you ought to think about selling," interrupted the spokesman.

"Who's we?" I retorted.

"The people we represent," he replied, looking very unruffled. I was beginning to get the idea of what was happening. All the while his other friend just stood there, chewing on a toothpick and looking ugly.

"Now whaddya say you make this easy and just tell us what you want for the joint?" said Mr. Nice Guy.

By now I was feeling really impatient. I finished my blow job and, turning to face both of them, spat out, "Okay, I'll take $8 million. Now get the fuck out."

Mr. Nice Guy grinned and raised one bushy eyebrow. "I wouldn't be so cocky if I were you, sonny. You know, some Saturday night, someone might just throw a stink bomb into the joint with everyone in it. That wouldn't be too good for business now, would it? So why don't you just think it over? We'll be back in a week." And as unceremoniously as they had arrived, the two pallbearers left.

The visit of the men in black was disturbing, to say the least. We had just gotten free of police harassment, and now something even more sinister seemed to be threatening us. I thought back to the preopening days of the Continental, when we were warned that you just don't contemplate opening up such an operation in the city of New York without the proper *protection*, police and *otherwise*.

Well, we had dealt with the police, so now I guess it was time to deal with the *otherwise* . . . but how?

* * *

Saturday morning found me at Joe's barbershop in lower Greenwich Village, getting my hair cut by my favorite barber whose name was—you guessed it—Joe. It seemed as though a lot of important people and places in my life at that time were called Joe: Joe's restaurant; Joe Iannone; Joe Scuro, my agent; and of course Joe, my barber.

Those were the days when you told your barber everything that was going on in your life, and what you didn't tell him, he had already heard from another patron. Joe knew everything about me and the Continental, so asking me how business was going, he sensed that something was wrong.

I confessed that I had a problem that I didn't know how to handle, which was a big admission for me.

"What's the matter, kid, tell ol' Joe the problem."

As Joe masterfully trimmed my neckline with a straight razor, a lost art today, I related the events of the previous evening, adding that I had only till the end of the week to come up with a solution.

Joe was the only one I ever trusted to trim my mustache; and as he held the blade over my lip, he came real close to my face and whispered, "Look, you come back here Monday morning, 10:00 AM sharp. I gotta regular customer comes in for a shave who might be able to help you out. Brighten up, kid, leave it to Joe till then."

Then with a flourish, he removed the barber's smock from around my shoulders, dusted me off with a large whisk brush, and, sharing my reflection in the mirror, said, "You're lookin' good, kid, see ya Monday, eh?"

"Sure, Joe, *grazie . . . ciao.*"

* * *

It was early Saturday night, and Joe Iannone and I were sitting in the back office of the Baths. It was deserted now. Helen and Ernie, my accountants, would not be back till Monday. I was filling in Joe on what was happening and about my haircut when there was a knock on the office door.

"Yeah, who is it?" Joe yelled out.

"It's me, Tommy," was the reply. Tommy was one of our best customers. He was a hairdresser and usually came in on Saturday night and didn't leave until Tuesday, when the beauty shops reopened.

"We're kind of busy, Tommy, having a meeting. Can it wait?" was Joe's reply.

"I got a problem, Joe, and I need some help, now."

"Oh, let him in, Joe, our problem won't go anywhere," I said, and with that Joe opened the door, and Tommy came rushing in.

Tommy was a good-looking boy. A little feminine perhaps, but then he was one of the best hairdressers in New York. Nothing ever embarrassed Tommy, but for now he was a bright shade of pink as he stood in the middle of the office, clutching only his towel around him.

Joe raised a quizzical brow. "What's the problem, Tommy?"

Tommy searched the office with his eyes to make sure no one else was there. Then somewhat reassured, he said, "Well, you see, Joe, I was in the Orgy Room upstairs, and this guy kind of sidled up to me, and before I knew it, he was giving me a blow job."

"So what's the problem? Wasn't that what you were there for?"

"Well, yeah, Joe . . . but you see, it was dark, and I couldn't see anything."

"It's always dark in the Orgy Room, Tommy, you know that."

"Yeah, I know, but you see this guy had a wad of chewing gum in his mouth."

By this time I was starting to see the point and couldn't help breaking out in a grin, which I tried to hide. In the meantime, Joey was getting more and more impatient.

"Yeah, so the guy was chewing gum, so what's the problem?"

"The problem is this," Tommy said as he threw off his towel, exposing what had obviously been a luxuriant field of black pubic hair but was now a field of gooey pink chewing gum.

Joey and I both convulsed in uncontrollable laughter, especially welcome after the heavy session we were having.

"Come on, you guys, it isn't funny. How am I gonna get this stuff off?"

"You're right, Tommy," said Joey, fighting to control himself. "Bring your dick over here."

Joey got out the first aid kit we kept in the office and, with the help of some methylated spirits, a tweezer, and a pair of scissors, went to work on the problem.

The sight of Tommy sitting naked on Joe's lap, dick in hand while Joe completed the surgical procedure, is one that to this day breaks me up.

But then it *was* Saturday night at the Baths.

Chapter 17

Mr. X

Somehow the weekend passed, and then mercifully it was Monday morning. As instructed, I walked into Joe's shop at exactly 10:00 AM.

As I opened the door, the little bells rang, and Joe gave me a silent nod to sit down. Taking the indicated seat, I shot a furtive glance at the customer in Joe's chair, whose face was entirely covered with a steaming white towel. Looking in the mirrored wall opposite the barber chairs, I could watch Joe massaging the man's face and whispering in his ear. This went on for quite a while.

Finally Joe spoke to me. "Steve, I understand you're looking for a good lawyer," he said, nodding his head up and down.

"Well, yes," I replied.

"Jus' so happens Barry here is the best," Joe said, raising the hydraulic chair so that Barry was sitting upright. He then removed the face towel revealing a bright, good-looking young man no older than me and of obvious Jewish descent.

"Hi," said my new lawyer. "I'm Barry Slotnick. Joe told me about your operation. Sounds fascinating. How about we go there, have some lunch, and talk?"

Joe, all smiles, patted Barry's face with aftershave, brushed him off, and in no time at all, we were cabbing our way uptown.

The cab conversation was genial and casual. No reference was made to the problem. Barry said he lived only two blocks from the Baths on Seventy-sixth Street and had a new wife and a child in the making.

Once at the Baths, I gave him a VIP tour of the operation, none of which seemed to faze him. He had heard that we put on great shows and asked if he and his wife could come down some Saturday night.

"Sure," I said. As it turned out, Barry was a stargazer. He had a fascination for performers and loved hobnobbing with them.

"Okay, Steve, let's get down to business. I'm your lawyer now. I'm a specialist in criminal law, but my office will handle all your legal work from here on. How's that with you?" he said, handing me his business card.

"Sure, Barry, but did Joe tell you about the problem, and the two—"

"Oh yeah, well, if and when those guys come back, just show them my card, and I don't think you'll have any more problems . . . you see, I represent a lot of important people, trust me."

Well, I had nothing to lose. Fred had retired, and I did need a good lawyer. Barry seemed bright and on top of things, and also very accessible, being right around the corner.

"Okay, great, Barry, we got a deal."

Barry smiled brightly as he shook my hand. "You'll hear from me next week, but call me if anybody bothers you."

Exactly one week to the day, on Friday, the two pallbearers came back as promised. This time, Joey didn't even bother to announce them but just escorted them to where I was doing my same preshow ritual.

"So, kid, do you see the light now? You've had a week. Maybe you'll be more reasonable now, huh?"

They could have been a vaudeville team, except that they were for real. Mr. Nice Guy and Mr. Toothpick Chewing Ugly. What an act—right out of *Guys and Dolls*, although I didn't think they would sing and dance too well.

Without being bothered to look up from my beauty preparations, I took out Barry's business card.

"Here, go see my lawyer," I said, thrusting it at them.

I thought Mr. Nice Guy, on seeing it, was going to have an apoplectic fit. He turned red under his starched collar, shoving the card in front of his friend. Mr. Ugly spat out his toothpick; and the two of them turned about-face, Mr. Nice Guy pausing only to say, "We're real sorry to bother ya, fella, have a nice day."

And they were gone.

* * *

It was Saturday morning, and I was back in Joe's barber chair for my weekly appointment.

"So, Steve, what's new?" he asked.

"Joe, you know everything is okay. Who the fuck is this guy Barry?"

I can still see Joe's smiling face in the barbershop mirror as he said, "Oh, he's Joe Colombo's lawyer, that's all."

* * *

That night, Linda was bringing down the house, and the Baths took on the aura of a Baptist revival meeting. Linda's voice rang out true and loud, sweet and soft, clear and husky. You name it, every color and passion the human voice is capable of was at Linda's command.

After I had made the final announcements and closed the show, the disco came on, and there on the floor was Barry and his lovely wife, Donna.

I burrowed my way through the frenzied dancers to greet them.

"Hi, how did it go?" Barry asked with his bright smile.

"You know very well how it went, Barry. They just took off like they were on the wrong planet."

"Oh well, they just know who's boss, I guess. Oh, by the way," Barry said, excusing himself from his wife for a moment, "my friends who I represent would like to do a little business with you."

Oh shit, I thought, from the frying pan into the fire.

"What do you mean *a little business*, what kind of business?"

"Well, now that we've kind of established the territory, they would like to take over the garbage removal, the cigarette machines, the jukebox, and any other vending machines in the place."

"What do you mean *take over*, Barry?"

"Well, whatever deal you got now they'll give you 5 percent more, plus you'll get better service and newer machines."

"So what's the catch?" I said incredulously.

"No catch, they're just good people to do business with; and not only that, you'll also have a friend as a bonus. See, they like nice clean cash operations like vending machines and things."

Apparently they do their own laundry, I thought.

"Okay, I don't see why not."

"You won't be sorry," said Barry.

And you know what? I never was.

Chapter 18

The Continental Kibbutz

Joanne and I had a favorite restaurant on Seventy-second Street called the Sacred Cow. It was an informal duplex affair that featured the best beef in New York City. We would have dinner there two or three nights a week, either indulging in the sirloin or the prime ribs. I had asked Joanne to meet me for lunch at the Cow, which itself was unusual since Joanne knew that I almost never stopped to have lunch but usually grazed on the run all day till dinner. She must have sensed that something was wrong.

It was a bright sunny day, so we chose to sit at one of the outdoor tables. Joanne had taken great care to get herself together, and on this occasion, I don't think she ever looked prettier. Gone were the dungarees and sneakers she had taken up of late, mistakenly thinking I would like her better as a tomboy; and in their stead was a floor-length pastel sundress, full makeup, and white high-heel shoes.

"Okay, Winchester, what's up?" Winchester was Joanne's nickname for me as she thought I resembled the model in the Winchester cigarette commercials.

"Well, hon . . . I find this very difficult, but I feel that I have to sort of go my own way."

"And what does that mean, Winchester, *sort* of go your own way? You've been *going* your own way for years now."

"What I mean is I need to have my own space and live away from home."

"But you're always at the Baths anyway, so why the need now?"

The waitress came to take our order, and I could see that Joanne was upset. But I think I was even more upset. This was one of the hardest things I had ever done in my life.

"Joanne," I said after the waitress had left, "I think we need to separate for a while and see where we're going."

Joanne was silent, and this was unusual for her. Joanne always had an answer. It took a while, but then she said, "And what about the kids? They need a father too."

That hurt, and she knew it. I had never really been a very attentive father, although I truly loved my kids. I just found it hard to relate to children and had once said to Joanne, "Introduce me to them when they're twelve," jokingly of course. But now we were not joking.

"You know I'll always be there for them and for you. Nothing much will really change. But I have to start living a new life."

"Are you trying to tell me that you're gay? I mean, come on, Winchester, what else is new?"

"Well, that's part of it," I said.

"And how long will this separation be for?" Joanne asked, mercifully not probing further.

"I think we ought to try six months and see how it goes."

I knew I had hurt Joanne and by doing so had hurt myself. I had such mixed emotions that all I could do was look at Joanne and cry. I did love her, I always did, and always would, but I was just not *in* love with her, and I felt I needed to be in love.

The waitress brought the food, and it stared at us from the table. Suddenly we both knew we weren't hungry.

"Can I walk you home?" I said.

"No, Steve. I can find my own way, thank you."

As I saw her walk away from me, her proud carriage belying the hurt she felt inside, I broke into uncontrollable sobbing.

* * *

Having made the break at home, I moved into the Stanhope Hotel on Eighty-sixth and Park Avenue. The Stanhope was at that time one of the most fashionable hotel residencies in New York City. I had an executive suite comprising a living room, dining room, bedroom, and kitchen, although I never bothered with the latter, having all of my meals sent up from room service. I felt like the Earl of whatever and enjoyed pampering myself.

But after about six months of living at the hotel, the novelty wore off, and the bills started to mount, especially as I was carrying two households. There was no doubt that I had to make a decision. Joanne was quite comfortable with me in a hotel because that was a temporary thing as she saw it.

I was also beginning to miss all the good things Joanne and I had shared. It's funny how, when you are away from someone, you tend to forget why you left and remember only the good things. At least that's how it was for me.

Joanne and I had become better friends now that I had been away. The six-month trial period was almost over, and Joanne kept asking me, "Steve, when are you coming home?"

Not having a defense, I said, "Okay, let's try it again."

So back I went, but it didn't take more than one night for me to understand why I left in the first place. Joanne having been brought up in a strict Catholic house believed that sex was only for procreation, and we already had all the family we could handle.

It wasn't till many years later that she really found herself and became chaplain of the Los Angeles Prison System. But that's another story.

The tensions grew; the kids felt it too, and before long I was out of the house again, determined to set up a permanent home base for myself.

Well, where better for me to live than in the good old Ansonia? Old man Starr was spending less and less time at the hotel, so my association with Allen, his son-in-law, paid off again.

As luck would have it, a fabulous apartment had just been vacated on the fourteenth floor. But it had fourteen rooms! It had once been occupied by the great Russian bass Feodor Chaliapin. I didn't know what the hell I would do with fourteen rooms, but the moment I entered the semimansion, I knew that this was where I was to call home.

The ceilings were sixteen feet high, as they were in all the Ansonia apartments. The entrance foyer could have been a three-room apartment by itself almost anywhere else. It was really of old-world proportions and exuded a rich and wonderful history and tradition. The apartment had a circular music room with polished hardwood floors and a whole semicircle of floor-to-ceiling French doors that opened onto a small but ornate balcony looking straight down the Great White Way.

The kitchen could have been built for an ocean liner, so grand were its dimensions and appointments. There were no less than three bathrooms in addition to the en suite master bath. The rooms were designated as such—kitchen, music room, living room (replete with fireplace), formal dining room, servants' quarters (three rooms), pantry, library, office den, and four additional bedrooms.

Being so enormous, the hotel had decided to break it up into smaller apartments if it proved difficult to find a tenant for the whole lot. "Nothing doing," I told Al, "it's mine."

We struck a deal to include the apartment in the basic Baths lease so that it would be a business expense. Although the apartment was listed at $600 a month, by saving the hotel the expense of altering and subdividing, I got it for $300 a month, a phenomenal bargain in those or any days.

Of course, I immediately got Richard Ohrbach to work on it, and he decorated it in a wonderful mixture of old-world charm with a fresh modern outlook. The furniture was all custom-designed to fit each room.

In the kitchen, a giant square center island was built housing a chopping block and every modern kitchen appliance. A square overhead rack suspended from the ceiling accommodated a galaxy of copper pots, pans, cleavers, tongs, and enough other culinary paraphernalia to cater to an army.

Track lighting was installed in all the public rooms, highlighting fabulous oil paintings both modern and traditional. All the oak floors were polished to a rich patina except for the living room, which featured a midnight blue Oriental rug. Velvet sofas of deep purple took the entire wall space.

A massive mahogany dining room table was specially built, with twelve hardwood tapestry chairs lining it under a crystal chandelier. All the bathrooms were renovated, while still maintaining the wonderful black and white marble tiles and the original gold fixtures. The servants' quarters were made functional and inviting. And as the pièce de résistance, I installed my beautiful blond mahogany Bösendorfer grand piano in the music room.

To justify the apartment as a business expense, I decided to install part of the crew from the Baths in the six extra bedrooms. Pedro, who was a bath attendant in the daytime, became my cook in the evenings. Manny, the towel boy, had his own room; and Don Scotti, my beautiful and talented assistant who was very active in the shows, shared a room with Paul, another assistant manager. I still had some vacancies, which I designated as guest rooms for "VIP," or as Scotti put it, Very Impregnable People.

What was actually created was a communal style of living and working. A "compartmentalized" life, with people to fill all your needs. It was an unwritten rule that anyone living in 14177 was open to conjugal visits by any other of us who was lonely, troubled, or just plain horny. And all this, with the Baths just below us—what more could anyone ask?

Joanne and our daughter Maria

Chapter 19

Doing the White Thing

The Baths was now an institution. Political leaders, local congressmen, fundraisers, charities, dissidents—you name it, they all wanted a platform at the Baths.

One of the most cutting and acidly honest black comedians of the time, Dick Gregory, was a welcome entertainer at the Baths. Of course, the gay community had always taken black performers to their hearts: Melba Moore, Patti LaBelle, Sarah Vaughn, Linda Hopkins, Etta James—they were all favorites.

But Dick Gregory didn't just entertain. His caustic wit and genius at satire did more to raise the consciousness level of white people and advance the cause of blacks than any posturing politician. He gave birth to a whole genre of black comedians, Richard Pryor and Eddie Murphy being some of the better known, with Chris Rock following in their path.

Back in the '70s, the politically correct expression when white people were talking about black people was the term "colored." It was only the blacks themselves, and comedians like Gregory that could jest at themselves, using the word "nigger."

The three most incendiary words in New York City at the time were "nigger," "kike," and "spic." If you used any of these words, you had better be sure you were on your own home turf.

In the eyes of the more vulgar of the population, kikes were money-hungry zealots, spics were despicable, and niggers . . . well, niggers were illiterate and smelled bad.

But like everything else in the gay world, such terms of endearment took on different connotations. Kikes were circumcised, spics were macho, and niggers all had big cocks and fabulous bodies.

Me being a bifaggot kike, I was attracted, as were many of my ilk, to the romanticism of the Latinos and the physical and spiritual beauty of the colored.

For a long time, bathhouses tended to be polarized. If you wanted to find a Jewish clientele, mixed with Slavic and Russian, you would go to the St. Marks Baths in the East Village. The Everard Baths on Twenty-eighth Street had a mixture of midtown businessmen and a sprinkling of Latinos from the downtown ghetto area. The Continental was for much of its reign held to be elitist, catering to fashion designers, yuppies, artists, photographers and their models, hairdressers, and others from all the performing arts.

But for me, a sojourn into Upper Harlem to the Mount Morris Baths was the height of eroticism. Scary, yes, and not every taxi would take you there, although getting a black driver to take you back was usually no problem.

But once you entered the age-old premises, you were immersed in a sea of darkness where only the glint of teeth and the gleam of eyes could be used as landmarks. In these portals, it was me who was trash—white trash. And boy, was I sought after.

Whereas in my own club, the mere sight of me was enough to put everyone off—"Oh, that's the owner." Here, I was a dove in a cage of bats. But bats can see in the dark, and I couldn't, so I had to rely on touch and sensory perception. And let me tell you, it was fun.

It wasn't until many years later when the city's economy took a nosedive that democracy took over, and the Continental, with its $1 disco, became a safe haven for every ethnic in town. We didn't make as much money, but with a bathhouse full of exotic Spaniards and black stallions, this white kike had a ball.

Chapter 20

Captain Cooked

The Baths being in vogue, I was approached by a local radio station, WINS, to host a radio interview and talk show. It would be called *Steve Ostrow Presents, Live from the Continental*. It really wasn't to be broadcast from the Baths but would feature some of the luminaries and artists who were appearing there.

I accepted on the condition that all editorial content was to be at my discretion, with no interference from the station. What I wanted was to have the opportunity to deal with current and pressing issues, as well as just presenting entertainment.

The program began with the "Continental Band," which was really a recording, playing the overture "The Continental." Then a taped announcer would say, "Good evening, ladies and gentlemen. From the bowels of the Ansonia Hotel, WINS now brings you, the world's most exciting showplace, and its founder, Steve Ostrow . . . Live from the Continental!" There would be sounds of steam, followed by a waterfall, and then I would come in.

During the run of the program, which lasted over a year, I presented many of the leading luminaries of the day. But the one I recall most vividly was an interview with a police captain, whose name shall remain anonymous. The captain was head of the New York Vice Squad and was known for his right-wing sentiments and conservative outlook. It's doubtful he ever accepted the fact that homosexuality was now legal in the city of New York.

He arrived in full uniform, all six feet two inches of himself bristling with medals and decorations and badges and tassels. After some introductory pleasantries to establish who he was and to get the discussion rolling, I said, "Captain, have you ever had sex with a man?"

Well, I thought he would take out his gun and shoot me.

"Of course not," he proclaimed apoplectically.

"Do you think you could ever be excited by a man?"

"Never!"

"Well, if you ever *did* have sex with a man, or a man got you excited even once, do you think that would make you gay?"

"No one could have sex with a man unless he *was* gay," he insisted.

"Okay. Do you think a man could ever arouse you sexually?"

"Of course not! What are you getting at?"

"Well." I persevered. "Let's say, just for argument's sake, that you are in a dark room, no lights on at all."

"Yeah," said the captain, eyeing me suspiciously.

"You're in this black room, and all of a sudden your fly is opened, and your penis is being sucked by a warm, moist mouth."

I could see the captain turning red again, but this time with embarrassment, not anger.

"Do you think you would get a hard-on, assuming just these given facts?"

The captain looked as though he would have liked to have been almost anywhere else in the world but that studio. Finally he gulped. "Er . . . well, I don't know. I guess it's possible. After all, I'm not impotent. But I would never let that happen in the first—"

"Never mind that," I interrupted. "Let's just deal with this hypothetically. You're being sucked by a warm, moist mouth. Your shaft is being licked, and you can feel the tongue rimming the head of your penis, and you have an erection. You agreed that's possible."

The captain was speechless.

"Now," I continued remorselessly, "the lights go on, and you see that you are being sucked by a cat. Do you think that makes you a bestialist?"

"Why, of course not. I didn't know what it was."

"Okay. It's not a cat. It's a dog. What then?"

"Same thing," the captain replied, feeling more secure.

"A goat."

"No way!" Now laughing.

"Okay. The lights go up, and it's . . . a man."

The captain was no longer laughing. In fact, the captain was no longer there. The last question had catapulted him out of his chair; and with not even a wave, he was out the door, gone! Now alone in the studio, I wound up the show. "Thank you, ladies and gentlemen. This has been Steve Ostrow, live from the Continental Baths, leaving you with this thought: the next time you have sex in the dark, maybe you should turn on the lights. Think about it."

Chapter 21

Jess

Even with the support of 14177, there was still something missing. It was that indescribable feeling of being connected to someone very special to you. Joanne, even though we were separated, was emotionally satisfying one half of me; but there was still a part of me that yearned. It seemed that all my life I would be destined to walk that tightrope, trying to balance the need to be with a male and a female.

It was summer. The city of New York is not a very pleasant place in summer, and in fact, anyone who is anyone is usually out of town by July and doesn't return until after Labor Day in September. The Hamptons get all the social butterflies, the really well-to-do are out of the country, and Fire Island gets all the gay yuppies invading the sacred turf of the established gay literati and otherwise talented.

But now there was another option, mainly for those who were stuck in the city during the week for whatever reason, and that was the sunroof at the Continental. So popular had it become, in fact, that we had to employ a full-time elevator boy just to ferry people up and down the seventeen stories from the fun to the sun. Although I must admit we did build a sort of fenced maze area where you could kind of play in the sand and still keep your tan.

Having always been a sun worshipper, I made it a daily routine to work out in the gym, then take the lift to the roof, grab a bit of sun and whatever, and then back down for a swim in the pool and a massage.

On this occasion, I had summoned the lift; and when it arrived, the door opened, revealing a lovely vision of a boy. He was of medium height, obviously of Latin descent, and was possessed of a dreamy demeanor. He seemed quite shy, and we didn't engage in any conversation. His eyes were hidden under thick glasses, but even without them, his wavy black hair seemed to provide a veil of mystery.

As we made the ascent, his body never ceased to flex and pose in those special movements peculiar to a ballet dancer. As the days went by, I found myself looking forward to my celestial voyage with even more interest than normal, and always with the same shy but seductive youth to guide me on my journey. After a while, I believed that we had entered into some sort of relationship, although what it was I was not quite sure.

One day, trying to locate the boy's eyes behind the glasses, I introduced myself. He answered, "Hi, Steve, and yes, I know who you are."

"Well then," I continued, "as you seem to know who I am, how about telling me something about yourself?"

"I'd love to," was the reply, "but this is your floor, and you have to get out, don't you?"

"For now, but I'll be coming back down, won't I?"

Again the graceful choreography of the boy's liquid body as he held the lift door open for me to exit.

Once up on the sunroof, I found that my thoughts still centered on this gentle but mysterious boy. Jorge and I were now on a somewhat formal basis, and I felt a huge void where that relationship had been.

I was on the roof thinking about Jess while the sun slowly sank into the Hudson River, with the industrial haze that was the New Jersey skyline producing the most gorgeous of sunsets.

Gathering myself up, I rang for the elevator, and soon my nubile dancer was at my service.

"Hi, Jess." I said. "How would you like to join me for dinner?"

There was no hesitation. "Sure, what time and where?"

"Eight o'clock in my apartment, 14177."

"I'll be there," said Jess.

And another saga was to begin.

Other than with Jorge on Fire Island, that night with Jess was the first time I had ever slept with a boy from night to morning in "real" life. It had just happened, and it felt so natural. From then on, Jess was to become a regular visitor to 14177, always spending the night with me, much to the chagrin of Pedro, who had to fix breakfast for us both.

Jorge on meeting Jess had thought, *Just another pretty face*, I'm sure. But even he was surprised at how fast and deep I was going into this relationship. To my amazement, Jess and Joanne would become fast friends. Whereas with Jorge, Joanne had never relaxed, it all just seemed very natural with Jess. Even my children, Maria and Scott, were drawn to him.

And so it happened that Jess, Joanne, and I became guests on Pat Collins's interview show. Pat Collins was a prominent TV personality with her own daytime television interview program, very like the Barbara Walters show that came later. Both she and her film director husband, Herb Danska, were interested in doing a documentary on the Continental and my life. They were fascinated by my avant-garde lifestyle and felt the rest of the country would be also. There was much talk of this, but nothing really materialized.

Pat did however ask Joanne, Jess, and me to be the guests on her interview program. Our segment was to be called *A Man, His Wife, and His Lover* and would be broadcast nationwide on NBC television to satisfy the public's curiosity about alternative lifestyles.

This was in the era of live TV when what you saw was what you got. Jess had stayed overnight with me and at 6:00 AM that morning took a Quaalude to calm his nerves. He had just begun a hairdressing course at the Vidal Sassoon School and was going to color and perm my hair for the 9:00 AM broadcast.

By 7:00 AM, I was a strawberry blonde, with my hair standing straight out from my head in frizzy, curly, Shirley Temple ringlets. It was too late to calm it down, so off to the studio we went, stopping only to pick up Joanne.

By 8:30 AM, the Quaalude had really kicked in, and the TV crew plied Jess with multicoffees trying to keep him awake. I learnt later that he had also been sniffing a rag soaked with ethyl chloride, a '70s recreational fad, which together with the Quaalude would have knocked over a Lipizzaner stallion.

At 9:00 AM, they had the three of us, waxen smiles on our faces, seated in chairs facing the camera.

"Mr. Ostrow," Pat began, "are you gay or straight?"

"Well, I think those are labels, and I believe labels are for suits. When I'm gay, I'm as gay as anyone else, and when I'm straight, I'm as straight as anyone else, and sometimes I can get excited with just tight underwear or on a trolley car."

Pat was now trying to smile politely.

"And there are other times," I continued, "when I'm just tired. For me it all depends on the person. My philosophy is, why give up 50 percent of the population?"

Having heard enough from me, Pat turned to Joanne, asking, "Joanne, how is it for you with your husband also seeing a young man?"

Joanne replied, "Oh, it's no problem for me; it kind of takes the pressure off."

At that point, Jess was semicomatose; but when he heard his name, he came back to this planet.

"Jess." Pat was now directing her question to him. "What can you give to a man that a woman can't?"

"Well . . . you know," Jess replied laconically, "a man and a woman get married, and then they have children, and the woman gets busy with the house and the kids, and pretty soon she forgets what it is that turns a man on in the first place." And then speaking directly into the camera to millions of housewives across the nation, he purred, "And I *never* forget."

I thought Pat would drop the mike, but somehow she kept her composure.

"Well, thank you, Joanne, Jess, and Steve. Ladies and gentlemen, that's our show for today. I hope you found it interesting. I'm sure I did. Have a good afternoon."

Daytime television had truly come of age, and it was twenty years pre-Oprah.

Chapter 22

"Could It Be Magic?"

Back at the Baths, I soon promoted Jess to being an alternate disc jockey, a job that he did really well. Indeed, the discothèque was so popular that we had taken to doing Continental disco nights in other venues in the city just to keep up with the new craze. We took over theater lobbies, shopping malls, arcades, and even turned the hallowed halls of the old Pan American Airlines building on east Forty-second Street into a dance hall during lunch hour. Wherever we hung a disco ball, set up the Bose speakers, and turned on the pulsating lighting, the crowds showed up.

It wasn't long before other dance clubs, patterned after the Continental, started to mushroom. First there was the Tenth Floor. Then the Garage, started incidentally by Larry Levan, our first disc jockey. There then followed in quick succession the Flamingo, a private dance club founded by Michael Fusco, who had run the Ice Palace in Cherry Grove for many years; and one of the most attractive, Les Jardins, run by John Addison, an ex-model who took over two full floors in the Diplomat Hotel on west Forty-third Street turning it into a white paradise. Walls, ceiling, furniture, floors—everything was white, interspersed only with mirrors. Les Jardins was truly glamorous. You had to be chic, and you had to wear white, or there was no way you could gain admittance. A fabulous verandah on the third floor invited outdoor dancing and romancing.

Glamour had returned to the city, a gift from the queer, gay, faggot—call it what you will—community. The blacks had given us rhythm; the Latins, machismo; the Jews, moxie. But we gave glamour. For too long, the United States had been caught up in tawdry skirmishes in inaccessible places for unfathomable causes. The Korean War and the Vietnam fiasco had demoralized and divided the country in the '50s breeding the flower-child generation of the '60s.

But the '70s offered a respite from the tacky and a chance to worship idols. The Hefners, Warhols, and Rubels built dynasties and palaces for the masses to practice their idolatry. And to no less a degree, the Continental was an offspring of this generation, offering a fantasia of unprecedented opportunities to a hitherto repressed minority. And boy, did they jump on the merry-go-round.

When the sun set, the fun started. Everybody had a statement to make. Style was not a matter of fashion dictated by a few international gurus but was an expression of who *you* were at that very moment. And not only that, but also who you wanted to *be*. What nature had not provided, you improvised. And that with which you were blessed, you maximized.

With the rescission of laws against homosexuality, we were liberated.

But not all of us. There were those whose genes had trapped them in bodies that belied their emotional proclivity. And while some of us came out of the closet, others went back in and came out in a frock.

Paints, feathers, sequins, rhinestones, silks, leathers, furs—you name it. Male, female, and in-between; gay, straight, and campy queen—all did their thing with no holes barred. And the world was a more fun place by far.

Whether it was in food, fashion, or lifestyle, gays were turning the city into a *Fellini Satyricon*. Everyone was into looking good. High-tech gyms were opening up all over the city, and the male torso was reinvented, certainly not as steroid-pected as today's pumped-up gladiators, but grace and beauty of physique were the attributes that everyone coveted.

And then there was the androgynous look, personified by the likes of Michael Jackson, Mick Jagger, David Bowie, and Boy George. The sultry look of Sal Mineo, Marlon Brando, John Garfield, James Dean, and Montgomery Clift appealed to all genders. Posters of James Dean hung in every gay bedroom in the city. The greatest stars of the era—Judy Garland, Bette, Streisand, Diana Ross, Elizabeth Taylor—were gay icons whose every inflection was copied by hundreds of lip-synching drag queens in every gay bar in town.

On the other end of the spectrum, there were the super "butch" or "clones" as they were called. Their drag were jeans, flannel shirts, leather belts, crew haircuts, mustaches, and army boots. Add to that a red handkerchief hanging out of your right or left rear pocket to signal whether you were a top or bottom, and you were ready to hit the "scene."

Forget gay Paree. New York had become the gay capital of the world. It was the best of times. The city was exciting; there was energy in the streets. Broadway was booming. And the Continental was the gay flagship of the world.

* * *

Barry Manilow, who had been Bette's accompanist at the Baths, had gone on to become her music director on all her tours. Barry had also supervised most of Bette's best albums and was also gaining popularity and prestige in his own right. But he had yet to produce his own recording for, being more of a musician, composer, and arranger than he was a performer, no record company would take him seriously.

Barry came to me one day and asked, "Steve, how would you feel about letting me have the Continental for an evening?"

Since that first day when he had been traumatized by the sight of hundreds of nude and seminude bodies parading past the stage of the Continental while he was rehearsing the band, Barry had started to acclimatize to the new freedom at the Continental. So much so that one New Year's Eve at a party we had held at the Baths, with literally thousands of naked men wearing party hats and dozens of nude girls frolicking in the pool, Liz Torres and Joey Bishop got him to do the unthinkable. With them showing the way, off came his black suit, white shirt, jockey shorts, and socks; and the three of them had jumped stark naked into the pool.

"I'd like to do a whole evening of my own songs, with my own band, and with just me performing." Barry went on.

"You'll clear out the whole house, unless you do it in drag," I remarked jokingly.

"Come on, Steve, I'm serious. I want to invite every theatrical agent and major record producer in the city. I want them to see and hear what I can do."

Barry at the Baths. Well, why not? I thought. "Sure, Barry, I think it's a great idea. If it'll help you, we'll do it. You pick the evening, and the place is yours."

In true perfectionist mode, Barry got right to work on the project, putting together a band of the best studio musicians in New York City. He installed a special sound system, hired Bette's Harlettes as background singers, and rehearsed for two solid weeks. I have always observed that the really great talents like Bette and Barry leave nothing to chance and work their asses off to achieve what on the night seems so effortless.

Although it was to be a by-invitation-only kind of evening, we put a small announcement in the papers so that the house would not only be record executives and their lot. After all, we did want to have some real people to play to.

Much to our surprise, over seven hundred people turned out on a weekday night including everybody who was anybody in the music business. It felt strange for me to be sitting in the audience like any other patron. But this was Barry's night, and the Continental took on the aura of a concert hall. Dressed in a white suit, shirt open at the collar, and long hair flowing, Barry appeared unannounced, sat down at the piano, and signaled the band to start.

He did a great job; and even I, who was familiar with his talents, gained a whole new respect for the man as a multifaceted musical maestro. His performance skills, though yet to be fully developed, revealed an engaging personality capable of pulling at the heartstrings of an audience with his sincerity and humility. His sweet, unassuming voice was cleverly underpinned by his understanding of the craft of composing. Even then Barry knew how to construct a song so that it had a beginning, a middle, and then a great sweeping emotional climax. Through his technical knowledge of orchestration, a song would gently tempt, then nudge, and finally carry the listener to magical heights with the expertise of a modern-day Puccini.

When the last song finished, the applause echoed for long after. Another star had been born. The evening was a great personal success for Barry, and I was happy that the Continental was instrumental in making it happen.

Oh, and incidentally Bell Records called the next morning to offer Barry a contract to produce his first solo record album featuring the song "Could It Be Magic."

Bathhouse Betty

features "My One True Friend"

Chapter 23

Bette, Buns, and Balls

Bette had done her Carnegie Hall concert, which had been a rave, and had just opened in her first Broadway show *Clams on the Half Shell*, a two-hour extravaganza featuring Bette and the Harlettes, her backup singers, Melissa Manchester being one of the original four Harlettes.

Melissa had called me one day a few years before and had asked for an audition. I thought she was talented but didn't think she was star material at that point in her career. But she did live only three blocks from the Baths, so I put her on to Bette, who grabbed her and put her in her backup group the Harlettes, and the rest is history. Melissa then went on to develop a great career of her own as her talents expanded.

Clams on the Half Shell was riotous fun. Bette showed herself in all her different moods, and the production values were fantastic for the time: much feathers and sequins and outrageous sets. The opening number had Bette suspended from the ceiling in a giant clamshell, singing her Continental theme song "You've got to have friends." From there she launched into all her trademark songs from the Baths, interspersing them with some brand-new material featuring Elton John's "The Bitch Is Back," and a new song from Paul Simon, "Gone At Last."

Teamed with the great Lionel Hampton on the vibraphone, she did a medley of forties hits, playing on the nostalgia. But it was her insane freneticism and the elaborately ornate and tacky costumes that drove the audience wild.

Of course the audience was mainly her "KY circuit" followers. In fact, there were so many of our patrons there that I felt I was back at the Baths and almost ran up unto the stage to grab the microphone. The only difference was that the Minskoff Theatre where it was playing was not underground, although they were both on Broadway.

It was years since Bette had started at the Continental, and now that I had used up all my options, her fees were outrageous. Seeing Bette backstage after the opening of *Clams*, I said, "Bette, how about doing one more show at the Continental for old times' sake, after this show closes?"

Feeling great after her victorious opening, she looked at me in her old-time way. "You mean you want me to sing in a steam bath?"

We both laughed, hugged, and agreed. "Yeah, let's do it."

* * *

The Baths, already known around the world as a gay mecca, was now achieving recognition as an entertainment phenomenon. Mainstream media such as *Show Business*, *Variety*, and *Backstage* were now regularly reviewing our shows.

The night Bette was to make her triumphant return to the Baths, I was more than a bit worried. The fire department had begun checking us out on show nights. We were approved for a total of two thousand people to be in the Baths at any one time, but that was meant to be distributed on three floors of which we now had ninety thousand square feet of space.

On the night of Bette's return, the line outside the Continental stretched almost to Lincoln Center. It was made up of a diverse mixture of celebrities, paparazzi, and just people who considered themselves Bette's "friends."

Of course the smart set had already checked into the Baths as towel customers, ensuring not only entry but something to sit on, both before and after.

I was frantic as usual coping with all the logistics of putting on the show. Barry; the band; Pinky, our lighting director; her lover Cheryl, our stage manager; the Continental crew; cashiers; managers; towel boys—we were all flat out.

By this time, the Baths boasted a fully licensed bar and cocktail lounge under the management of none other than Barry Cross, my former Beneficial Finance boss. How the tables had turned! Barry had retired from Beneficial, and I grabbed him up. He was a natural behind the bar, and as straight as he was, the boys loved talking to this George Raft throwback.

The best estimate I was able to come up with was that there were some four thousand people in line at the Continental to buy tickets to the show, enough to have filled the opera house at Lincoln Center. We sold two thousand five hundred and then had to stop. Those who didn't get in camped outside hoping for a glimpse of the action after the show. At the last minute, we installed a loudspeaker on top of the tin entrance canopy, so Bette's followers could at least hear the event, along with everybody else who lived on Seventy-fourth and Broadway.

With Barry Manilow at the piano, hair now down to his shoulders, and Joey Mitchell beating on the drums, it was like the first night Bette appeared, only this time you can be sure I was not paying her $50.

Bette's entry on the theme "But you've got to have friends" set everyone into a frenzy, but there was absolutely no way to move. For the first time, I was actually scared at the sight of a crowd. There was no room for anybody to budge. Packed in, they covered every bit of floor space on the entire lower level of the bathhouse. In the event of a fire, I didn't know what would have happened. The only solution would have been for everyone to strip down naked and stand in the pool until help came. That would have been a hilarious sight, but at least the thought of it calmed me down.

I was locked onstage as the MC. Bette had just finished her opening number, and I was ad-libbing, allowing her time to get into her next costume. As I looked out at the audience, my eye caught the back wall, and I froze. My worst fears were being realized. Standing against the wall were two firemen in full uniform. I don't know to this day how they got in without my knowing, unless they had checked into the bathhouse in civvies and then donned their uniforms.

I was sure they were going to stop the show and empty the house. Could you imagine refunding two thousand five hundred people their money and sending them home? Not to mention the one thousand five hundred or so serious bath customers who were floating around the upstairs areas listening to the show over the PA system.

While I was trying not to dwell on these dire possibilities, Bette exploded on stage with the Harlettes behind her, doing her Andrews Sisters Bugle Boy bit. But from behind the curtain, I had only eyes for the two firemen, who to my amazement were smiling from ear to ear and applauding madly.

As festive and outrageous as the show was, there was overall a tinge of both déjà vu and sadness. We had seen it all before. But now we were aware that we might never see Bette again in this sort of ambience. After her success on the Johnny Carson shows, her concert in Carnegie Hall, and the Broadway hit *Clams on the Half Shell*, Bette made a conscious decision to seek a broader audience. She no longer wanted to be identified as being a fag hag. Much like Streisand, she sought an international career.

There are those who say that she turned her back on her gay following, which is pretty risky business. But in 1999, Bette reidentified with her roots and came out once more via a new CD, *Bathhouse Betty*.

Mercifully the show came to an end without incident, written into the history books to the accompaniment of thunderous applause.

The disco went on in a cloud of dust till 10:00 AM the next morning, when the last souls departed to the strains of Bette's recorded voice singing "Sweet Marijuana."

It had been another Saturday night at the Baths, and we had come full circle.

# Bette's Back

with her new CD:

Warner Bros. 1998
(Thanks as always to crazed fans Steve Weiners and George Anshutz for the above altered scan.)

Bathhouse Betty!

Her first on Warner Bros.

Chapter 24

Close Encounters of the Third Kind

One bright sunny morning, a bright sunny boy who resembled Puck from *A Midsummer Night's Dream* materialized in the kitchen of 14177. He was no more than nineteen and had a happy countenance that just glowed from within. He was holding a large earthen pot in which a beautiful green plant flowered. The plant was larger than he was, and I thought for a moment that I was hallucinating.

"Hello," was all I could think of saying.

"Hi," he replied energetically, a sweet innocence surrounding him like a halo.

"Would you like to put that down?" I said.

"Oh, great. Thanks. Would it be okay if I left it here for a while? It would look great in your music room."

"Well, I'm sure it would, but whom does it belong to?" I said, wondering how he had already seen the music room.

"It's mine," he smiled.

"And who are you?" I asked lightly.

"Oh, don't you know me? Joe hired me about a week ago. I'm a friend of Pedro's. I helped him clean the apartment, and now I'm going back downstairs."

"And what do you do for us?"

"I'm working in the snack bar from 12:00 to 8:00."

"Well, I must come down for a coffee soon. What's your name?"

"Chula. I'm Jamaican, but I took the name from the Topis American Indian tribe."

And so he looked. I could easily imagine him standing in full native gear, one foot poised over the other, spear in hand. He was lovely: earthy, alive, spirited, and, above all, real. No pretension, no gay bitchiness. Just . . . Chula.

"Look, Steve . . . is that okay, that I call you Steve?" I nodded. "Well, I had to leave my flat because I didn't have any money, and to tell the truth, I've been staying with Pedro in his room, but there's no place for this plant of mine, so I thought I'd decorate your music room with it, if that's all right with you."

What else could I say to this ingenue but, "Sure, it's okay. Are you any good at decorating?"

"Well, that's what I really want to do. I'd like to talk to you sometime about brightening up the Baths for show nights."

"What do you mean?"

"Well, I think each show should have a special theme, and I could do it up each Friday for the weekend and change it the next week."

"And how much would you need to do that?"

"Well, let's see . . . flowers, balloons, streamers, posters, cutouts . . . I have very good connections to get things cheap. I could do the whole job for $50 each weekend."

I almost collapsed. The last time Richard Ohrbach had decorated the Baths, it had cost $250,000.

"Well, I guess we can afford that," I said. "Let's give it a try. When would you start?"

"Now!" His crisp body was coming to attention.

"You got it. Go for it . . . but bring me all the receipts," I said, handing him $50.

Throwing me a salute and about-facing, off he went with his plant in tow. I gazed affectionately after him, not realizing then the amount of beauty and depth of feeling this nature boy would bring to me and the Continental, in his far-too-short life.

* * *

Some of the celebrities who came to the Baths on show nights tended to make an entrance. They were there to see and be seen. But others came and went so discreetly that even I didn't know that they were there. One day I not only witnessed a surprise visitation but also got a graphic lesson.

In the gay world, where physical beauty counts so much, it is hard not to be self-conscious about your shortcomings. For example, I am a terrible swimmer; and for many years, I didn't get into the pool because I thought everyone would be looking at me, saying, "What a terrible swimmer," as they laughed.

But on that memorable day, a grotesque, overweight man with balding hair, spectacles, and a belly that overhung his private parts, but not enough that you couldn't see how private they really were, waddled out of the pool. Most people, looking like that, would never come to a bathhouse, much less take off their towel to swim.

Then slowly, a buzzing was heard from around the pool as all the beautiful people got together and gaped.

The portly individual paid them no mind and, with perfect aplomb, lit up a fat cigar and lovingly exhaled a cloud of smoke. Now their assumptions were confirmed, and there was a hush of awe. But one boy echoed the silent thought, "There goes Alfred Hitchcock."

And nobody saw the fat man anymore. What they saw was a genius. Visions of James Stewart, Grace Kelly, Cary Grant, and Audrey Hepburn—all embodied in the aura of this man.

From that day on, I have never refrained from jumping in the pool.

* * *

I have never been much of a partygoer. I abhor small talk; and although I adore a one-to-one discussion, as soon as there are groups of people smoking and drinking, I look for the nearest exit. Paradoxically I am quiet at home, and never happier, than when on a stage with hundreds, even thousands, of strange people in the audience.

But the '70s was a party era. Whether it was on a public or private level, parties were the in thing. There was even one fashionable New York lady who had built her whole life and fortune by doing nothing else but arrange and throw wonderful parties. An invitation to one of Elsa Maxwell's parties, whatever the theme, was like getting your name in *Who's Who*.

On the opposite end of the spectrum, however, was a cult figure that rivalled the reputation of the great dame as a party thrower, but for totally different reasons.

Andy Warhol was the brat of the era, the Picasso of avant-garde, the purveyor of the trite and the trivia. An invitation to a Warhol party carried with it the dubious distinction that you were one of those people who were so out in society's eyes that you were in.

My first and only sojourn into one of Andy's divertissements remains in my mind as a surrealist foray into a Fellini-like world of the obscene and the depraved. I remember climbing up an interminable, rickety set of stairs in SoHo, which finally delivered me into a smoky loft that seemed to float on the pungent odors of tobacco, incense, and pot.

There, lolling on pillows and mattresses, were the nebulous shapes of androgynous people clothed in the anonymity of their ubiquitous garb, which seemed to comprise robes of flowing fabric. A cherubic young blond with Botticelli features and wearing a diaphanous white negligee greeted me with a friendly hello without ever leaving the massive lap of a black-haired siren of cruise-ship proportions who was sniffing coke.

As I wafted through the immense room, I could make out the famous faces of the Warhol Club: Poutaasa, Holly Woodlawn, Scavullo, Capote. Photographers, writers, models—they were all there. Transvestites, transsexuals, and the entranced—all in attendance and paying tribute to the wizard of the odd.

The man holding court, Andy Warhol himself, reigned from his throne deep in the murk of the dense clouds that wafted around him. There were works of art strewn around the floor and mounted haphazardly on the walls. But the crowning touch was the famed Campbell's Soup can, which hung on a space all to itself, like the *Mona Lisa* in the Louvre. Only *she* never took herself seriously.

Limbs and mouths reached out from hidden corners to offer hallucinogenics or genitals—take your prick. And I soon lost all bearing as to where I was.

After drifting through a maze of people, I knew that if I ventured any further, I might never be heard from again and my remains would probably be cannibalized. I finally hit a wall and, hoping that there would only be four of them, traced my way for what seemed to be an eternity until, mercifully, I found the place where I had entered.

The same grotesque coupling of Beauty and the Beast that had first welcomed me gazed at me with sadness as they saw that I was leaving.

For all I know, they're still there.

* * *

It seemed that no matter where I looked, there was an article in the media on either Bette, Barry, the Baths, or me. The public seemed to have a great fascination for what really went on in the basement of the Ansonia.

I was constantly being interviewed by the gay and straight press. *Rolling Stone* did a sixteen-page feature article titled "King Queen" on me and my personal life, with a front-page picture of Joanne, Jess, my two kids, my Afghanistan hound dog Taj, and, oh yes, of course, me.

The popular magazine *After Dark* did an in-depth story called "What Makes Steven Run?" on how I was being touted to be the next mayor of New York City—more on that later. *Forum*, a mainstream magazine that focused on how to have a better and more satisfying sex life, interviewed both Joanne and me in an article titled "Open Marriage."

Women's Wear Daily did a three-page story on the Baths and its effect on setting fashion in the city. *The Saturday Review of the Arts* did a wild story entitled "Steve Ostrow's Satyricon," and the gay press ran ongoing stories about my life and loves, most of which was very scantily based on any facts, but it sold papers.

Incredulously I was invited by a Dr. David Kahn, a noted reality therapist, to be a panelist on an adult seminar he was giving for the New School of Social Research. It was titled "Alternative Lifestyles," and I guess he thought who better to embody it but me.

The audience was comprised of some two hundred housewives who looked like they had come in on a bus from the suburbs, all brandishing their notebooks and shopping bags.

Dr. Kahn started off the lecture in a rather dignified way, going into the history of human relationships and the sociological implications of changing ideas and attitudes. Several large horseflies were droning lazy circles in the ceiling above the lectern, and I could see everyone's attention focusing on them—that is, except for those who had buzzed off themselves.

"Thank you for your attention," Dr. Kahn concluded. "I would now like to introduce our very illustrious panelist, Mr. Steve Ostrow, founder of the Continental Baths and discoverer of Bette Midler and Barry Manilow. Please feel free to ask him any questions that you have in mind."

It was quite an experience for me facing that sea of suburban matrons. Most of the questions they asked were pretty unexciting and were just to satisfy their curiosity as to my family life and such. Then a courageous gray-haired woman stood up and asked me what I thought was the most important thing in a relationship. She said that she and her husband had been married for over thirty years, and in all of those thirty years, she had never been satisfied sexually and for that matter didn't really know if her husband was either. She was a brave woman, and I felt great compassion for her and those lost thirty years.

"Thank you, madam, for being so honest," I said, and then addressing the entire group, I continued. "Look, guys, I probably have had more sexual encounters in the last week than most of you have had in your entire life, but I think the most important thing in any relationship is communication.

"We are all afraid to tell our partners what it is that really turns us on. A man goes to a prostitute and says, 'Look, this is what I want,' and gets it. But when it comes to our own partner, we feel ashamed to say what we want for fear of being thought crude, dirty, or whatever. This lack of communication also prevents our partners from telling us what they want.

"The basic rule I learned from the good doctor here is that the more honest I can be in a relationship, the more I permit my intimate other to open up to me. Sometimes it can be as simple a thing as saying, 'You know, dear, if you would just move your finger one half inch higher (or lower), it would make all the difference.' But no, we suffer in silence, too timid to express our wants, and so thirty years may indeed go by unsatisfied when a half inch in one direction or another would have made all the difference."

The standing ovation that I received from those lovely ladies meant as much to me as a curtain call at the Met. As we left the lecture hall, Dr. Kahn said, "You know, Steve, when those ladies go home tonight, their husbands are going to be in for a shock . . . By the way, how many encounters *did* you have last week?"

Chapter 25

Friends of the Family

It was always exciting to discover and then nurture new talent, but one of the greatest joys for me was to be able to present to the Batherazzi legendary performers at the zenith of their powers.

This was possible at times because we ran a late show, and very often I was able to negotiate with the artists' managers to put them on after they had finished a gig in one of the major hotels. I always kept my eye on who was appearing at the upmarket showrooms for that reason. It worked out well for both us and the artist, who was able to parley the evening into something more profitable, as I usually paid cash for the appearance.

Just such an opportunity arose when the fabulous Sarah Vaughn was booked into the Persian Room at the Plaza Hotel. Sarah was rumored to have been battling a drug-related problem and was known to cancel at the last moment. As I always paid in advance to make it more attractive, this was a risky undertaking, but Sarah Vaughn had been one of my idols for years, and no way was I going to miss this opportunity.

I was only able to book her for one night, a Friday. With the contract in my hand, I sent press releases out to all the gay press, put ads in the *Times*, the *Post*, and the *Daily News*. The tickets went on sale the morning of the show; and by twelve noon, we had sold out the house, one thousand five hundred tickets at $12 each. Helen and Ernie worked their little fingers off tallying up the receipts to make the three o'clock closing at the bank to deposit all the money.

"Have a great night, guys," I sang out, and off they went with $18,000 in cash.

I had no sooner gone downstairs to watch the band rehearsing for the night's show when I was urgently paged on the PA system to come to the reception desk. When I arrived, I could see Joey, my manager, in a heated discussion outside with a tough-looking lady in a frumpy skirt and jacket. Out in the street, I could also see about a dozen very officious-looking guys surrounding the entrance. The line of patrons had already started building up for the evening.

"What the hell is going on?" I said, running out to the street.

"Who are you?" the lady barked.

"I'm Steve Ostrow. I own the place. Who are *you?*"

"We're the New York State revenue agents, and *we* own the place until your back sales tax of $17,000 is paid," she proclaimed, handing me a writ of execution indicating that she was empowered to take whatever action she deemed proper to ensure payment.

We normally paid our sales tax quarterly, and I had always instructed Helen and Ernie to wait till the last day and then take the check right to the tax office so that we would earn interest on the money until the last moment.

"When was the deadline for payment?" I demanded.

"Yesterday, but we waited until twelve noon today before getting a writ," the tax lady sternly replied.

"Hold everything," I said. "I'm sure my accountants have taken care of the payment." And with that I ran to the back office.

I was now frantic. This was to be one of the biggest nights in our history. The whole house was sold out and the performer paid up front. I couldn't believe this was happening. I broke out in a cold sweat; surely there must have been a mistake.

I rummaged through the office, and then I saw it. There, there in the desk drawer, was the tax statement, all completed and a cheque drawn for $17,000, payable to the New York State Department of Sales Tax. Helen had obviously prepared it but, in the excitement of the ticket sales for the Sarah Vaughn show, had forgotten to take it to the tax office.

I grabbed the statement and the check and felt the panic subsiding in my body as I ran back out.

"Here, call off your blood hounds," I said, pushing past the state marshals blocking the entrance and then shoving the check and the statement in front of her. "Here's your money. Now back off."

"This is a cheque," she announced imperiously. "It would have been accepted yesterday or before 3:00 PM today; but now that the banks are closed, there's no way we can verify that the funds are there to cover it."

"What does that mean?" I asked incredulously.

"It means, mister, that these premises are closed for business until Monday morning, when you can present the check. Either that or we'll take the cash now."

"But you know the banks are closed. You just told me that. How do you expect me to come up with $17,000 in cash?" I protested, thinking miserably of the $18,000 worth of ticket receipts that Ernie and Helen had just taken to the bank. If only they had waited.

"That's not our problem, that's *your* problem," she said, signaling her crew who proceeded to rig a heavy metal chain across the entrance to the Baths, to which she affixed a padlock.

I couldn't believe this was happening. Surely not in America, the land of the free.

"Give me one hour," I pleaded. "Otherwise, my business is ruined. One hour, that's all I'm asking," and then added in desperation, "Sarah Vaughn is booked to appear tonight."

I'll never really know for sure, but I believe I struck a responsive chord with Sarah's name. At least I thought I could detect a softer tone when she replied, "One hour?" And then looking at her watch, she said, "We'll wait till 4:30 PM, and then we go . . . but the chain stays on till it's paid."

With the line of customers waiting for admittance backed up onto Broadway, it reminded me of the days of the police raids. But this was no time for reminiscing. I ran back into the office and grabbed the phone.

When Barry had introduced my new *friends* to me, they had given me a number to call in case there was ever any difficulty. They had been meticulous in all their business dealings with me and indeed had updated all the vending machines with the latest technology and even given us brand-new garbage bins. I had no complaints. But now I did have a desperate problem.

"Hello," was all I got when I dialed the number.

"Hi, this is Steve Ostrow from the Continental."

"Oh, yeah . . . Steve, sure, how are you, this is Angelo," said the gritty voice. I didn't know Angelo from a hole in the wall, but he obviously knew me.

"Well, I'm fine, but I got a problem."

"Wassamatter, kid, talk to me."

"Look, I've got the state agents padlocking my place and demanding cash for back sales tax or they close the place down. Now there's plenty of money in the bank, but they won't take a check, and the banks are closed, so I can't get the cash out, and I got a big weekend happening and—"

"Hey, take it easy, kid. Just tell me what you need."

"I need $17,000 in cash, and I need it in one hour."

"Hold the phone . . ."

By this time, my panic and the cold sweat had returned, and it was all I could do to hold on to the telephone. I was thinking how nice it would be to live in a country with no governmental agencies.

"Steve, you there, kid?" I was jolted back into reality.

"Yeah, Angelo."

"Okay, wait outside," he told me. "We're sending one of our drivers. Look for a black Cadillac. He'll hand you a package to take care of things till Monday. Got it?"

"Yeah, Angelo, thanks a lot. But I only got till 4:30 PM."

"Don't worry, eh, have a good weekend." And with that the phone clicked off.

The line of patrons waiting to get into the Baths now stretched beyond my vision. Grabbing Joe, I told him to serve free coffee to everyone in line, including the gestapo and Madame Göering. That done, I positioned myself by the curb to await what would be either a limousine or a hearse.

I had never realized before how many black Cadillacs there were in New York City. It seemed to me that every other car that came down Seventy-fourth Street was either black or a Cadillac or both. It was getting closer and closer to 4.30 PM when finally one of them screeched to a halt in front of me.

"Steve Ostrow?" came a voice from the driver's seat.

"That's me!" I yelled, running to the car.

"Who's your lawyer?" the voice asked.

"Barry Slotnick," I replied.

"Who were you speaking to before at the office?"

"Angelo."

"Here. Angelo says he'll see you Monday when the banks open," the voice with the dark glasses said, thrusting a brown paper bag out the window.

"Tell Angelo thanks!" I shouted as the car sped away.

Again a brown paper bag was playing an important role in my life. I took a fast look inside the bag; and there, in neat stacks of $100 bills, was an awful lot of green money. It's 4:28 PM. No time to count it.

"Here it is, all $17,000!" I yelled, running up to the good madame and shoving the bag into her hands.

"What's this? A bag of groceries?" she said derisively.

"No, but it will buy an awful lot of them. Open it up," I insisted. I remember the look of incredulity on her face as she said, "Let's go in your office."

The money had been arranged in seventeen stacks of ten $100 notes. It didn't take her long to do the accounting, at which point she turned to me with the hint of a smile.

"Sarah Vaughn, huh? She's one of my favorites. Here's your receipt. You're back in business. Don't forget to tell her who made the show possible."

If you only knew, I thought.

The luscious sounds of Sarah's voice permeated the room, painting every inch of every surface with a liquid purple hue. We were all in awe, aware of the privilege of being so close to one of the greatest performers of this or any other time.

The lady herself was humble and unpretentious, as is so often the case with the truly great. For the most part, she would just sit on a stool and let that magnificent instrument of hers play with a melody line, dipping down into a chocolate chest register of unbelievable depth, and then ascending to lustrous heights, but always in the service of the music. At the end of each selection, she would acknowledge the thunderous applause, head bowed, with a simple

"Thank you, thank you, ladies and gentlemen. Thank you very, very much." That was all she would say, but then she had said it all in song.

After the events of the afternoon, it was a joy just to relax and enjoy the wave of love that flowed from her to the audience and then back again.

That night at the Sarah Vaughn concert, as I looked at Jess in the glass DJ cage, ready to start the disco, I suddenly felt intensely aware that he was an embodiment of all the things that I longed for: music, art, beauty, warmth, grace. His very countenance seemed more out of some Greek mythological time than the present—so much, indeed, like Mary Renault's "Persian Boy" that I felt like Alexander the Great in his presence. For me, Jess was the perfect androgynous combination of male-female that I had been yearning for.

Back then, the idea of men living together in a relationship was new. Society disapproved of gayness in general, in couples or not. Casual sex was rampant; experimentation and partying, yes. But entering into a meaningful relationship with another male was frightening as it meant living in a real world with *middle-class* values and giving up the sexual freedom that had been so hard won. Everyone was happy playing; however, *this* was serious stuff.

"Okay, Steve," Jess said when I proposed we enter into a serious relationship, "let's try it and see what the *feelings* are." Jess always made fun of me for talking about *feelings*, which was the new buzzword of the psychotherapeutic '70s.

We clicked coffee cups, gave ourselves one week to think about it, and then see where we wanted to go from there.

But what *would* that life be like? The new buzzword in the gay world was relationships. Everyone wanted to get into the act, and for some, it was just that. Not having role models of our own, gay couples could only pattern themselves after what was heterosexually proper.

The problem was that most straight relationships didn't seem to be working either. Straight society certainly did not provide for the pent-up sexual energy of gay people who did not necessarily equate sex with love, much less commitment. Baths, beats, parks, warehouses, trailers, trucks, sand dunes—you name it, they provided an emotionally safe haven for our hell-bent hedonism. But *relationships*, that was really scary.

Still, there was a yearning for a coming together of the soul, for some deeper meaning that no amount of promiscuity could provide. If meaning could be measured by quantity of semen or frequency of ejaculation, then we had it all. *But it wasn't enough.*

Steve Ostrow
presents
Sarah Vaughn

at The
CONTINENTAL BATHS
230 W. 74th St., N.Y.C.
(212) 799-2688
Wed., Dec. 19th at 10:30 P.M.

November Saturday Schedule
Nov. 3   Boobie Knight and The Soulsciety
Nov. 10 Sally Eaton and Cliff and
         Cliff Grisham
Nov. 17 Laura Kenyon
Nov. 24 Dawn Hampton

Limited Number of Seats Available!

Chapter 26

Putting on the Ritz

The New Year found me caught up with a fascinating new project, a Broadway musical called *The Ritz*, involving a murder and a Mafia gunman who gets trapped in a gay bathhouse called the Ritz.

The play was written by Terrence McNally, who originally titled it *The Tubs*—guess where he got that from—and who opened it as a "straight" play at the Yale University Repertory Theatre during the 1973-4 season. This was the same Terrence McNally whose brilliant play *Master Class*, an epic realization of Maria Callas during her Juilliard teaching days, was now touring the world to standing ovations.

For the New York opening, McNally changed the main character into a heterosexual businessman who hides in a gay bathhouse to escape his murderous mafioso brother-in-law.

I was approached by the producers to cooperate with the production, to which I agreed, and then they said that they were still looking for more backers. The Broadway scene had been floundering, and musicals were a big risk. The Ritz was to be one of the first productions to be offered like a stock issue, with lots of investors having a piece of the action. I called Eric Marks, my Israeli contractor who had built the Baths for me. He was hot to be on the inside track of a major Broadway show, and together, we became part backers of the production.

Rita Moreno was cast in the lead role, a fabulous sort of Spanish Bette Midler called Googie Gomez. She would go on to win a Tony Award for her performance, although I always thought Liz Torres could have done just as well or perhaps better.

Everyone knew of course that *The Ritz* was just a facade for the Baths and that Rita's character was a polyglot of all the risqué comedian singers we had ever had at the Baths. After all, no other baths in the world, other than the Caracalla, had ever had entertainment. So who were they kidding?

Opening night was a sellout; and I had invited everyone involved: cast, crew, producers, tech—you name it—plus a host of other luminaries back to 14177 after the show to await the reviews. Even with fourteen rooms, you could not move. Every inch was planted with one bright star or another. Rita arrived to thunderous applause, and the party was truly on.

I had the entire affair catered by the Stage Door Delicatessen, a New York icon. The night was uproarious. The music played on, and the food never stopped. Great bowls of champagne punch were policed by bath attendants to make sure no one dropped any acid in them, a '70s practical joke. Everything was perfect except that Jess hadn't been home in three days, and I was near frantic. He hadn't been seen in any of his customary haunts, but some had said they had seen him with a good-looking guy with a mustache. Well, we did say we would *think* about our new relationship.

Being the host, I was trying to keep calm and enjoy the festivities when Scotti came up to me with a quizzical look on his face.

"Steve, you have two more guests at the door."

"Well, let them in, what's the big deal?"

"The big deal is that it's Jess, but he's with a guy called Noel that looks like Burt Reynolds. I've seen him working in his father's hardware store; did you invite him?"

"I damn well did not!"

"What do you want me to do, Steve?"

"I'll take care of this myself, Scotti, thank you."

I was furious. This was *my* night. How dare Jess have the audacity to flaunt some new guy in front of me and my friends! As glad as I was that he was okay, no way was I going to let that happen. News travels very fast in the bath world. I had always preached to everyone that if a relationship is based on sex or money, you're always vulnerable, because there will surely be someone who will come along with a bigger dick and more money. But if the relationship is based on feelings and communication and trust, you need never fear losing it, although it might change in time to a different level.

With a full head of steam, I managed to push my way through the merrymakers to the front door. Expecting Jess and his new friend to be in full party gear, I was taken aback at seeing them both in jeans and old sweatshirts. Even so, I had to admit they made a stunning couple. So if this guy didn't have more money than me, that left only one other possibility.

Before I could utter a nasty word, Burt—I mean Noel, whom I recognized as a bath customer, and who obviously knew me, took the wind out of my sails saying, "I'm sorry, Steve, I didn't know about the party."

For damn good reasons, I thought. But I was even more surprised at what he said next. "Look, I know you must think Jess and I are fabulous lovers. But the truth is, we just don't get along. I mean, he's sexy, and I like him and all, but I just can't deal with him. He's too moody. All he talks about is how you two guys communicate and discuss feelings. Well, I guess I just can't handle it, so I'm bringing him back to your doorstep. Good night."

With Noel gone, the forlorn creature that was now Jess looked at me plaintively, saying, "Well, can I come in, or should I go back on the streets?"

Well, we all know that the streets of New York City are no place for a pretty young boy to be after midnight.

"Sure, come in," I said. "There's always room at the inn."

By 3:00 AM, the early morning edition of the papers had arrived. All the reviews were favorable. Clive Barnes of the *New York Times* wrote, "I laughed a lot, and who could ask for anything more?" Indeed, I thought, with Jess still in my bed, who could ask for anything more?

The funny season begins
when you check in for a night at The Ritz.
THE RITZ
...a hideout for hilarity.
A RICHARD LESTER FILM "THE RITZ"
JACK WESTON RITA MORENO JERRY STILLER KAYE BALLARD
TERRENCE McNALLY ADELA HOLZER
TERRENCE McNALLY DENIS O'DELL
RICHARD LESTER

Chapter 27

It's Rudy! Men, Tarry!

The raucous sounds of feminine voices emanating from the reception desk told me that something was going on. Not only that, but I was sure I recognized the voices as coming from Joanne and Marie, Gabe's wife.

What the heck could they be going on about? I thought as I raced out from the back office. Sure enough, the two of them were harassing Gus, the cashier.

"Gus, honey," Joanne was saying, "surely you can do this for me?"

"And for me too," Marie chimed in.

"Well, I guess it's all right. I don't think Steve would mind, although it's kind of a breach of confidentiality."

"What wouldn't Steve mind?" I demanded, arriving on the scene.

"Oh, sweetheart, we just want to borrow a couple of sheets and pillowcases from the laundry." Joanne's voice was oozingly seductive, as she lovingly caressed the linen in the basket.

"But that's the dirty linen basket, my love," I said incredulously. "You for sure don't want to be taking any of that home." But neither Joanne nor Marie looked very surprised at my edification.

"Okay, what's going on, guys?" I said, now wanting to be in on the game. Silence.

"Well, if nobody's going to talk, then suppose I just take this dirty laundry downstairs and throw it in the washer," I said, grabbing hold of the basket.

"No!" screamed the two of them, making enough noise to stop the action on the third floor, which, believe me, is no easy feat.

"Okay, Gus, suppose you tell me what's going on, or would you rather go back to cleaning toilets?"

"All I know is that it came out of the room of some redheaded dancer."

"Look, it's not Gus's idea," said Joanne, now looking sheepishly at me. "Well, Steve, if you must know, Rudolph Nureyev stayed here at the Baths last night. Jess tipped us off, so we ran down just in time to see him check out.'

Nureyev had been a patron of the Baths for some time. He always checked in whenever he was doing a performance at Lincoln Center. I was well aware of this but never publicized it.

"Yeah, so what's that got to do with the dirty linen?"

"Well, you see," she stuttered, "Marie and I wanted to keep the sheets and pillowcases from his room as a kind of souvenir," and with that the two of them started to giggle. "Imagine," Joanne continued, "imagine having the very bed linen that Rudolph Nureyev slept on!"

"And would you like to have them autographed?" I quipped.

"No, but we for sure will never wash them," Joanne retorted, as she and Marie both grabbed the linen out of the basket and made a run for it.

Gus and I rocked with laughter. *If they only knew the real Rudy,* I thought, *they'd not only wash that linen but burn it.*

I had often seen Nureyev running through the bathhouse at odd hours, always mercurial. For a moment you would see his unmistakable, beautifully etched body, pale as milk and topped with reddish hair (he was a true strawberry blond, take my word for it); and then before your very eyes, he would disappear as if vaporized.

Here was the enigma: the highest-paid entertainer in the classical world, running loose in a bathhouse, looking for the roughest, blackest trade he could find—none of whom, incidentally, had the faintest idea who he was. I shuddered to think of the misfortunes that could happen to him.

One Saturday I was surprised to receive a call from his New York manager.

"We are the managers for Mr. Nureyev, who we understand is a patron of your . . . health club."

"Yes, what can I do for you?" I immediately thought that there might be a problem. After all, he was the hottest property they had.

"Mr. Nureyev is doing a run of *Romeo and Juliet* at Lincoln Center and unfortunately is not able to come to your emporium."

Well, I thought, *how quaint. We're now an emporium.*

He went on to request that we have our masseur come to the Tower Suite of the Waldorf-Astoria that night to give Mr. Nureyev a rubdown before the show.

"Why, certainly. We are flattered," I replied. Tony, our masseur, was known for his iron hands. He was the strongest in the business, and when he gave a deep tissue massage, you either yelled in ecstasy or passed out. Tony had told me that Rudy liked his massage about twice as strong as most people were able to stand.

"There is one other thing," the manager went on. "As you know, Mr. Nureyev is very artistic."

"Yes, I am aware of that."

"To put him in a proper mood for Romeo, he would like to have a very pretty boy to look at while he gets his massage."

"Oh."

"Do you think you could handle that?"

He must have sensed my hesitation.

"Mr. Nureyev would *certainly* make it worth his while."

I'm sure he would, I thought.

"Yes, leave it with me, and I'll send the boy with the masseur."

"That's very kind of you. Also, as I am Mr. Nureyev's personal manager, I know his preferences. Could you please have the boy come to *my* room first, as Rudolf is very particular, and I must be sure that the boy suits him aesthetically."

I was now starting to get the whole picture. "I'll give the boy instructions."

"Thank you very much, Mr. Ostrow. Rudolf will be very grateful. And I will take care of the finances."

What to do? Nureyev was Jess's idol. I knew if I kept this from Jess, he would later find out and probably never forgive me for depriving him of the chance of a lifetime, to meet and to be with Nureyev. Yet my own feelings of jealousy and possessiveness were running rampant as ever. But then there was Nureyev, and what better package could I give him to gaze upon than the idyllic Jess?

I didn't know what to do. Jess and I had now settled into a comfortable relationship, one that worked for the both of us. We were there for one another, taking care of each other's needs. The deal was that we did our own thing during the day, Jess taking dance classes and working at the Baths in the evening as a disc jockey and me looking after my burgeoning business empire, which now included Tiger-Mite Health Food stores, Hi-Lite Wines and Liquors, Super-Rite Markets, and of course Uptight Boutique, now with a branch in Greenwich Village.

Most of the times, we would meet up for dinner and then continue on our separate ways. We had our favorite restaurants: the Isle de France, the Red Baron on the West Side, Joe's in the Village, and, on special occasions, the Forum of the Twelve Caesars. Lutèce, which was and maybe still is the finest restaurant in the city, was so intimate and inviting that even though it was outrageously expensive even for those days, it became like a second home to me, eating there at least once a week with Joanne or Jess—separately of course.

When I had checked in the midnight shift, Jess and I would go upstairs to the apartment. After a leisurely nightcap, we would go to bed together. Once I had fallen asleep, Jess was then free to quietly get up and go do whatever twenty-one-year-olds do in the wicked hours of the night. It was always on the understanding that, come what may—and I'm sure it did—by morning, when I woke up, he would already be back in bed. This way there would be no reason for a repeat of the Noel interlude.

Now, this might sound like a strange arrangement to some people, but it worked for us, and nobody had written a rule book as to how a gay relationship should be structured. And even if they had, I doubt if anybody would have followed it in the '70s. This, after all, was the *me* generation, where everybody wanted everything and didn't want to give up anything else to get it. So in keeping with the me generation, I did think about keeping the Nureyev thing a secret; but after all it being in the interest of art, I knew I would have to leave the decision to Jess.

When I explained the request and the arrangement, it didn't take Jess long to get the idea.

"Wow, what an opportunity!"

"Then you'll do it?" I said, my heart sinking, for not only did Rudy have more money than me, but he also had a bigger dick, I can assure you.

Jess was silent for a moment and then said, "Steve, I honestly would love to do it, but I'm thinking I want a serious career in ballet, and someday I may meet up with Nureyev professionally, and I . . . well, I just would feel he wouldn't take me seriously after that."

Of course he was right; I hadn't even considered that. What a relief!

But now I needed to find someone else, and suddenly it hit me—Vince! He was my assistant chef, a well-built, dark, and very handsome boy, about twenty-five and quite macho looking, as opposed to Jess.

"Rudolf who?" Vince replied when he heard the name.

"Rudolf Nureyev, the ballet dancer."

That still didn't ring any bells. I told Vince that all he'd have to do is go with Tony and be in the same room during the massage.

"And I get paid for this?"

"Real well," I said.

Vince went off with Tony, and I went on to get ready for that night's show.

The Saturday night show would prove to be a real tearjerker. After an opening act featuring Jane Olivor, a rising young singer who was the Continental's answer to Edith Piaf, the great Lillian Roth then took the stage.

Lillian was a small dark-haired, kind of medium-built lady with intense charisma and verve. Much of her life and art paralleled that of the great Judy Garland. Aside from her fabulous career, Lillian was now immortalized in a major motion picture, *I'll Cry Tomorrow*, starring Susan Hayward. The boys at the Baths identified with her longtime struggle with alcoholism, and they had cheered her from the moment she walked onstage till long after the last note had faded away.

So busy was I with the show that I never even noticed that Vince hadn't returned. It wasn't his shift till Sunday afternoon, so I didn't give it a thought although he usually stayed for the show. Vince was also a kind of hi-fi and TV freak and had one of the first video cameras. With my permission, he was building a library of the Continental shows and had captured Bette's final performance at the Baths, which I have recently seen on a commercial video, although how it got there I do not know.

I was seeing the last few disco dancers out and welcoming the Sunday morning shift when I felt a tap on my shoulder. Turning around, I could see no one. And then, as if by magic, Nureyev appeared in front of me, towel beclad and smiling, surely a major event.

"Mr. Ostrow."

"Steve, please, Rudy."

"Okay, then. Steve," he said in his Russian-inflected voice. "I want to thank you for the most wonderful evening. That boy, Vince! He was fabulous. Could you send him to my hotel room again tonight?"

I said that Vince was supposed to work a shift at the restaurant.

"I will pay double for his replacement," Rudy said.

I assured him that that wouldn't be necessary, that I'd find someone.

"Thank you," he said and disappeared into the vapors. Or so I thought.

Suddenly he reappeared out of nowhere, like an apparition. But by now I was getting used to this. "Steve, I want you to be my guest at the ballet when I dance Romeo again tomorrow night."

"Why, thank you, Rudy, I would be honored."

He promised to leave a ticket in my name at the box office. Then he asked, "What are you going to do this rainy afternoon?"

"Oh, Sunday afternoons I usually spend with my wife and kids."

"Oh . . . well, I thought maybe you and I could go to a movie together."

Here was one of the most famous entertainers in the world, a man who had just played to four thousand screaming idol worshippers the night before. And now it was the morning after, and he was a mere mortal, alone in a city of millions. I have never forgotten how sad I felt for him then.

"Can you tell me," he asked, "are there any good porno movies in town?"

I went to get the gay papers to check for him, but by the time I had returned, he was gone. Someone had probably caught his fancy, and I was sure it wasn't Juliet.

Just as promised, there was a ticket awaiting me at the box office when I arrived at Lincoln Center. The new complex was indeed beautiful, and the magnificent Chagall murals flanking the entrance were strikingly highlighted. The alfresco restaurants and coffeehouses giving a new dimension to what had been a dreary collection of West Side derelict buildings.

The old Met, on Thirty-ninth Street and Broadway, had been a landmark both for the city and in my life. My brother Marshal and I had spent countless evenings together in the standing room section hearing the likes of Milanov, Bjoerling, Merrill, Del Monico, Peerce, Pinza, and countless others who never made the transition to the new house. The richness and warmth of the old Met would never be duplicated.

But the new arts center, a four-block cultural oasis located between Sixty-second Street and Sixty-sixth Street west of Broadway, gathered together the New York City Opera, the New York City Ballet, the New York Philharmonic, the Drama Theater, and the Metropolitan Opera, all in close proximity, linked to one another by beautifully landscaped promenades.

With these golden memories flowing through my consciousness, I sat back in my seat, anticipating the experience of seeing Nureyev as Romeo. The evening was to be even more special as the Juliet that night was to be none other than Dame Margot Fonteyn. Admittedly she was not thirteen years old—as Juliet had been—but once she started dancing, I would dare anyone to challenge the image she conjured of fervent youth and desire.

The audience itself radiated glamour and style. One could always tell the difference between an opera audience and a ballet audience: the former was primarily made up of white-haired septuagenarian matriarchs, sometimes reluctantly accompanied by slumbering seniles; the latter, ballet sycophants and aspirants, flouting the latest fashions of their trendy designers.

A hush fell over the audience when the conductor in the pit raised his baton to commence the overture. But before Prokofiev's music flooded the house, my gaze fixed on a solitary figure in a parterre box, stage right, usually reserved for royalty and the like. There, perfectly coiffed and handsomely tuxedoed, with a white contrasting bow tie, was none other than Vince, my assistant chef.

Well, who the hell is watching the store? was all I could think. Vince always worked on Saturday night.

The dazzle of the first act, the brilliance of the fight scene, the poignancy of the young lovers—all wove their spell in an evening of sheer magic. Nureyev was a vital force that had not been seen since Nijinsky. He was the embodiment of everything that is sexual, sensual, and visceral, taunting the forces of gravity with that magnificent twisted smile.

And Fonteyn! Well, she flowed. She was liquid; she was limpid; she was girl; she was woman. She took life from Nureyev's ardor as Eve had done from Adam.

And then to the last act, the final scene where Romeo, thinking Juliet dead, gathers her up and carries her from one side of the stage to the other. Nureyev's face was a portrait of pathos and utter, utter tragedy. As he literally dragged the seemingly lifeless body of Juliet across the stage, her feet dragging, I have never experienced an expression of such urgency and yearning as Rudy manifested. Even Romeo's futile death by his own hand came as an anticlimax to what we had already witnessed.

I gave up counting how many bows were taken at the final curtain. Still shaken by the experience, I almost didn't hear my name being called as I walked through the lobby.

"Steve, how did you like it?" There, looking like Robin in cape and costume, was Vince. I'd almost bumped into him, so engrossed in my thoughts was I. "He and the old lady dance pretty good together, don't they?"

"Yeah," I said. "Maybe I should book them into the Continental. By the way, who's working your shift tonight?"

"Oh, didn't Joey tell you?"

"Tell me what?"

"I quit."

"You quit? Just like that? Why?"

"Well, Rudy has hired me as his personal secretary, and he's taking me on a world tour for one year right after these performances are finished."

"That's great, Vince," I said glumly. But really, I was happy for both of them. "You *will* drop me a postcard, won't you?"

"Sure, Steve," he said and then with a wink, "as soon as I learn how to write."

Postlude

That night, Rudy came back to the Baths to swim and sin. Not even the macho Vince could clip his wings. Catching him by the disco floor as he surveyed the scene, I grabbed his hand, more to hold on to him than anything else. I didn't want him to pull his disappearing act again, at least not yet.

"Rudy, thank you for tonight. It was a magnificent experience."

"Oh, so you liked it, yes?"

"No, Rudy, I didn't like it. I loved it. But please, you must tell me one thing."

"What is that?"

"When you were dragging Juliet from one side of the stage to the other, your expression was so intense, so tragic. What was going on in your mind while you were doing that?"

"Oh well, I was thinking how hungry I was and how soon I could get off the stage and go for dinner."

I stood there, my eyes tearing from laughter, my hand grasping his. At least that's what I thought, till I looked and could see . . . he was gone.

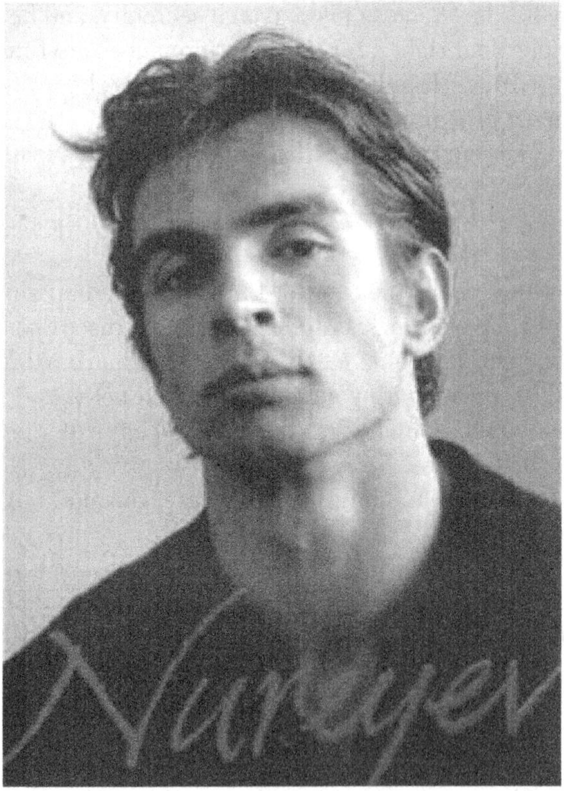
Nureyev

Chapter 28

Fire!

The fire came out of nowhere. Jess, his friend Gary, and I were sitting in the music room of 14177. We were having a late coffee—or at least, I was. The two boys were smoking a joint and doing in a bottle of Nuits St. Georges. From the enormous bay windows, we could see all of Broadway, from Seventy-fourth Street down to Times Square and beyond. It was a clear starlit night with the Great White Way competing with the galaxies, a blend of heaven and earth, with one fusing into the other.

But as I was admiring the beauty of the evening, a thick, viscous cloud began to block out my view. *Must be a storm brewing,* I thought. But no, the cloud was rising from *below* the windows toward the sky. And then all hell broke loose. An alarm bell went off in the hotel, and the shrieks of fire engines could be heard piercing the night.

"Hey," I yelled, pointing out the window, "that's no cloud. That's smoke! Come on, guys, there's a fire in the building."

All the elevators had been shut down, so by the time we made it down fourteen flights of stairs to the street, there were hundreds of residents bustling around in disarray. Looking up now at the building, we could see copious smoke and tongues of flame shooting out of the second-story windows.

"Shit, that's the top floor of the Baths!" I screamed, grabbing on to Jess and Gary.

"Yeah," Jess said, looking at the flames with a glazed expression. "Aren't the colors pretty . . . all that red and orange and yellow."

I could see that they would be of no help, so I ran into the building alone. The firemen were everywhere by now, putting up ladders and rolling out hoses.

"Hey, where are you going?" one of the firemen yelled, stopping me.

"That's my club that's on fire," I said.

"Well, you can't go in till we get the fire out."

No sense arguing with him, I thought, and ran around to our Seventy-fourth Street entrance on the ground floor.

"What's going on?" I yelled to Joey, who was at the desk giving instructions over the PA system.

"Fire on the second floor, Steve, in the room area. I got all the guys down by the pool." And sure enough, downstairs were two to three hundred of our towelled patrons, all stacked in the pool should the fire come their way. Thank God it wasn't a show night. I ran up to our second floor, but the water from the fire hoses coming in through the windows prevented me from going any further.

"Did everyone get out from the upstairs area?" I screamed to Joe.

"Far as I know," he said in his usual cool manner.

It was three in the morning before the fire was completely out and the firemen let me upstairs. Fortunately the fire had been contained in one area of about forty rooms. All of the cubicles were steel and survived, but the walls and ceiling of the building were a soggy, charred mess, and the chemical smell of burnt foam from the mattresses was overpowering.

"Was anybody injured?" I asked the fire captain, who was cordoning off the area.

"No firemen," he said.

"Thanks. What about patrons?"

"None that we could find."

Reassured, I went back down to the pool area. The huddled masses looked like Israelites foraging through the Red Sea.

"Okay, guys," I announced, "you can come out now. Joe, coffee and cake for everyone, on the house."

God must have blessed his wayward flock, for no one was hurt. But all that night, I had to solace those sad customers who made their home at the Baths. "Where will we live?" they asked. I had never fully realized how important the Baths were as a home for the lost and exiled of our clan, for whom no family existed.

Much as the young and hopeful of the theater world would pilgrimage to Hollywood, so did the lonely and outcast come to the Continental as the gay mecca of the world. For them, the bastions of the Baths provided a haven from the persecution and ridicule they had experienced in rural America. *Midnight Cowboy*, with Jon Voight and Dustin Hoffman, one of the first mainstream films with homoerotic overtones, poignantly depicted this forlornness and estrangement.

With the fire out and the panic over, I called Eric Marks, my contractor, at 4:00 AM, waking him up.

"I'll be there with a crew first thing in the morning," he muttered in between yawns.

At 8:00 AM, Eric and a dozen construction workers stormed the Baths; and believe it or not, by the 4:00 PM shift, we were cleaned, painted, and refitted, with business as usual. What could have been a catastrophe had only brought us much closer together.

Chapter 29

The Golden Girl

After all his years in show business, Ted Hook, my PR man, was still starstruck. Ted was always enthusiastic; in fact, he was a bundle of unbridled energy and optimism. He loved show business, every aspect of it. He had started out as a chorus boy and had hoofed his way through dozens of musicals, never achieving any great acclaim but always doing a committed and fully professional job. But now his terpsichorean days were over, so he was thrilled when he got the chance to bring Gladys Knight and the Pips to the Baths. They were doing a Saturday night show at the Plaza, and afterward they would head uptown to do a one-night late show gig for us. Ted wanted to do a big ad in the gay press and also in the *Advocate*, but I vetoed his plan. I didn't want to build our room on star names, preferring to have people think that there was *always* something good going on at the Continental. But Ted kept begging, excited as he was at the idea of booking Gladys Knight, until I finally relented and let him run a teaser saying, "Fabulous Mystery Guest this Saturday night at the Baths."

"Well, if that's what you want, I'll do it," Ted said, picking up the telephone. "But we're missing a big opportunity to cash in on her name."

It had been a strange week. Barry Cross, my old-time martinet from the Beneficial Finance days, was now running the club bar for me; but he had not been seen all week. All my calls to his house were unanswered. Barry was a very meticulous man when it came to business and appointments, so I feared that something really radical was wrong.

I was doubly worried because Barry had been losing his cutting edge over the past few months. When I tried to draw him out to get at his problem, he would just shrug me off. Finally he confided to me that he had overplayed his hand on a gambling spree and as a result had built up a large debit account with some rather unsavory characters. I had offered him some money; but Barry, being very proud and independent, merely said, "Thanks, kid, but no thanks. I'll work it out."

I hadn't thought much more about it until he failed to show up at the bar. Alarmed, I grabbed a cab and went to Barry's hotel apartment, on the east side of Manhattan. As soon as I saw the ambulance in front of his building, I knew the worst had happened. The cleaning lady had found Barry's dead body that very afternoon. The ambulance driver said he had apparently died from a massive heart attack, and the next day, the coroner's report mentioned that two men had been seen leaving Barry's apartment the day he was found. There was no question in my mind that they had been collectors and that Barry, unable to pay, had died of the fright at whatever punishment they had threatened.

I felt awful. Barry had been a longtime friend, and I would have done almost anything to help him. In the end, it was his pride that killed him.

So that Saturday night, I was looking forward to a big show to take everyone's mind off the tragedy. The *surprise guest* announcement was packing the house. Before I got dressed for my emcee role, I checked as always to see that all the night's acts were on board.

"How we doing, Ted?" I said, seeing him in the dressing room.

"Well, the band's all here."

"Yeah."

"And the lighting crew."

"Yeah."

"And the DJ is ready."

"What are you trying to tell me, Ted?"

"Gladys."

"What about Gladys?" I could always tell when Ted was hedging. Usually he'd be talking in run-on sentences. Something had to be wrong for Ted to be taciturn.

"Well, no one has seen her, and she left her Plaza gig over an hour ago."

"Shit . . . call her manager."

"I did, but there's no answer."

"Well, call *her*." By now I was starting to steam. It was twenty minutes to showtime, and people were already in their seats.

Ted looked at me sheepishly. "I don't have her number, and there's no listing for her. I already tried."

"Okay, Mr. Hook. You better get on that stage and do a soft shoe till I figure out something to do." Ted often warmed up the audience before the show started and then would introduce me as "Mr. Continental."

Back in the office, I racked my brain. In all these years, I had never had an entertainer not show up. But tonight it looked like the unthinkable was happening.

Acting on a sudden impulse, I picked up the phone. "Plaza Hotel? Can you please connect me to Gladys Knight's room?"

"And who shall I say is calling?" So . . . she *is* staying at the Plaza. Why the hell not? We should have thought of that first thing.

"Her manager," I said. She would certainly talk to him.

"Hi, hon, what's up?" came the silky, sultry voice. "I'm in the bath."

"What's up is that this is Steve Ostrow of the Continental Baths. I believe we had a deal for you to be on our stage right now."

"Oh yeah . . . my manager told me something about that. But listen, honey, I'm just *toooo* tired, and this is the only bath I'm gonna be in tonight."

I could have sworn I heard a splash, but before I could even say, "Well, what about the Pips?" The phone went dead in my hands.

Cursing, I got dressed, racking my brain for a way to salvage the evening for the huge crowd that awaited our mystery guest.

"Yes, ladies and gentlemen, it's going to be a great night here at the Continental." I could hear Ted's voice through the office speakers. Showtime had arrived, but not our Gladys, and Ted had started his warm-up.

I knew we had a few moments as Ted loved to ham it up and then talk about all the acts that we had planned for the rest of the month. He always cased the audience beforehand and would take great pleasure in pointing out stars and celebrities.

I hurried down to the show area.

"And last but not least, we're thrilled tonight to have with us in the audience . . . the one, the only . . . Freda Payne, the Golden Girl!" Applause, stamping, whistling.

"Freda," Ted continued, "please stand up and take a bow!"

"Come on, Ted," I said, now on the stage and grabbing the mike from his startled grasp. "Freda is too beautiful just to take a bow. Let's get her up here for everyone to see."

Freda Payne was the Whitney Houston of the seventies, with a solid gold hit record and the number one song on the disco charts, "Band of Gold." Flashing a bemused but luscious smile, Freda started the walk to the stage.

Throwing the mike back to Ted, I jumped down into the audience and chivalrously escorted her up the stairs à la the Oscars. The applause for this dazzling lady, dressed in a tight-fitting number with sequins and rhinestones for days, would not let up.

Once on stage, I grabbed the mike again from Ted. "Well, guys, are we gonna let Freda go without singing her hit song?" The thunder of bare feet stomping the floor and the screams, whistles, and hoots gave the good lady no choice. "We *do* pay, you know," I whispered as I nuzzled her ear.

"Well, I do have my professional standing."

"You're on, lady, go for it."

The night was a fabulous success. Freda sang her top chart numbers, and afterward we played Freda's dance album right through to morning. And guess who were the last two on the dance floor?

We must have made quite a couple, Freda and I. She in her sequined silver gown and me in my one-piece white jumpsuit with gold chains galore, the iridescent disco lights glinting off our gyrating bodies and the gathering clientele forming a circle around us while in the background sylvan bodies of all sexes slipped in and out of the deep blue pool. Fellini at his best could not have improved on this scene, that very special Saturday night at the Baths.

* * *

Not only had Freda saved the show, but she captured my heart that magical night. When the Continental lights were flickering on and off, the signal for all those not in towels to exit, I asked if I could escort my elegant dance partner home.

"Why, that would be very chivalrous of you, Mr. Ostrow," Freda said. "You must be a throwback to another era."

"No, I just know a lady when I see one."

I signaled Scotti and told him to have a stretch limo at the entrance in fifteen minutes. Scotti was a gem. Not only was the limo awaiting us, but as we entered the rear compartment, we found an ice bucket chilling my favorite champagne, Dom Perignon, and a large crystal bowl of glistening beluga caviar, garnished with lemon wedges.

"Where to, madam?" I asked as I popped the cork.

"Well, I'm staying at my manager's apartment just on East Eighty-sixth Street . . . hardly far enough for us to properly enjoy all this."

"I totally agree. Driver, take us for a ride in the park . . . a long ride."

As we shared the champagne and caviar, Freda told me her sad story, being brought up in poverty in the Deep South, where her grandparents had been slaves. She was raised to be a good Baptist girl under the strict guidance of her parents. She said she was never really comfortable with all the success and preferred her hometown to the big city.

Freda was going through a very hurtful time. She had become infatuated with the debonair Omar Sharif, and they had had a whirlwind jet-set romance, which had taken them to Monte Carlo.

Omar, she said, was an inveterate gambler. Once in a casino, he would pay her no attention. She soon tired of this and left, brokenhearted. I could now see why she appreciated my being gallantly old fashioned. Freda was a romantic, as I am.

After we finished the food and drink, we continued to circle Central Park, watching the city come to life slowly of a Sunday morning. This lovely woman was now in my arms. We made love to each other through our eyes, our hearts, and our body contact. Here was a sensuous and warm human being sharing her body and soul with me.

The sun was fully up by the time I showed her home. Morning had come in all its verdant glory. The bells from the city cathedrals competing with each other for attention, but it was the sweet singing of the birds in the park that orchestrated our rhapsody.

"Thank you, Steve," the gracious lady said as I opened the car door for her. "May I see you again?"

"Please. I'd love that." And then she disappeared into the canopied East Side residence in the charge of a liveried doorman.

* * *

Freda and I had met at the right time, and I became her gentleman escort in New York. We did all the trendy discos: the Tenth Floor, the Garage, the Loft, Hollywood, Les Jardins. Yet the best times were when we were just by ourselves, picnicking in the park, quiet dinners in intimate restaurants, and—the highlight of it all—the Central Park horse and buggy ride, when we were like two little kids.

But Freda was yearning for a complete relationship. She had been brought up with traditional Baptist values and was still a very proper lady.

We hugged, we necked, we kissed, and we loved; but Freda's virtues were never compromised. Freda wanted a husband, a family, and children, even more than a career. I respected her for this; and knowing that I would never divorce Joanne, our relationship had a beginning, a middle, and sadly, an ending. And all in three weeks.

The Golden Girl left as she had arrived, still shining and untarnished. But perhaps with an even deeper glow.

Chapter 30

The Ritz Continental

With the tremendous influx of gay yuppies being spawned by the in society, I upgraded the Baths to rival any five-star hotel. Well, let's say that we were at least a five-star baths. After all, we were housed in what was considered to be the second most famous building on the Upper West Side after the Dakota, described by many as the city's most European building. Built by Graves and Duboy for builder William Earle Dodge Stokes, the two-thousand-five-hundred-room building, erected between 1899 and 1904, had been home to the likes of opera stars Geraldine Farrar, Feodor Chaliapin (in 14177, no less!), Lauritz Melchior (who practiced archery in the one-hundred-ten-foot corridors), and Ezio Pinza; musicians Arturo Toscanini, Igor Stravinsky, Mischa Elman, and Yehudi Menuhin; impresarios Florenz Ziegfeld and Saul Hurok; and a host of authors and artists, together with athletes Jack Dempsey and Babe Ruth, among others.

In his book *Upper West Side Story*, Peter Selwyn relates that Stokes, heir to the Phelps Dodge copper and manufacturing fortune, was determined to build the world's grandest hotel. On the lobby floor were an ornate ballroom, several cafés, a tearoom, a writing room, a palm court, and a lobby fountain with *live seals*. And in the basement—guess what? A Turkish bath and the world's then-largest indoor swimming pool. If Stokes could have only seen what good use we put those facilities to.

Having been so anointed, how could we fail to be the world's grandest bathhouse? To ensure our five-star rating and accommodate our international clientele, I installed such amenities as a beauty salon for men, an in-house library, a resident podiatrist, a travel agency, and a concierge station. We also became the first bath operation ever to accept credit cards, and indeed you could also buy one—to three—to six-month coupon membership books at a 10 percent discount. Up till then, no one would ever have dared leave their right name or credit card number at a bathhouse. Everybody always used aliases when they signed in during the raid era and indeed still do in some venues.

But the pièce de résistance was a small nondenominational chapel that we built for those who chose to meditate in between fornicating. Surprisingly it proved to be very popular, and it wasn't long before we had alternating clergy offering services on Sunday mornings. Not satisfied with our twenty-four-hour fast-food counter, I designated an area of the downstairs as a gourmet dining room, replete with Lutèce-type wicker chairs and glass-topped tables. Lush green ferns provided privacy, but not enough that you couldn't peek between and enjoy the continuous floor show of bathing beauties.

Bookings were essential for the Continental Room; and I offered the job of maître d' to, of all persons, Noel Cohen, Jess's past paramour. His Burt Reynolds persona, enhanced by a tuxedo, lent just the right air of elegance to the enclave.

The Baths was now at the height of its popularity, so much so that Levi Strauss and Wrangler competed to open a boutique in the club. One of our customers had just bought the Wrangler franchise for the Upper West Side, and so the Wrangler Continental Boutique was launched to great success.

With every convenience and everything done for you, except to wipe your—you were free to concentrate on your mission. And at the Continental, nothing was impossible, not even finding someone to do the above.

Chapter 31

Room Service

I had just bought a new red Cadillac Eldorado Biarritz convertible with white leather upholstery. Scotti, who tripled as houseboy in Fire Island and part-time personal secretary and chauffeur in New York, had taken delivery of the *vehicle* (not to be considered just a *car*) and, after putting it in the hotel garage, came to collect me for a run.

When we got to the garage, we were greeted by an empty space. The *vehicle* had gone for a run, but with someone else who obviously also appreciated its flashy looks. So much so that it had indeed been carnapped, a rather unusual occurrence in New York City in those days when crimes tended not to be petty. Armed robbery, assault, murder, and rape were the preferred order of the day.

The police put out an alarm, but the Biarritz was so spottable that whoever committed the dastardly deed deemed it more feasible to strip it down and sell off its parts. A week later it was found: stripped, burnt, and abandoned. Not unlike some other relationships I have been in, although at least in those I got to have a good ride along the way.

That day, Scotti and I were sitting by the pool commiserating over the *vehicle* and discussing the plans for a new type of show, one which would not feature stars but would be uniquely ours, almost a Continental stage show, cast with our own talent, original choreography, and music. The concept was exciting. Scotti was very much a Joel Grey sort of person, and we both had been very impressed with the hit show *Cabaret* and the film version.

Then as we conversed, it struck me. "Scotti, do you smell something awful? Or is it us?" I asked, pushing my seat back from the table.

"Whaddya mean, Steve?" Scotti said, big brown eyes kind of hurt under long silky eyelashes. "Oh no, you're right! It smells like shit!" he exclaimed, his nostrils now dilating.

"Shit would smell a lot better, I think. Let's check it out."

It was not unusual for one of our angel-dusted divas to plop in the pool or steam room and not even be aware.

"No, it's not from the pool, Steve," Scotti said as we investigated.

Following the scent like two hound dogs, we ended up near the new rooms we had built on the downstairs level for beachfront patrons. Door by door we sniffed, but the smell seemed to cover the whole area.

"Steve, look at this." I followed Scotti's gaze. The door to room 50 had no less than three overdue notices on it. We checked people in for eight hours, and then if they didn't reregister, we posted a notice on the door.

"Get Joey right away," I said. Joey was always calm in any emergency, but even he was flustered by the stench as he held his nose with one hand and tried to search out the master key with the other.

When we got the door open, we all just stared.

There, lying facedown on the steel bed was the fattest man we had ever seen. He was not only obese, he was obscene. The layers of flesh flowed untethered under the prone body, stretching to the floor by its own weight like sodden strands of spaghetti.

After a rudimentary but quite unnecessary check of the man's pulse, Joey said, "He's gone."

The pallor of the man's skin had already told us that. But it was the pool of vomit and excrement that was creating the stench. In all the years the Baths had been operating, we had never had a fatality, nor even a serious accident.

"Wait, what's this?" I said, spotting an open bottle on the floor with capsules spewn about.

"Probably uppers," said Scotti in a knowing tone that belied his age. "He probably OD'd on amphetamines on top of amyl."

"I don't think so," said Joey, looking closer at the bottle. "It's a prescription from a doctor—digitalis capsules."

"Shit—he had a heart attack," I said, thinking, *How inconvenient*. After all, it *was* Saturday, and soon it would be showtime.

"What do you want me to do, Steve," Joey asked, "call the police?"

I thought for a moment. Police! They would disrupt the whole evening, unless they just carted him out.

"Stay here until I call Barry. Don't let anyone know what's going on. No one."

"Yeah, Steve, what's up?" I was happy to hear Barry's laconic voice on the telephone.

"Some guy's dropped dead in his room—looks like a heart attack. What do I do?"

"Well, as your lawyer," Barry said drolly, "I can only tell you what you're supposed to do."

"And what's that?"

"Call the police."

"Yeah, I figured that out myself. And what will *they* do?"

"They'll cordon off the downstairs area, station police around the Baths, and wait for the coroner to arrive."

"How long does that take?"

"Well, let's see. It's Saturday . . . no later than Monday."

"What!"

"Unless it's an emergency, like a murder or something. They'd probably get him out quicker if you said you'd killed him. Coroners usually don't work on weekends."

"Thanks *a lot*, Barry. I'm really glad I called you."

"Have a good weekend, Steve. By the way, who's on tonight?" And I could hear the mirth in his voice. He of course knew I never listened to attorneys or accountants when it came to a business decision.

Now after all, the guy was dead, obviously of natural causes. There was nothing to be gained by losing the whole weekend with police in and out of the place, and surely they had better things to do in a big town like New York City. So, really, I rationalized, it boiled down to a simple business decision.

"Okay, Joey. Get a crew together. Don't disturb anything in the room, but seal it off. Get large sheets of plastic and cover the ceiling, the door, the walls—everything. Encase it all so the stink stays here."

"And then?"

"Evacuate the area and fumigate it. Move anybody in this section to the upstairs, and don't rent any rooms here for the weekend. Tell them we're renovating."

"What about the police?"

"We'll call them in the morning once we check people out. I'll tell them we just found him. Our friend won't mind, I'm sure."

And he didn't.

For months afterward, room 50 would never rent. Somehow the word had gotten out, as it always did. We finally solved the problem by demolishing the room and installing in its place an exercise bicycle with a little bronze plaque that said,

In memory of room 50

They also serve who merely die and wait

Chapter 32

Decadence

The idea of staging our own Continental show continued to captivate me. I wanted it to incorporate all the things that appealed to me artistically. I had built the Continental following my own instincts. Of course I did have a BA, but I'm sure it didn't stand for Bathhouse Administration.

The premise that I followed was, if I created an environment that was more beautiful than what existed outside—which was not hard to do in New York City—then people would want to be in that environment.

Having done that, I now wanted to fashion our own individual show that would express who we really were. A show that would go beyond drag and cabaret, bringing together music, dance, and the arts. Sure, we had developed and fostered many great original artists. But the idea of our own total concept show, now *that* was a new challenge.

I had written a poem called "Sonnet to a Prude," which had been published in the gay press and been received with great interest. Wouldn't it be fabulous now to have it set to music and choreographed!

The poem was inspired by an encounter I had had in Puerto Rico with a beautiful boy named Raies in the void between my relationship with Jorge and Jess. It opened with a prologue that tells it all and then proceeds to the sonnet.

> Because the skin was smooth, yet taut, because the tone was gold.
> Because the eyes were life and truth.
> Because he gave and wasn't bought.
> Because he was a boy, a youth.
> There is a surge of life and love that only is expressed.
> In naked, turgid, rigid strength that cannot be suppressed.

And if the tenderness beneath the trembling, burning need
Is softly stroked and cupped in hand
Then life will send its seed.

Sonnet to a Prude

You'll think of it as waste, you prude
You'll think of it as perversion
But don't forget, you've done it too
Except in your own version
There cannot be but mystery in what becomes of youth
It grows through joy and ecstasy in futile search for truth
And if, along the way, a man can show that he can care
And if, along that way, they stop to live and love and share
Then how can that be bad, my friend, and how can that be wrong?
Just 'cause you read it in the books and no one sings its song
Remember, God begot His one and only son, and Adam came
Upon this earth as man, yes, but human first
And Eve came later through his rib
Now is that any way to have a kid?
So nature had to stop and pause and find a better way
For Man and Woman to reproduce
And now, in later days
A man must with a woman be
To bring into this world
A someone who, if he loves me, you would consider soiled
But I take love from where it comes
And that's where I will go
And I will offer anyone
Me to get to know
So don't hold back
And don't attack
Just let whatever be
And maybe, you and I
Together
Can be
We
So laugh and jeer, you faceless prude
But just remember this:
You will have lived and loved and died
And know not Raies's kiss

I discussed the idea with Jess, who of course was aware of my Puerto Rican idyll. He thought it was a great idea and would love to choreograph it. He knew two fabulous dancers from the New York City Ballet: Vernon, an Adonis of a man, and Irene, a statuesque blonde Amazon. They would dance the parts of Adam and Eve.

Jess of course would dance the part of Raies, with one condition. He insisted that where it said, "And know not Raies's kiss," it would be changed to read, "And know not *Jess's* kiss."

Well, that seemed a small price to pay for a première danseuse, so we started to work in earnest.

The sonnet became part of our new concept show, which we called *Decadence*. The show would open to a bare stage, gold curtain drawn. Then Scotti would peek out from behind the curtain and burst onto the stage in a 1930s bizarre Berlin costume à la cabaret, complete with face makeup and rhinestone-studded walking stick.

After captivating the audience with a dance routine combining grace with grotesquerie, he would announce the beginning of the "new era of decadence." The curtain would then go up, revealing Jess's prone body on the stage, dimly lit.

I would then be fixed with a spotlight, and in full tux would recite the sonnet. The strains of *Pachebel* were the cue for Jess to rise and begin the dance.

The sonnet was greeted with a standing ovation. The show continued with Jane Olivor doing a vignette of Edith Piaf songs as only she could, very much in the French tradition but in a piquant style that made her appear fragile and vulnerable, where Piaf was earthy and gutsy.

Then eight members of the American Ballet corps in dance briefs performed an American Indian tribal ritual in which a young American Indian man is sodomized by a warrior as an indoctrination while the rest of the tribe dance around them.

This was followed by Caleb Stone *being* Judy Garland and our own Pedro doing his Carmen Miranda bit with a fruit salad on his head. A full company musical revue finished the entire performance, everyone staying in their original character and costume.

The crowds became as large as any that Bette had commanded. Michael Giametta from *Michael's Thing* and the theater editor from the *Advocate* loved it; but I wasn't prepared for the rave reviews of the sonnet in the straight press, for this "highly original, homoerotic interpretation of an age-old theme executed with great sensitivity and style," as Rex Reed of the *New York Daily News* put it.

PBS (Public Broadcasting Station) asked to do a documentary on the show and then video the performance. I entertained the idea but, wanting to keep the mystique of the Baths intact, rejected the request. There were other obstacles too: Jess and the ballet dancers didn't want to come "out" on public TV, and of course, there was the sanctity of our own patrons' identities to be considered.

And so, after a run of about six months, *Decadence* became history.

* * *

Soon I was involved in brokering a different kind of decadence, not for myself but for Bette. Barry Slotnick had just been elected president of the board of directors of the Westchester Premier Theater. He wanted to launch the premier season with a major star to set a tone that would attract other artists to play the theater.

"How about Isaac Stern?" I suggested.

"That's just the thing. Most people think that because we're in Westchester, we're old fuddy-duddies. We don't want to compete with Carnegie Hall. We want a broad type of entertainment."

"So who're you after?"

"Bette Midler."

"Well, you certainly picked the right broad. Go for it."

Barry went on to explain that they wanted her for eleven shows over a ten-day period. The theater held three thousand five hundred people, and the ticket price was to be $20. But Aaron Russo, Bette's manager, wouldn't even consider their offer, saying that she was too busy working on filming *The Rose*. So Barry wanted me to talk to Bette, though I told him that I hadn't spoken to her in months. He begged me to give it a try, promising me 10 percent of the fee if I signed her on.

I never wanted to be anybody's agent or manager, least of all Bette's. But I couldn't really turn Barry down. Still, I had to know what I was getting Bette into, so I told him, "I've got to see the theater first. You may have to put in a steam room."

"Let's have dinner tonight at the theater restaurant," he said. "They make great steaks. Bring Joanne."

"Who's footing the bill?" I asked.

"The theater, of course."

"Oh, good. I'll be very hungry, and you know I only drink Château Lafite Rothschild 1959."

After dining with the board of directors, a real stuffy lot, Barry and I left the girls while we took a tour of the theater. It had an immense parking lot and two restaurants, one formal, one casual. The theater itself was rather mundane, having no particular charm other than it was very wide, almost like a stadium in design—surely not an intimate showplace. I did a fast check of the sight lines in the theater, looked over the tech equipment: lights, sound, stage machinery, and checked out the dressing rooms. It seemed well equipped. Then my eyes fell on the candy counter, which featured the usual sweets *and* a huge machine that spewed out fresh buttered popcorn.

"Well, it's certainly not the Tubs, but we'll see what we can do." I said.

"Then you'll talk to Bette?" Barry said hopefully.

"You Bette," was my flippant reply. "But she won't come cheap. She's just finished Mr. Kelly's in Chicago, Carnegie Hall, and she's on her way to the Palace. The only way I can talk her into making a detour to this dump is to call on our friendship . . . and guarantee her big bucks. Do you want her that bad?"

"Let's put it this way. I've kinda . . . given my word that we can get her."

"Well, you know her theme song," I reminded him. "Well, you've got to have fri-e-e-ends."

Bette's house on Barrow Street in Greenwich Village was quaint and old fashioned, much like her idea of couture in those days. As I pressed the bell, I couldn't help laughing at the remark she made when I called her: "Steve, you're not going to ask me to go back to the Tubs, are you? You know I'm really a nice Jewish girl from Hawaii."

Bette had only recently moved from the Upper West Side, where she had flatted on West Seventy-fourth Street with her friend Michael Federal, a bass guitar player.

"How do you like the house?' she asked me. "Some people go up in the world, and I came down. Next stop: the Bowery."

But it was obvious that she loved the place, and it was to be her New York home for many years.

"Well, babe," I said, giving her a big hug after stumbling over a spaced-out body clutching a guitar, "it reminds me of Grandma."

"Grandma. Who?"

"Grandma Moses. Very original," I said, noticing the eclectic paintings and hangings on the walls.

"Okay, what brings you to the classy part of town? You're a West Side derelict."

"You, my dear."

"Oh, Stephen! You've gone straight! And just when I was beginning to feel safe with you!"

Briefly I ran through the proposition while Bette poured lemonade, the hardest drink in the house. It wasn't an easy sell. "Why would I wanna sing in Westchester for some old grey-haired farts and their fat wives?" she asked.

I was winging it now.

"'Cause I asked you to. And because I can swing a great deal."

"What's the great deal? Remember, I'm a career girl now."

"How about a hundred percent of the gross ticket take? That's $577,500, on a sold-out house."

"You're kidding! You're nuts! Who's gonna agree to that?"

"The grey-haired old farts."
"Am I *that* good?"
"No, but they think you are."
"Can you swing it?"
"If you say yes."
"How?"
"I'll leave them with the parking lot, the concessions, the vending machines, the liquor . . . oh, and the popcorn."

* * *

"You're out of your mind," Barry protested as soon as I told him of the offer.
"No, Barry, *you're* out $577,500. But think of all the popcorn you can sell."
"I'll run it by them."
"Great! Oh, by the way, we're going to need a few perks to seal the deal."
"She wants a Mercedes-Benz like Janis Joplin?"
"Yeah, but only for the gig. You can have it back after that. But make it a stretch, with a twenty-four hour chauffeur."
"Anything else while you're hallucinating?"
"Yeah, a suite in the Westchester Hilton for Bette and her entourage."
"Can we have that back after the gig too?"
"That's negotiable. After all, we don't want to be unreasonable."
But the board of directors accepted the terms.
The run was a complete sellout. Bette, being the shrewd businesswoman she really is, took out a full-page ad in the *New York Times*. It cost ten grand, but the entire house sold out in a day. She made a bundle; the grey-haired old farts had the time of their lives, with Bette heckling them mercilessly each night; the theater was firmly put on the map, and they bonanza-ed out on the money from the concessions.
"Nice going, Steve, you made me look real good," a smiling Barry said as he handed me a cheque for my fee. "I don't know how you did it."
"Ah, Mr. Slotnick," I said, pocketing the cheque, "you must never underestimate the power of popcorn."

Chapter 33

Queen for a Day

One day I received a call from a young girl who said she was the niece of a lady who was a fabulous talent and that I should audition her. I said I would be glad to. "Send her down in the afternoon."

The girl then said that her aunt hadn't left her room in weeks and almost never went out.

"Why is that?" I asked.

"Because she's too fat," was the reply.

I was kind of intrigued and told the girl that I would taxi up to see her aunt the next day. As it turned out, the address the girl gave me was in upper Harlem, so I had the taxi driver wait for me while I ran up six flights of rickety stairs to see this wonder.

And a wonder she was. Reclining on a mattress from which she never got up while I was there, the lady in question almost filled the entire ten-by-ten-feet room.

"And what is your name?" I asked.

"Queen Yanna," she answered in a rich, deep voice.

"I understand you're a great singer, and I'd love to hear you."

"Hmm," she replied. And then, without getting up, obviously a major event, she took off into a medley of blues, jazz, and gospel that ran the gamut from Ella to Sarah to Mahalia herself. I was floored. Well, she was too, so we were even.

I invited her to open the show that Saturday as we were having Tiny Tim as the star attraction, and it would be a great combination. She was very grateful, and we discussed logistics. I would have a car pick her up, and she would have her whole family do the same.

Somehow it all came off. Once we got her on stage, in an upright position, she was an epic. She wore a jacket of bright yellow brocade over a black tent dress. And on her head perched a virtual crown, in keeping with her regal status.

"And now, ladies and gentlemen, Queen Yanna!" I announced.

Well, she mesmerized the audience, her pealing tones cascading off the concrete walls. The crowd wouldn't let her go, and I was getting a bit apprehensive as Tiny Tim was pacing backstage. And then the unthinkable happened.

Queenie threw a furtive look to me backstage and then grimaced. I just stared in disbelief. Having been on too long, she had defecated right on to the stage. Now we're not talking delicate turds here; we're talking big time. Luckily the dress hid all from view except from those on stage level, like me.

Yelling to Pinkie and Cheryl, my two lesbian stage managers, I said, "Bring the curtain down *now*!" We three then managed to get Her Highness off the stage and on to a proper throne. The crowd was still stomping their feet, but I really didn't think we needed an encore.

A quick cleanup, and Tiny Tim finally took the stage. He tiptoed through the tulips—quite a feat, considering—but no amount of his prancing and whistling could enchant the audience. He was a caricature, and they had just had an audience with a real queen.

Queen Yanna returned triumphantly on many more occasions, proving that even regal bugles blow.

Chapter 34

Stuttgart

For the closing performance of *Decadence*, from whatever motive of artistic integrity that persuaded him, Jess told me to give the sonnet its original ending: "But you will have lived and loved and died / And know not *Raies's* kiss."

As he ran off the stage that night, still clad only in his G-string, a good-looking blond man of regal bearing came up to him and, taking off his sable coat, enveloped Jess in it. We were all sort of stunned. The man after all was Prince Egon von Furstenberg, who was a well-known patron of the arts and the Baths.

On a previous occasion many months before, Egon had professed his attraction to me, of all people, and had asked me to consider becoming his lover. I had attributed that to his being intoxicated or high—whether he was or not, I don't know—and never thought any more about it. So I was even more taken aback by his dramatic gesture to Jess as, after all, we bore no resemblance to each other.

Anyhow the prince disappeared with Cinderella for the evening, having found the perfect fit for his sable, or the perfect sable for his stable.

Surprisingly Jess was there in bed when I awoke the next morning.

"How do you like royalty?" I asked.

"It can be a pain in the butt," he replied. "But look what becomes a legend most!" as he lolled in his newly acquired fur. Sadly the legend didn't last for long as, four nights later, the fairy prince asked for his coat back.

* * *

Jess's role in *Decadence* had made him a celebrity. The great Bob Fosse himself had come over to me after one of the performances to say, "That boy could become a star. Tell him what I said."

It was obvious that Jess was born to dance.

I had seen a notice in the *Times* saying that John Cranko, the artistic director of the Stuttgart Ballet, would be auditioning young dancers for entrance into the company's prestigious ballet school. Cranko was renowned for having made the Stuttgart Ballet into one of the world's finest and most acclaimed ballet companies. His settings of both classical and modern ballet, but especially the traditional story ballets, had revolutionized the dance world.

I encouraged Jess to audition for Cranko, with mixed feelings, of course. The thought of Jess being away was scary, yet I knew that the drug scene and the party life of New York would always be too tempting and would eventually destroy him. When he was accepted, I rejoiced—one of us was going to have his dream become a reality.

The school provided food and accommodation and was subsidized by the German government. It was a brilliant opportunity as graduates were eagerly sought by major ballet companies as well as having a toehold in the Stuttgart Ballet.

All Jess would need was spending money, and money for dance clothes and gear. I set up an international account for Jess where he would receive $50 a week automatically while he was in school. We packed him up and kitted him out and then put him on a Lufthansa flight to Stuttgart from JFK.

* * *

In his first weeks away, Jess had sent only a few vague letters, so I was surprised one day to hear that he was on the line from Stuttgart—collect, of course.

"I want to come home," he told me.

To begin with, he explained, the school was very strict, like a monastery. Most of the kids in the school were younger than Jess and were European. His only friend was George Bailey, the dance repetiteur, whose aunt Hattie McDaniel had played Mamie, the maid in *Gone with the Wind*.

"I'm just not cut out to lead this kind of life," he said. "Up at five thirty, in bed, lights out, by nine. You know me, I'm just the other way around. Can I come home?"

"Look, stick it out another week. I'll grab a plane and come visit you . . . would that help?"

"Yeah . . . I guess. Can you bring me some dope?"

So that was it. "No," I said. "But I'll bring a bottle of Château Margaux."

"Okay, I'll get the cheese." And as ever, I took the bait.

* * *

I would return to Stuttgart three times during the year that Jess was there. Being an opera singer as well as Mr. Continental, I was readily welcomed into the artistic set. One of my great disappointments, however, was that John Cranko had tragically perished in a plane crash just before Jess arrived in Stuttgart. I did however get to meet Glen Tetley, the new head of the ballet, as well as Richard Cragun and Marcia Haydee, the company's two premier dancers who were having a tumultuous love affair. Marcia eventually took over the company, and Richard took on a male lover, so there was much drama going on both and off the stage.

But the highlight for me was to see the Stuttgart Ballet Company perform the modern works of the great avant-garde French choreographer Maurice Béjart. His use of the dancer's body in a new way that combined the classical with the abstract was electrifying to watch, and the Stuttgart Ballet Company was spurred on to even greater heights by his inventiveness.

Béjart, his male companion, George Bailey, and I were enjoying an afternoon coffee in the garden cafe of the Schlossgarten when the subject of *Death in Venice* came up in conversation. We had all seen the film, based on the short story by Thomas Mann, and I was saying how the boy who'd played Tadzio, the object of von Aschenbach's obsession, had entranced me.

"You know, of course, that Visconti had searched the whole world to find such a beauty," Béjart said.

"Yes, but whatever happened to him? I've never seen him in anything since the film was made," I said wistfully.

"Well, I have," Béjart replied.

"Where? When?" I demanded.

"In a plaza in Athens, a known pickup spot for rent boys."

Béjart went on to explain that the boy, whose real name was Bjorn Anderson, was found by Visconti on a farm in Denmark. He had no dramatic training and never spoke a single word in the film, while Visconti just shot the whole film around him, like a tone poem. The most beautiful boy anyone had ever seen, he was a total innocent. But during the shooting of the film, for which he was paid a pittance, he got caught up in Visconti's world. By the time the film was over, he had developed a drug habit, but there was no more money coming in to support it.

"Yeah, but what happened when you saw him in the square in Athens?" George pressed. "Because, honey, I've been to that square, and I never did see the likes of *him*."

"Well, I actually took the boy home," Béjart continued, relishing our fascination.

"And?" we all said in unison.

"And . . . nothing happened."

Stunned silence from all of us.

"Oh, it wasn't that I didn't want it to. You see, the boy was so drugged out that it would have taken someone twenty-four hours a day, seven days a week, to bring him back to life. All I could do was stuff some money in his pocket and take him back to the square."

"That's all?" we chirped.

"Well, I must admit, I did give him a bath first. After all, one must be kind in these matters . . ."

Béjart's story heightened my fascination for the film, and while in Germany, I tried to obtain the rights to do an opera based on it at the Continental. I got as far as reaching Thomas Mann's widow, who advised me that she had already been approached. Benjamin Britten was negotiating with her and the Mann estate to present the opera at the next Aldeburgh Festival.

Disappointed but not thinking I would be in the running, I let it go. Years later, Britten's *Death in Venice* premiered at the Metropolitan Opera. It was a masterpiece.

Congratulations, Benjamin, but whatever *did* become of Bjorn Anderson?

Chapter 35

Legends

Starstruck as Ted Hook was, he was shocked when I told him about the legendary entertainer I wanted to bring to the Continental.

"But he's 100 percent straight, Steve!" Ted protested. "We've never had a totally straight man play the Baths before. And does *he* know what he's getting into?"

"Oh, I don't think he's *that* naïve, Ted. I mean, he's been around a long time."

"Too long, maybe," Ted retorted.

"Now, Ted, let's not be catty. He's a legend, and we should be proud that he's playing the Continental."

In fact, Cab Calloway was doing Cab Calloway when I was a little boy. He was famous for his fast-paced chit-chatter, the original rap artist before it got political. His "Minnie the Moocher" and "Za Zuh Zaz" were classics.

We had hosted many legendary female performers such as Margaret Whiting, Julie Wilson, Sarah Vaughn, Morgana King, and Lillian Roth, but never a male star of Cab's magnitude. He had just finished a stint on Broadway doing the *Bubbling Brown Sugar* show; and now he had one night free in New York, between a gig at the Palace, a cameo in the film *The Blues Brothers*, and a European tour.

The only problem was that we would have to use our own band: Barry, Joey, and the Continentals. *And* there would be no time for rehearsals. Could we get it together in time? His agent sent us down the band charts as soon as we signed the contract, and I turned them over to Barry. If there was anyone in the world who could work it out in an afternoon, it was him.

Barry worked the boys all day till they were dripping. After a grueling session, they jumped in the pool and just had enough time to blow-dry and dress for the show.

Cab himself arrived only about an hour before, a lovely, polite white-haired gentleman who presented like a Southern Baptist minister. Cordially greeting the

CONTINENTAL BATHS CLUB

Olympic Pool
Steam Room
Sauna
Restaurant
Sun & Sky Club
Overnight Accommodations

★ MEN ONLY ★

OPEN DAY and NIGHT
All Year 'Round!

799-2688

230 W. 74th St.
off Broadway

CONTINENTAL BATHS
and
STEVE OSTROW
Present

"The Best At The Baths."

such names as

- Bette Midler
- Liz Torres
- Linda Hopkins
- Pat Suzuki
- Daphne Davis
- Dawn Hampton
- Lee Anthony
- Betty Rhodes
- Scott Jarvis
- Cab Calloway
- Rosalind Kind
- Jill Corey
- Donnybrooke Alderson
- Manhattan Transfer
- Joanne Beretta
- Delores Hall
- Tiny Reed
- Tally Brown
- Jackie Curtis
- Holly Woodlawn

and many more...
Showtime Midnight
General Admission $4.50
Ladies Admitted 11:30 PM But Are
Requested To Leave After Show
230 West 74th Street
Tel.: 799-2688

Announcing
CONTINENTAL SAUNA CLUB
Every Saturday Evening
at 10:15 PM
You Are Invited To An Exciting
Lounge Show (Ladies Invited)
111 West 56th Street
Tel.: 489-8124
"The New After Theatre Spot
That Provides
The Pause That Refreshes..."

band, he disappeared into our glamourless dressing room and didn't reappear till I made the announcement. "Ladies and gentlemen, the Continental Baths is proud to present the inimitable Cab Calloway!"

He then came out costumed in a glittering tux that almost seemed to have mirrored lapels. The tux threw off every color in the rainbow as it played with the spotlights. He took the stage and, grabbing the mike, ran from one end to the other in a blaze of iridescent energy. The man was a supercharged sexagenarian dynamo. That famous grin seemed to start at one ear and go to the other while teeth the size of headlights blazed between red rubber lips.

Cab performed for over two hours, the longest show we ever had, but never once fatiguing or taking his foot off the gas. He floored us. The man, his charisma, his delivery, his presence, they showed us that you didn't have to be gay to be a star.

Barry and the Continental Band, inspired by his professionalism, never missed a beat. There wasn't a bun on a seat in the place as, together with the band, they gave him a standing ovation that rings in my ears to this day. We called a cab for Cab who had a plane to catch, but not before he did a final encore of "Sweet *Georgie* Brown."

What a man!

* * *

Some stars are so legendary that you can hardly believe that they still walk this earth.

Such was the case with Josephine Baker. I had heard stories about her having been the Queen of Camp in Paris, but I thought that was before the revolution. I had seen pictures of her in various articles from time to time, but they were always in black and white or rotogravure in the era before color, so it was easy to assume that she predated my era and was now extinct. But no, Josephine was one of the nobility that continued to reign into semimodern times.

Josephine's name had come to my attention by chance as I was dining out with Chula one evening. Chula and I would often go to dinner now that Jess was not around; we were good buddies and enjoyed each other's company. Chula was happy-go-lucky and easy to be with, so it was natural to assume that he was uncomplicated and had it together. At least that's what the rest of the world thought.

Chula had started to confide in me more and more. He was the kind of boy who could not be alone with himself for a moment, as a result of which he was constantly surrounded by friends and hangers-on. Chula could not go for a newspaper alone but had to have someone accompany him. He had a loving mother and four great brothers, none of whom knew he was gay, Mom excepted—this was when being gay was still considered a disease. But he never talked about his father—it was as if he didn't exist.

Chula had a big hole in his heart that only being around people could fill. It was one of the reasons he was so gregarious. But he and I had a special relationship. No matter what facade we chose to show the world, Chula and I shared what was really going on for us inside. We never pretended; we never had to be on. We were always real with each other. In our relationship, there was no bullshit. I hadn't planned on digressing so much but just felt that this was the time to tell you more about Chula, one because he was so very special and two because he personified so many self-ostracized young gay men at the time.

So here we were, Chula and I, trying out a brand-new restaurant called Josephine's that had opened on the West Side. There were oodles of money spent on this one, and it was run by another legendary woman who simply went by the name of Bricktop. Now Bricktop was famous for having run the trendiest nightclub on the rue Pigalle in Paris back in the twenties and thirties. It became a refuge for many expatriate Americans such as Gertrude Stein, Cole Porter, Ernest Hemingway, F. Scott Fitzgerald, and others, not the least of whom was Josephine Baker. It wasn't long before Bricktop became Josephine's confidante and pseudomanager.

The new restaurant, Josephine's, had opened with no less a personage than Mabel Mercer, doing her thing at the piano. Mabel was an interpreter par excellence, someone whom composers wrote songs for and others came to hear how those songs should be sung, the kind of singer that Frank Sinatra came to listen to. Mabel's voice had long since lost the fluidity it had in her youth, but it didn't seem to matter. Her way of speaking the lyrics on pitch managed to inflect every word with just the right intent.

After enjoying both the meal and Mabel, I asked the waiter if I could speak to Bricktop and gave my calling card. It didn't take but moments for the lady, famous for her red hair on top of a chocolate complexion, to come to our table. The hair was sparser now and the complexion a bit mottled, but the most striking feature were the green eyes. Now I don't know whether she was wearing contact lenses—remember, this was back in the early seventies—or the eyes just had it. In any case, you knew you were in the presence of someone who has seen and done it all.

We hit it off instantly, Bricktop and I. We were both promoters at heart. Bricktop levelled with me, saying that she was running the restaurant for a black international syndicate who had fronted all the dough. She and Chula were a hit too as Chula let his Jamaican jargon jive with her Parisian patter.

Bricktop knew right away who I was and what the Continental Baths was all about, and so I got straight to the point.

"Was there really a Josephine Baker?" I asked. "And if so, why hasn't anyone done a movie about her?"

"My dear Stephen," she said in her husky, drawling tone that managed to be silkenly seductive at the same time, "Josephine not only existed, but she's still bigger than life."

Bricktop went on to tell me that Josephine was indeed alive and had devoted the last decade of her life to orphaned children. She had converted her villa in the south of France into a home for these abandoned kids of all colors that she called her Rainbow Tribe, and such was the need that she was now working together with UNESCO for the improvement of the lives of underprivileged children all over the world. She was facing an immediate crisis as the payments on the villa were hopelessly in arrears, and she had exhausted her own fortune.

"When was the last time she gave a performance?" I asked.

"Josephine has not been well herself over the last few years and so hasn't performed at all. The children take all her energy."

"When was the last time she was in the United States?"

"I can't remember. It's been a long time. You know of course that Josephine was never really appreciated here in her own country. It was only when she went to Paris, where they idolized her, that she became the legend she now is." And now painfully, but strangely without bitterness: "We both left in those days because of the discrimination. People forget how it was for black folk back then."

"How do we get her back?" I asked.

"You must be kidding, honey. Josephine here in America after all these years? What for?" And suddenly we were back in the Deep South, all traces of her polyglot accent gone as she zeroed in on me. "The only thing that would get Josephine to go *anywhere* would be for the kids."

"Look, Bricktop . . . do I call you Bricktop?"

"You can call me anything you want, honey. Just put your cards on the table."

"Okay. Look. I've got some powerful friends in this town who would love to do some good work."

"Go on, I'm listening," she said, taking out a long gold cigarette holder and lighting up an even longer brown cigarillo.

"What I'm saying is, I would like to sponsor Josephine Baker coming back to the US for a special concert to raise money for her kids."

There was a long silence as Bricktop contemplated my offer.

"You mean *you* or the *Continental* would like to sponsor Josephine?" she finally asked.

"I *am* the Continental," I said grandly, with a debonair smile, prejudging the impact.

"Well, that may be a problem," she said, bursting my balloon. "Now Josephine's no prude—and mind you, she was queen of the camp crowd before Bette Midler even had any friends. But this is for the kids. Besides, she has a manager, who by the way just happens to be in town."

"Talk to him for me, Bricktop," I urged. "For the kids."

"You know," and then fixing those green eyes exclusively on me, itself an honor, "I really do believe you. Come here tomorrow, same time. Have you eaten?"

"Not yet, and I'm hungry," Chula piped in, understandably.

"Tell me how you like the food," Bricktop said, disengaging herself from our table.

"It can't be any better than the company," I said chivalrously.

"Yeah, but it's expensive, and I come cheap," was her earthy reply.

"So do we," said Chula, and we all had a chuckle.

* * *

"You know we're talking serious money here."

We were seated at the same table as last night. Bricktop had made the necessary introduction and then left us with our drinks.

Josephine's manager was a dead ringer for Lawrence Fishburne as Tina Turner's husband in *What's Love Got to Do with It*, complete with a black mustache, dark business suit, flash tie, and diamond cuff links, only he invented the drag first.

"I know serious people," I replied.

"It's got to be done big time."

"That's the way I do things."

"Josephine's not gonna haul her ass over here to do a gig for the Continental Baths," and then seeing my raised eyebrows, he added, "No offence. It's just that if it's for the kids, we have to find a prestigious sponsor."

I suggested that he and I coproduce the show and get UNESCO to sponsor it.

"Ha! That's a joke," he said without smiling. "We've been that route before. They'll take the money, but they won't put up a dime."

"That's what I'm here for," I said grandly.

"You gonna foot the bill for Josephine?"

"Me and my friends."

"Well, I don't know who your friends are, but you better have a lot of them. Josephine travels in style."

I had read about her fabulous costumes and that she would use dozens of them in her act. She'd need a hotel suite for her and her dogs and a full-time chauffeur and limo. "And there's one more thing," he told me. "Look here, let's talk real time. Josephine is a sick woman. Remember, she's sixty-three, and it's been a fast life."

I felt he was talking to me as a friend for the first time, we having gotten over the first hurdle.

"Go on," I encouraged.

"She doesn't perform anymore 'cause no one will take the chance."

"What chance? Her name alone would draw a crowd."

"If she shows. But it's a fifty-fifty shot that she'll just cancel."

"Even if it were for the kids?" I asked.

"That might make the difference."
"Let's go for it," I said, clinking empty glasses with him.
"You might lose a wad on the theater booking and advertising."
"Gotcha."
"She might not come at all."
"We'll take the gamble."
"Your name and the Continental will have to be in small print."
"That's okay, we wanna do it."
"*Real* small print."
"I don't care if it's in hieroglyphics."
"Let's eat."
And another adventure was about to begin.

* * *

Incredibly, La Baker had said yes, forthrightly warning that the show was conditional on her being well at the time.

I was to handle the logistics: the theater, advertising, publicity, and so on. Her manager was to handle Josephine. I guess that's what he took "coproduce" to mean.

Now to find a venue. There was no way we could stage the event at the Continental. We needed a large legitimate theater but not so large that Josephine's act would lose its intimacy. She was, after all, a one-woman show, not a rock band.

After racking my brain, I came up with a grand old Rococo theater called the Beacon, which was directly opposite the Ansonia, on Broadway between Seventy-fourth and Seventy-fifth. The Beacon had once been a live entertainment palace when the West Side had been in one of its cyclical peaks of vogue. It was now used exclusively for films. But when they heard who the performer would be, they agreed.

The Beacon held about three thousand eight hundred people, and we had planned two shows, a matinée and an evening performance. With everything in place, I approached UNESCO. Not surprisingly, when they heard it was Josephine Baker and that they could only make and not lose money, as my people were footing the bill, they agreed to sponsor her return under the UNESCO banner. It would be a great international—and risk-free—coup for them. It was truly *an offer they couldn't refuse*.

Josephine was supposed to arrive ten days before the concert. The hotel was booked, the flight arranged, the publicity ready to roll. And I had placed a full-page ad in the *New York Times* à la Bette Midler. Now I was getting a little nervous.

Finally the day came. The flight from Paris was delayed. We waited at JFK for over three hours. Mercifully the Air France Airbus eventually arrived. The demure small slender lady who came through the arrival gate totally dressed in unadorned black with matching sunglasses would have fooled me for sure.

"That's Josephine," her manager said, running to embrace her. La Baker had arrived.

The name Josephine Baker was magic even after all these years. But hardly anyone knew anything about her. After all, she predated Piaf, and no one had actually seen her perform. The big question now was no longer *would* she, but *could* she? And even if she could, how good was she?

The press had a great time interviewing her. They dug up that she had done undercover work for the French Resistance during World War II. Born in 1906 in the slums of St. Louis, Missouri, she had grown up sleeping in cardboard shelters and scavenging for food in garbage cans. No wonder she had an affinity for the poor children of the world.

Josephine had her stage debut at the age of thirteen at the Booker T Washington Theater and went on to the Ziegfeld Follies before leaving for Paris at nineteen. There she transformed herself onto a bigger-than-life black sex goddess and became the toast of the town.

UNESCO jumped onto the bandwagon as if it had all been their idea. They put up banners all over Broadway leading to the theater and had fund-raising tables set up in the lobby. We sold out the two performances in a matter of hours after they'd gone on sale, due more to curiosity than anything else. People wanted to be able to tell their children that they had actually seen Josephine Baker live, although I'm sure the kids would just stare and say, "Who?" Even today I get that from some of the younger generation when I talk about Bette Midler, who's still out there stomping the boards.

Still, there was always the chance that she would back out. If she failed to appear, all ticket moneys would have to be refunded; all bets called in, and I would have to sell a lot of soap and towels to recoup the expenses.

I had had an opportunity to talk to Josephine at the airport and on the trip back to her hotel, after which she went into seclusion. All my preconceived notions were wrong. I don't think I have ever met a more down-to-earth, unassuming woman who at the same time was arrestingly intelligent and worldly wise. She wore no makeup under the dark glasses, but you could see the fabulous bone structure of her still-beautiful face although she took no pains to hide her age.

Contrary to my expectations of endless possessions packed in Vuitton luggage, she had arrived with one steamer trunk, presumably containing her costumes, and her own personal overnight bag. Given her diva status, I was prepared for tantrums, temperament, and theatrics. But Josephine saved all that for the stage.

That moment finally arrived. The house was full, the orchestra arranged for by her manager, playing the songs that Josephine Baker had made famous long before Chevalier and Piaf.

And then the metamorphosis happened. Gone was the demure, unassuming grandmother I had met at the airport. In her place was a great, winged peacock bird with feathers spread in a vast fan of silver and blue plumage. She wore a feathered crown of crystal so high that you wondered if it was supported by invisible wires from the rafters. Around her neck was a necklace of diamonds so large and brilliant that you might think they were powered by batteries, which indeed they were.

In the midst of all this was the face, that flawless face now with makeup to die for. Eyelashes that curled upward to the heavens. Eyes so bright and wide, you could see her pupils from the last row. And the legs, the famous Baker legs. So long that you wondered how there would be room for a body above them. And all this perched on glistening glass high heels that put the Eiffel Tower to shame.

How she managed to maneuver in that creation was surely one of the great mysteries of the world. But manage she did, electrifyingly delivering one dynamite song after another in a clear, beautiful musical voice that was ageless. Costume change after costume change, each outdoing the last, would wreak havoc on the by-now blistered palms of the audience.

And then, for me, came the most magical moment of all. Having done a string of encores at the end of the show, Josephine emerged onstage, sans costume, sans jewelry, *sans* wigs. Just her simple beautiful self. She took the handmike, and as we sat in stunned silence, she actually descended the stage steps into the audience. She walked among us, showing herself to be a mere mortal like the rest of us. She talked about her children, the needy children of the world. She talked about her life: her struggles, her highs, her lows. She went from row to row, shaking hands individually with as many people as possible.

And then back on stage, she sat down on the front lip, feet dangling, and asked what we would like to hear her sing. She was so generous with her art that the matinée show threatened to run over into the evening performance. With hardly a break in between, she ran the whole gamut again that night.

Not bad for a sixty-three-year-old grandmother, a wonderful, wonderful woman whom I no longer think of as black and white or rotogravure. To me *she* is a glorious rainbow.

Josephine Baker died in Paris six years later at the age of sixty-nine, four days after the opening of *Josephine*, a show based on her life. Her funeral took place in her beloved France, the country that she had adopted as her home.

"Josephine—coffee skin, ebony eyes, legs of paradise, a smile to end all smiles."—Pablo Picasso.

Chapter 36

Twinkle, Twinkle, Little Stars

Along with the famous, the flashy, and the legendary, there were many artists who appeared at the Baths who, although not well known at the time, and possibly still, were quite remarkable in their individuality and their talent.

Laura Kenyon was a singer with every attribute needed to become a star. She had a rich and powerful voice with a full range of dynamics. Laura was a feisty young talent who got right down with the audience, as did Bette. She probably had a better voice but lacked Bette's poignant vulnerability. Some performers like Laura project right out into the audience, and that's fine. Others bring the audience right on to the stage with them—and that's magic.

As Stanislavsky puts it, it's the difference between seeking sympathy as a performer or seeking empathy. With sympathy, we feel sorry for the performer. With empathy, we share in their experience. And that is the kind of performance we remember long after we have left the theater, and what I always looked for when I auditioned talent for the Continental.

The Manhattan Transfer, as they were called, were a most unlikely group to have been successful at the Baths, one would have thought. But luckily I wasn't that one. I guess when they auditioned for me, I was captivated by their semiclassical approach to singing. Their signature was and continues to be a four-part harmony, based on the structure of the sax section of the great bands, like those of Count Basie and Harry James.

Two guys and two girls comprised the group blending soprano, alto, tenor, and bass. But it wasn't only their singing that made them popular with the Bath audience, it was their fresh-faced joy in what they were doing that made them irresistible.

Dubbed Queen of Cabaret by cult reviewers, Dawn Hampton had been beating the bushes in such New York City clubs as Tijuana Cats, Marie's Crises, and the Duplex, before she landed on our tacky stage in 1972. A singer's singer, she captivated the Bath audience not only with her artistry but with her sultry personality. She was everybody's Eartha Kitt, Bessie Smith, and Billie Holliday all rolled up into one compelling package. Dawn became a staple at the Baths for many years, and any night she appeared was a happening.

Another contender was Jane Olivor, née Linda Cohen of Brooklyn. Jane had patterned herself after the late great Piaf, and her quasi-French renditions of the classics were admirable. Jane also did a cameo for us in the *Saturday Night at the Baths* film.

And then there was Judith Cohen. Judith was everything a star shouldn't be: short, unattractive, and overweight. She had a white pallid face and a crown of scraggly red hair. When Judith would appear, she would pour out all her insecurities. She was never really on pitch, never in tempo, but nobody cared. All the guys emphatized with her. She was everything they didn't want to be, but were.

Lorna Luft, now *there* was a talent. If she had been anyone other than Judy Garland's daughter, she would have triumphed. And no, we never had Judy at the Baths, but that was only because she died in 1969, before entertainment was really in vogue at the Continental. But unlike Liza whose frantic intensity drove her to stardom, Lorna was a more relaxed entertainer, relying on musicality and subtlety. But the guys wanted to see a Judy reincarnation, and Lorna was just being Lorna. It didn't work.

I have read and heard reports that Whoopi Goldberg, then unknown, would appear in midnight concerts at the Baths doing backups and solos. But then I have also read that Johnny Carson would make incognito visits to the Baths to experience the real Bette, after her appearances on his television show had bowled him over. I can neither confirm nor deny either, although during show nights I was usually so engaged with the logistics of the entire operation that it could have eluded me. With Whoopi being an unknown at the time, it's entirely possible. As for Johnny, well, he was a master of disguise. What'ya say, guys? Were you there?

One of the most popular attractions at the Baths was Poutassa. Who? you're probably asking. Well, Poutassa was the preeminent drag queen of the era. She was black, she was beautiful, and she was wicked. If she got you in her sights, she would tear you apart from the stage. But nobody cared. Poutassa would whirlwind around like a ballet dancer, shedding one item of costume after another till little was left to the imagination; but what there was, was anything but little.

Poutassa's impersonation of Diana Ross was to die for. She would come out in a fabulous low-cut gown adorned with a bath towel over her shoulders like some fantastic shawl. She would then catwalk down the stage singing "Stop! In the Name of Love." The guys went crazy for her. But Poutassa could be real mean. Get her a little high, not a difficult task in those days, and she could claw your eyes out if you crossed her. But the memory of Poutassa, her exquisite body glistening under the stage spots, will remain with me and a thousand others forever. She was more than a drag queen, she was the Queen of Drag.

Not every performer however grooved on the unique Bath ambience. Some found it intimidating, others maddening.

Joanne Beretta was one of the latter. "I hated it, I hated everything about it," she later complained. "It was hot as hell in there, people were lying around almost naked, they were high, it was all unfocused."

A concert hall it was not, but for those who could accept the novelty of the Baths and embrace it, there was no better audience. The Baths was an enigma to the outside world. Much as they would have liked to believe that this subterranean satyricon harbored only sex perverts and deviants, how could they explain that the cream of New York society clamored to gain admittance and that the list of performers the Continental presented read like a *Who's Who* in the entertainment world?

Women's Wear Daily, the prestigious New York trade paper of the fashion world, sums it up beautifully in their article "Splish, Splash, I Was Taken to the Baths," February 11, 1972:

> "Why isn't there a place like this for woman?" the article asks at the end. Well, see chapter 41 and find out why.

Chapter 37

The Key to the City

By the mid-'70s, New York City was fast going down the tubes. The promised prosperity of the Lindsay administration had failed to materialize. Crime was rampant; and drugs, always a problem, were eating away at the fabric of life. On a national level, the Vietnam War was polarizing the country. The Nixon era of negativism had been no help; and New York City, always liberal and democratic, viewed him with distaste and national politics with contempt. Watergate had been the watershed.

The Continental had, by then, become the political pulpit for all but the squeaky-clean WASP politicians to lobby for the multisexual vote. What had long been the greatest city in the world was now caving in on itself. People were no longer proud to be a New Yorker. But people and their talents were what had made New York City great. The fear was that if they deserted the city, it would become nothing but corporate headquarters and slums. Something bold and new was needed; and out of the chaos, incredulously, I was asked if I would run for the office of mayor in the next mayoral campaign.

At first I scoffed at the idea, but then it kind of grew on me. Serious contenders like Senator Carl McCall and Percy Sutton encouraged me to run on their ticket, if not for mayor, then at least for borough president or assemblyman. Together we would have made an invincible trio.

But was New York City ready for a bisexual mayor? Well, to win an election in New York City, you needed the gay vote, the Jewish vote, and the black vote. With my Harlem friend Senator Carl McCall, respected for his political astuteness and having diplomas from Dartmouth and the University of Edinburgh, we had the black vote. With Percy Sutton, we had the solid Irish Catholic vote. And with me—well, I was a polyglot link to get the gay vote, bisexual vote, *and* the Jewish vote, which was all the opposition candidate Abe Beame could attest to.

There were myriad interviews in both the gay and straight press. *Rolling Stone* did a sixteen-page feature on me in May of 1976. It was titled "King Queen" with a half-page photo of me, Joanne, my kids Scott and Maria, and our two dogs Taj and Snoopy. *Mandate*, the nation's largest gay magazine, did a feature article titled "What Makes Steven Run?," written by Freeman Gunter.

What had started as a political and possibly a public relations ploy was now a serious possibility. Joanne, when interviewed, was asked how she would feel about living in Gracie Mansion.

"Well," she replied, "it's a wonderful house. I'm not sure who would be sleeping in what bedrooms, but the children would love it. I wonder if I could keep the horses there."

But when it came down the line, I opted out. Not because I didn't want the job or didn't think I could do it but because I knew that as soon as I was nominated as an official candidate, the press would have uncovered the federal fiasco, and there would have gone the chances for the city's first bisexual mayor. So what was the point?

Not having a strong-enough mayor, in 1976, the city of New York had to be bailed out of impending bankruptcy by the then governor of the state Hugh L. Carey. Sorry, guys.

* * *

One day David Buckley, who was just breaking into journalism, called to do an in-depth interview on the "Steve Ostrow for Mayor" phenomenon. Never one to turn down free publicity, I agreed—even though he was writing for his brother-in-law—Al Goldstein's publication *Screw*, the most outlandishly obscene magazine on the streets in those days.

In all my years of running the Continental, other than for the opening or a special show, I had never spent a nickel in direct advertising for the Baths, preferring to attract attention from the press and have the Baths be covered as news. So far it had worked, but I now felt that we could use a little publicity. Since we had paved the way for bathhouses to be recognized as legal operations, new investors, realizing the potential profit in the business, were beginning to follow our lead. We now had competitors.

One of them was my old-time friend Walter Kent, who couldn't take the heat back during the raids and had left my operation. I kept him on retainer for years as a sign of goodwill for having approached me with the original idea. But now Walter had severed all connections with us and opened up his own operation on the East Side, calling it the Beacon Baths. It was strictly a soap-and-towel operation to catch the conservative executive trade. I wished Walter the best of luck and even went to his opening celebration.

A more direct competitor was the Club Baths, a modern, up-to-date operation, which opened in the East Village. I kind of liked going there myself, as I could be incognito. Soon they franchised another branch in midtown. Both these operations and the many that followed them had the advantage of escaping the huge legal and protection expenses the Continental had suffered. But the Continental was still in a class by itself, since none of the others ran a show or provided the same amenities. So I gave David Buckley the grand tour—clothed, of course.

"You realize, David, you're only seeing the tip of the iceberg while you're not in a towel." David was a very attractive and charming man in his midthirties: tall, affable, and courtly in manner in contrast to the trashy paper he represented.

"Well, Steve, I'm really very straight although I may have taken a few curves along the way. But I really don't think you guys have discovered anything that we haven't done already."

After that, David started coming to the Baths regularly for the shows, each time accompanied by a luscious young brunette. On one occasion, I caught them sequestered in a room on a Sunday morning—not the province of straight people.

"Out, you traitor," I said in jest. "You're going to give the joint a bad name."

"You know, Steve," he joked, "I took a little stroll through the place last night, and I take it back. I really think you guys *have* made some new discoveries since the *Kama Sutra*."

David and I struck up a really good friendship, and before long, he came to me with the idea of shooting a movie in the bathhouse. It was to be a gay film aimed at a general audience.

"What are you gonna call it—*West Side Story*?" I asked.

"No—*Saturday Night at the Baths*."

Three months passed, and I had forgotten about the project until David showed up one Saturday night with his girlfriend in tow. I guided them to my special reserved table by the dance floor, and he dumped a thick bound manuscript onto it.

"Are you sure this isn't *War and Peace*?" I exclaimed, hefting the script.

"Believe it or not, it all revolves around one Saturday night show at the Baths. Give it a read."

The film script centered around a young pianist and his girlfriend. He auditions at the Baths to play for the show, and I hire him. The guy's ambiguous sexual feelings are brought into the open by the seductive show manager, and everything comes to a boil during a Saturday night performance of *Decadence*. The film dared to tackle the he/she/he theme, and the writing was very sensitive.

Interested, I asked, "Okay, David, who's going to play me?"

"You are."

"You're crazy."

"Look, Steve, this is a low-budget film. But we can make it happen. I'm willing to raise the money and do the work. You're in for half as coproducer, but my idea is that everyone in the Baths plays themselves. The only two professional actors will be the boy and the girl. You'll be great."

David was dead serious. I could see he really believed it could work.

I protested saying that I was too busy to be in the film and that maybe he could get Robert Redford to play me; after all, we were about the same age.

"We'll shoot around you and do all your scenes when you're free," David countered, ignoring my humility.

"But, David," I said, "you know how protective I am about the Baths and my clientele. I don't want anyone to feel inconvenienced, and everybody's privacy must be respected."

He said that he fully understood and that no one would be on camera if they didn't sign a written release.

"But," he said, "we're going to open up some major issues here: being queer, being straight, and being in-between."

"Yeah, David, I know. I read the script, and I like it, that's why I'm with you all the way. But just remember: the customer comes first."

"Hmm," mused David, "that may be an even better title."

"Screw you, David," I said affably, and the project was launched.

Our first task as coproducers was to brush up the screenplay. We called in a Professor Franklin Khedouri, who put the polishing touch on the final version. Next we hired Robert Aberdeen to play the straight guy and Ellen Sheppard to play his girlfriend, two quite remarkable young actors. Our own doe-eyed Don Scotti did a remarkable job playing the "male fatale" role of my assistant manager.

True to his word, David worked around the Baths clientele. A good deal of the film was shot on location in Greenwich Village, Central Park, and the East Side, giving it texture and ambience.

There were two hot love scenes: one between the girl and the guy that we shot in warm tones of amber and reds and the other between Scotti and the guy, which we shot in exotic shades of blue and purple. Both were really long and quite explicit for the time.

The *Decadence* show featured the Indian ritual dance, performed by members of the New York City Ballet Company, Jane Oliver, Caleb Stone as Judy Garland, Poutassa as Diana Ross, and even our own dear Pedro doing his Carmen Miranda bit. I played myself with my usual aplomb. I loved the opening scene, where I swim across the pool, never getting my coif even damp. Even Esther Williams couldn't do that without a bathing cap.

Basically the theme of the film was this: Boy 1 and Girl are having a great relationship. Boy 1 and Girl meet Boy 2—Scotti—and they all get along just fine. Boy 2 gets Boy 1 alone, and that's when the fun starts. Boy 1 then goes home to Girl, who asks what happened. Boy 1 then tells Girl the truth. Girl then

Scene from film Saturday Night at the Baths,
Don Scotti and Robert Aberdeen

asks Boy 1, "How does this affect us?" Boy 1 looks at her and says, "I don't know. I hope it doesn't." End of picture.

The movie ran ninety minutes and cost $120,000 in 1973 to make. We had a grand opening at the Fifty-seventh Street Art Cinema. The critics loved it; the public loved it. But that was New York City. When we shipped it out cross-country, not being distributors, we didn't know what we were doing. The cinemas would pay for one showing, then copy the film, never paying another cent.

Well, we got our money back but never saw another dime. For years afterward, whenever I traveled, I would find it playing in the strangest places. When I would want to see it, I would tell them it was my picture. They would say, "Sure, mister, buy a ticket, and we'll give you a free bag of popcorn." So much for being a movie producer.

After twenty-five years, I only recently found a video of the film and revisited it. Of course it reflects a pre-AIDS era, but you know what? The issues are still the same. It's a pretty good flick. If it's playing your way sometime, go see it. Tell them you know the producer. It may just get you a bag of popcorn.

Chapter 38

Triple Play

I had originally invited Jess to be in *Saturday Night at the Baths*, offering to fly him in from Stuttgart for ten days to shoot all his scenes. But he had fallen off his bike and torn a cartilage in his knee, which kept him out of action for two months. On one of his previous trips home, he had connected with a rather good-looking redheaded man, a Continental client, who really did resemble Robert Redford in his better days. Just so his recovery time wouldn't be a total loss, Robert, that was his name too, now took Jess to the south of France and Monte Carlo. Somehow the knee managed to make the trip, but I'm sure Jess prudently stayed off his feet a great deal of the time.

Being at loose ends, with the film in the can and things a bit subdued in the city as they always are in the summer, when everyone but the infirm and the interned have departed, I decided to take a trip to one of my favorite cities. Montreal has two seasons: August and winter. Having been there in winter, I thought I'd revisit it in August. I had also heard that a fabulous new baths called the Sauna Neptune, patterning itself after the Continental, had opened there. This I *had* to see.

So with Jess not around and Jorge seeing the innocuous Terry, I thought, *Why not take Chula with me?* Just as a buddy, of course.

"Montreal! Wow! Why not? Sounds great, Steve! When do we leave and for how long?" Chula eagerly responded.

"Let's do a week. We need to check out a few things. Can you be ready by tomorrow?" I said, enjoying the impulse of it all.

"I'm ready tonight, but tomorrow's just fine. Just gotta tell Mom what's going on."

Dorothy, Chula's Jamaican mom, was a sweetheart of a lady and a beauty in her own right. We got along just fine, and Chula was her pride and joy.

"Tell your mom you'll be in good hands," I said.

"I think she knows that already," was Chula's easy answer.

Chula and I had really become good friends. We played around and flirted with each other, but first there had been Jorge's and then Jess's vibrations floating around, and we just hadn't thought of each other *that* way. So it was free and easy to just pick up and go on a business trip together.

I really wanted Chula to check out the disco and baths scene with me. He would see it from the younger point of view, and me from—well, let's face it—a more mature viewpoint. At least that's what I was telling myself.

As usual I booked in at the Bonaventure Hotel, where they treated me as a VIP now as I'd been quite a regular. On this trip, I was given the Presidential Suite, a bit strange as Quebec had a premier and not a president. But there was no four-poster bed this time. Instead Chula and I had two double beds, discreetly separated by a table and a lamp.

We took a swim in the rooftop pool at sunset, watching the city lights come on to decorate the night like an inverted Milky Way. Racing back to our room, I buzzed down for cocktails then, when Chula was finished, took my turn in the shower.

While I was lathering up, I couldn't help thinking of how Chula had looked by the swimming pool. The boy was absolutely beautiful. He had an etched body of just the right proportions, skin the color of Baileys and cream, my favorite cocktail, tightly encasing a fine bone structure, and all interconnected by a sensually anatomical network of muscles, sinews, and veins. It was as though I'd seen him for the first time. But even so, I wasn't prepared for the sight that greeted me as I reentered the room.

The lights had been dimmed, and there was a whole new Chula once again. The glistening athletic swimmer of before had now changed his guise; and there, on the bed, was a reincarnation of the Persian Boy, clad only in a diaphanous garment of fine white filigree lace, the honeyed glow of his amber skin warming the room.

The expression on Chula's face was one of peace and serenity. He was seated on the bed, cross-legged as if chanting a silent mantra.

"You said you wanted to check out a few things in Montreal," he said in a tone neither coy nor seductive. Very gently, I eased the fragile garment from his golden shoulders. Like a timeless sphinx, the proud figure that lay in waiting didn't move or resist, letting me slowly savor each new sensation as I continued my exotic journey down the contours of his body.

When I had reached the sacred temple of all life, he rose, now unadorned, to his knees, and I the same. As if accompanied by a mystical lute, we danced in each other's embrace, coming together in what felt to be the most natural of all unions. We had come home in Montreal. From that moment on, no matter who else was in our lives, home would always be in the heart of the other.

We checked out a lot of things that night but never did leave the hotel room. The week in Montreal was productive, however. Montreal is one of the most romantic cities in the world, the combination of old and new, French and English blend to give it a special flavor unique in all of North America.

The next day, we visited the new sauna and met the owners, Lorne Halliday and Andre LaFlamme, a pair of French lovers totally mismatched, like *The Odd Couple*. They had poured a ton of money into the place, having been impressed with the Continental, which they had visited many times in New York. Chula and I loved it and wished them the best. They had only been open for one month, but business was booming. We did the discos and gay clubs, but they were still furtive and underground. The young people of Montreal however were very stylish and avant-garde. The city had glamour, but the gay scene still suffered under the reign of a conservative government, and homosexuality was still illegal in any public context.

Little did I know then how important this trip would later be; but my relationship with Chula, which was founded on friendship, would wind up where it began—in a swimming pool. By the time we returned to New York, we were so comfortable with each other that people tended to assume that we were longtime lovers.

One day, when we were swimming in the pool at the Baths, I decided to try to make it official, asking Chula, "What do you think about us being one to one with each other?"

"Are you ready for that, Pops?" That was Chula's favorite nickname for me.

"If you are, sure, let's do it."

I hugged him in the pool, our naked bodies rising to the occasion, and then we ran to my little latrine office to finish the "ceremony."

As I waited on the altar for my bride, Chula ran to get us towels; and when he didn't return immediately, I peered out to find him. There he was, naked and still glistening from the pool, having a conversation with Marcos, a young stud who frequented the Tubs. Then they both sat down at a table and lit cigarettes.

Now all my prior passion converted to anger. I felt cuckolded. Just as I was about to stomp out of the office and make a scene, Chula came back and readily discovered my shift of mood.

"What's wrong, Pops?" he asked.

"Chula," I told him, "you're my best friend."

"Yeah, so?"

"So . . . I just don't wanna fuck that up."

"You mean you're not ready for one to one, Steve."

"I don't think so, Chu. I'm too possessive."

"Wow! What a relief!" Chula said, and we held on to each other for a long time as we laughed and cried. Our one to one had lasted all of ten minutes, admittedly a long time for the '70s.

* * *

Comfortable as my relationship with Chula was, it didn't quite take the edge off my sense of loss over Jess. So naturally I turned to business to distract me.

New York City was in a mess. Crime was rampant, and the drug problem had escalated. The Baths was still popular, but the real trendy crowd that had been our mainstay was now frequenting some of the newer establishments. The Continental plant was slowly starting to deteriorate with age, whereas newer facilities had the advantage of modern plumbing and design.

In a bid to capture a whole new segment of the population, I instituted a mixed dollar disco night on Monday evenings, our slowest period.

Well, let me tell you, all of Harlem and Puerto Rico converged on us. It was a scene from *West Side Story*. Half of the boys who came in were real macho and created a whole new vibration in the club: colorful, noisy, sweaty, and *very* sexy. Some of our more genteel guests were a little jostled in the fray, but for the most part, it was very erotic. After the girls went home, some of the swaggering straight kids hung in later and eventually got into towels. And then the hunting season was truly on.

One of the boys, a rippled-stomached Puerto Rican youth of about nineteen whose tawny body was accented by a white shell necklace, caught my fancy. I had noticed him constantly playing pool with his friends and not really mixing.

I eventually went up to him and said, "Hey, my friend, you play a good game of pool."

"Yeah. You play?" he asked, his eyes fixed on the cue ball.

"Depends on the game," I replied with a straight face.

"How about snooker?"

Well, it wasn't the game I had in mind, but it was a start. It also wasn't hard to let him beat me, and after a few nights, Pablo and I became "pals."

Linda, a Marilyn Monroe look-alike, was a steady at the Baths on Mondays and show nights. An old friend of Jess's from dancing school days, she was a fag hag but was also known to be a swinger. Seeing her eyeing Pablo, I went over to her.

"You like him?" I asked.

"You bet!" she said. "He's hot!"

"Let me see what I can work out." And going over to Pablo, I said, "Hi, guy. That blonde is hot for you."

Pablo focused his green cat eyes on her. "I could handle her easy."

"Maybe I can arrange a little party for the three of us. What do you say?"

Pablo pulled back on the cue and suddenly blasted the black 3-ball into the pocket. "Sure. Let's fuck her."

It didn't take much to persuade Linda when I said we could all three go up to my apartment and have a ball. I copped a bottle of Dom Perignon, two candles, and three glasses and herded everyone into the master bedroom suite.

The soft glow of the candles and the heady aphrodisiac of the champagne soon had us all in a bonding mood. The sensual tension in the air would have turned on a community of Buddhist monks. Gently and lovingly, we placed Linda on the bed and removed her garments slowly, one by one. When she was stark naked, her legs flexed into the air and her pelvis gyrated as if she was having an orgasm just in anticipation of things to come, so turned on was she.

Pablo couldn't wait to get his clothes off. His body glistened, and all the strength in his supple body seemed to culminate in the throbbing cock that thrust from his young loins.

"Hurry, hurry, stick it in me," Linda was gasping. No time for foreplay here as she grabbed Pablo by his taut brown buttocks and ground him to her.

The sight and sound of that beautiful bronzed boy, like some sweaty construction worker hard at work with his jackhammer, pounding into her, had me so turned on that I literally ripped my own clothes off as I mounted the bed. Grabbing Pablo's shoulder, I thrust my own body on top of his and then, moving to Linda, straddled her face as she pulled my cock into her eager mouth.

The boy had the stamina of a stallion, and we kept rotating our positions, one of us fucking her and the other being sucked. I have never encountered a more sensually exciting experience in all of my life. Till this day, the thought alone of that all-barriers-down happening makes me giddy.

Linda was like a wild thing. She went from one of us to the other, wanting every orifice of her body to be penetrated. Finally, Pablo and I both came in her; and we all lay on the bed, exhausted but still pulsating, the room continuing to echo with Linda's screams of exultation.

"Let's take showers," I gasped, and off we went to the bathroom, where it all started again as Linda went from one soapy cock to another. While she fixed onto Pablo, I lathered him from behind, and it wasn't long before the good youth had come once again into her mouth as I came between his legs.

"I'm hungry," Pablo finally said after we crawled out of the bathroom into the kitchen.

"More champagne?" I offered.

"Nah. Got any Sugar Pops? I love Sugar Pops."

"You can have all the Sugar Pops you want, young man," I said as I poured him a great bowl of the stuff and set the milk in front on him. "You've done just fine. And you, Linda? What can we do for you?"

Linda just smiled her Marilyn Monroe smile and, reaching over, grabbed both our cocks. "You can do it to me all over again, guys."

The rest of the night was a haze. Sometime before morning, I escorted Linda back to the Baths. After a cursory check to see that all was well, I went back to the apartment to pass out. There, in the bedroom, was Pablo. The poor boy had given his all for the cause and had crashed on the bed, stark naked. Tantalizing as it was, even I was too tired to take advantage of the situation, which would have been clearly an act of necrophilia in the circumstances.

By morning, however, the juices were flowing again; and Pablo awoke with weapon full at the ready.

"Hey, where's the blonde?" he asked, staring unabashedly at his cock.

"Well, she's gone," I said, "but maybe I can give you a hand—after all, what are friends for?"

Thus, Pablo became my new macho bedmate who called me his "man." My other elitist residents—Scotti, Pedro, and Manny—were aghast at this ghetto kid sharing 14177. But Pablo was low maintenance. Give him a bowl of Sugar Pops, and he was happy. And he was just what I needed to fill the hole in the bed that Jess had left.

Chapter 39

The Met Comes to the Baths

Eleanor Steber was one of the most acclaimed American divas of all time. She had fashioned an international career, conquering all the great opera houses of the world. She was renowned for her quintessential interpretations of Mozart and for having created the role of Vanessa in Samuel Barber's opera of the same name. She was also the Met's first Arabella, Konstanze, and Marie in *Wozzeck*.

Madame Steber was an ebulliently lucid lady of imposing proportions, and as she lived in the very same Ansonia Hotel as the Baths, I often shared an elevator ride with her. This was always a happening as she was usually accompanied by her personal secretary and companion, who was even more heroic in physique, leaving the poor ancient Ansonia lift grinding in exhaustion as it took us on our journey.

Having by now realized many of my wildest fantasies through the bathhouse, the idea of bringing the Met to the Baths began to excite me. After all, we were both in the same business, really. I mean, entertainment can take many forms. And, as many of the Met audience frequented the Baths and vice versa, why not make it more convenient by putting it all together for an evening?

And so the idea hit me: Madame Eleanor Steber, Live at the Continental Baths.

"Madame Steber," I always called her that as she was undeniably friendly but appreciated the recognition her status amply deserved, "have you ever sung in a bathhouse?"

"Oh la la." Voluminous laughter emanated from her golden throat and then, composing herself—she did after all know who I was—said, "Well, yes, Stephen, I have actually sung at the Caracalla Baths in Rome."

My god, I thought. *Could it be possible that the world's greatest Mozartian soprano would give a live concert at the Continental Baths?* The mind boggled at the thought.

"You know, Madame Steber, that we have had some of the greatest popular performers of our time sing at the Baths."

"Yes, I know. I have seen your posters in the lobby."

Dare I go further? I had better; there were only three floors to descend before she would disembark.

"Would you consider doing a live classical concert at the Baths?" I croaked.

"Only if it were done with great dignity, style, and panache," she replied without hesitation.

"Believe me, it would be world class," I proclaimed.

I later found out that I had caught Madame at an opportune moment. Both Maria Callas and Renata Tebaldi, the other two women sharing prima donna status with her at the time, were having a ball with the press in a pseudo-contrived feud that kept their names in headlines in all the world's papers. Madame Steber was a shrewd lady, and well, she knew how the press would eat up such a bizarre happening.

"Then let's get cracking," she said. "My secretary will put you in touch with Joseph Rabb, my manager, and he'll discuss the possibilities with you. Tra la la," she vocalized as the lift halted with a thump on the ground floor.

* * *

Joseph Rabb was a very handsome and engaging man who ran one of the top management agencies in New York City. In addition, he was also an accomplished concert violinist in his own right. He agreed to meet me at the garden patio of Lutèce on East Fiftieth Street, which was, and probably still is, a great place for lunch under any circumstances. The white wicker tables and chairs set in a fern-greened, lattice-enclosed sanctuary made you forget the hustle and bustle of New York City. André Soltner, the gracious owner and chef, personally saw to all our wants and for our dessert prepared his celestial orange soufflé with clotted cream.

By the time it arrived, we were getting down to business.

"You know, Eleanor is a very gutsy lady," he told me, "and she's quite serious about doing this concert."

"I want to make it the artistic event of the year," I said.

"Will your patrons sit and listen to opera?"

I told him that we'd had politicians, comedians, drag shows, ballet, rock, and Broadway stars but never an opera singer. "They will be the most appreciative audience Madame Steber could ever hope for," I promised.

"Steve, let's do it," Joseph replied. "But let's do it real big. You know, Eleanor has a recording contract with RCA Victor. How would you feel about letting them in to record the concert?"

Wow! I thought. *Eleanor Steber, Live at the Continental Baths, on an RCA recording.* It would be the most unusual musical event of the year.

We clinked brandy glasses and then both got rolling.

As it turned out, RCA Victor was red hot to record the concert. We negotiated a deal whereby they would pay all expenses—the artistic fee, publicity, accompanist, setup, and catering, right down to the programs—and I would receive a royalty on every recording sold.

Once we had fixed on a date, I went full-out advertising the show in all the straight papers as a black tie, black towel event: the audience having a choice of being dressed in formal attire or getting into a luxurious black bath towel with the Continental insignia embroidered across it in white. I made a deal with Bloomingdale's to produce the towels for us in return for them featuring it in their boutique department at $25 each, which turned into a huge hit for them, selling out ten times over.

All of New York City was abuzz on the night of the concert. RCA had been in and out of the Baths for three days, setting up and testing the equipment as naked bodies trampled over the recording wires.

Madame Steber had come down to the Baths to rehearse that afternoon. No sooner had she started the opening aria from *Idomeneo* when the bulbs in the steam room exploded with a sound like a rifle shot. It had been rumored that Caruso's voice could crack glass. But we now knew for sure that Steber's voice could kick ass.

To transform the Baths into a concert venue, I had one thousand five hundred red-upholstered folding chairs placed, theater style, throughout the room. Brass stanchions connected by plush velvet ropes designated the aisles. Handsome, well-built young men, clad in black Continental towels with black bow ties to distinguish them from patrons, guided the audience to their seats, which were all numbered for reserved seating.

Chula blew his $50 budget, bedecking the whole area with bevies of flowers and ribbons, and the cream of New York society was present.

I took the stage in my tux and, addressing the audience, said, "This is a house of love. Love comes in many shapes and forms, and tonight we have love in the form of the beautiful voice of Madame Eleanor Steber of the Metropolitan Opera."

And then it happened. But I'll let the reviews of the next day's press speak for themselves.

> It was an affair to rank with the coming of Christ, the death of Garland, the birth of the blues, and the freezing of spinach! . . . The ushers are leading the tuxes to their $15 seats . . . Reverence is the order of the evening and Madame is feeding from the reverence and giving out schmaltz. (Arthur Bell, *The Village Voice*)

> Miss Steber appears from the steam room in a chiffon gown, loaded with diamonds and a black towel draped around her waist. Mrs. Leonard Bernstein, Suzy, Patrice Munsel, a lot of Metropolitan Opera stars and half of New York society love it. Miss Steber is in good voice, singing everything from *Tosca* to Strauss waltzes while boys yell, "Brava!" (Rex Reed, *New York Daily News*)
>
> The local music scene may never be quite the same again . . . The music was great, the performances magnificent, and the entire ambiance unique, happy and warmly wonderful . . . Miss Steber offered music of the highest quality—and the steamy atmosphere of the Continental resounded with gorgeous singing and rafter-raising cheers . . . Steve Ostrow is obviously too shrewd a businessman not to take advantage of a popular hit. La Steber (and, we dare say, others) will surely make music again at the Continental. (Byron Belt, *Long Island Press*)
>
> While togas and towels and mirrored walls gave the place Berlin-in-the-thirties overtones, the concert was serious. With the concert market dwindling, Miss Steber said the Baths provided "another outlook for serious music" . . . She received a thunderous ovation and the audience rose in tribute. The social season was underway! (Bernadine Morris, *The New York Times*)

But perhaps the most remarkable and historical was the telegram I received from the then mayor of New York City, the Honorable John Lindsay, which I read out to the assembled audience:

> I wish to extend my congratulations to the Continental Baths and Health Club on the occasion of your black tie, black towel concert. Your sponsorship of the appearance of an opera singer of the stature of Eleanor Steber is a wonderful opportunity for the community to enjoy her great talent outside the Metropolitan's halls. I am sure this festive event will herald a response worthy of your fine preparation. I wish you continued success in extending the benefit of great music to the people of our city.

I had done it. If I never accomplished another thing, bringing the Metropolitan Opera to the Continental and having the Baths raised to a status celebrated by the highest office of the city filled me with a sense of emotion and fulfillment beyond that of any other experience in my life so far other than fathering a child.

The reception that followed was one of the high points in the life of the Continental. Towels and gowns were dropped as bodies, male and female, plunged into the pool, such was the feeling of oneness that had been achieved through the power of music.

RCA Victor recorded the concert on a Red Seal label, their most prestigious disc category, titling it *Steve Ostrow Presents Eleanor Steber Live at the Continental Baths*, featuring "Impromptu Remarks by the Artiste and Mr. Ostrow." It quickly became a cult item.

For years afterward, I received royalties from sales of the recording but lost track of them as I later traveled the world. The only copy I now have is one I "borrowed" from the San Francisco public library in 1978. I would go back to San Francisco, but I'm afraid I'd be stopped from leaving the city until I paid the overdue penalties—presumably with interest—for over twenty years.

There are times when I wonder, did it all really happen? But then I go to the record cabinet, and there it is . . .

STEVE OSTROW
PRESENTS

ELEANOR STEBER

LIVE AT THE CONTINENTAL BATHS

(Recorded October 4, 1973)
WITH IMPROMPTU REMARKS BY THE ARTISTE AND MR. OSTROW

Side A

Mozart
Idomeneo: Zeffiretti lusinghieri
The Magic Flute: Ach, ich fühl's
Così fan tutte: Come scoglio

Charpentier
Louise: Depuis le jour

Side B

Puccini
La Bohème: Quando m'en vo (Musetta's Waltz)

Massenet
Manon: Scene and Gavote

Sieczynski
Wien, du Stadt meiner Träume*

Fields-Kreisler
Stars in My Eyes*

Ross-Lehár
The Merry Widow: Vilia;
I Love You So ("The Merry Widow Waltz")*

Puccini
Tosca: Vissi d'arte

Edwin Biltcliffe, *Pianist*
*Joseph Rabb, *Violinist*
Photos by Nick Sangiamo
Art Director: J. J. Stelmach
Produced by Joseph Habig
Recording Engineer: Paul Goodman
Timings: Side A—29:06; Side B—29:22 / Clearance: Side B, #3, 4, 5—ASCAP

TMK(S) ® Registered • Marca(s) Registrada(s) RCA Corporation
© 1974, RCA Records, New York, N.Y. • Printed in U.S.A.

Chapter 40

High Noon

> Steve, I've been offered a place with the Norwegian National Ballet as a member of the corps de ballet. It means leaving Stuttgart, but I think it's in my best interests. My knee is better now, and I'm back dancing. Robert has returned to Australia. I'll be living in Oslo and will be sending my new address and telephone number. Love, Jess.

My god, I thought, as I finished reading the letter. *He gets farther and farther away. Oslo, Norway. The land of the midnight sun. But he's doing his thing, he's dancing. And what am I doing? Running a sex palace for the deprived and the depraved. Sure, I am still taking lessons, but what happened to my dream?*

Earlier that year, the Lauritz Melchior Foundation had notified me that I was one of nine finalists worldwide. And at the sing off that followed in Carnegie Hall, I had come in second. Maybe there was still a chance for me.

I sent a cable—not to Jess but to the Royal National Norwegian Opera. It was like rolling the dice to see which way both of my most cherished fantasies would come up:

> Dear Interdant. I am a dramatic tenor, a finalist in the Lauritz Melchior Heldentenor Contest. I will be coming to Norway in the early part of October and would welcome an audition with your company at your earliest convenience. Your reply will be greatly appreciated.

Amazingly, in two weeks' time, I received the following cablegram.

> Dear Mr Ostrow. As it happens we are seeking a dramatic tenor to replace one of our long-time resident artists who has chosen to take retirement.

We will be very happy to see you on the 10th of October at 10 AM in the Opera House. Sincerely, The Royal National Norwegian Opera.

* * *

I had heard much about the Land of the Midnight Sun but didn't know what to expect at this time of the year.

The taxi ride from Oslo Airport into the city was breathtaking. The sky was ribboned with purple clouds through which a deep, egg-yolk sun glowed. Because of the proximity to the Arctic Circle, the colors of the great Norwegian pines—and indeed all of the foliage—were almost too intense to imagine. The air was crisp and tinglingly clear, and I felt the excitement of a new adventure.

The first thing I did after checking into the Coliseum Hotel was to call and confirm my audition appointment with the opera company. Jess had no idea that I was in Norway as I wanted to do the audition first and then surprise him. That gave me two days to myself to acclimatize and see Oslo.

Although having a population of less than four hundred thousand, Oslo was a very cosmopolitan town. The people were tall, blue-eyed, and fair for the most part; and all the men looked as though they had modelled for Tom of Finland: blond-maned stallions, handsome of face, with great wide shoulders on bodies tapering down to tight, narrow waists, and then long, muscular legs, booted for the most part, and all with crotches bulging from skin-hugging blue jeans. One could only hope they would all be gay—but alas, they only looked it. In fact, homosexuality was still illegal in Norway and would remain so until 1981. The underground clubs that did exist were frequented by gay guys who were usually short, fat, sloppy, and generally unattractive. So I spent most of my time sitting in the coffeehouses on the great Karl Johans Gate, perusing the pedestrians.

Once having seen the Ibsen Memorial, there was really no better sightseeing to do. Besides, I was practicing celibacy prior to the audition, which was rather commendable, I thought, although I didn't really know what other choices I had.

I did however visit the offices of Det Norske Forbundet, the national gay rights organization that dated back to 1948. The Continental was internationally famous, and they were happy to see me, making me an honorary lifetime member. They were fighting the good fight, but it wasn't until 1981 that a two-part antidiscrimination law forbidding all forms of public discrimination against gay men and lesbian women was enacted. As a result, homo—and heterosexuals there now have equal standing in the eyes of the law. Something that is still not universally accepted in the United States and many other so-called *democratic* countries.

* * *

"Steve, what are you doing here?"

I thought Jess would fall over when he saw me. I had gone to the Norwegian Ballet Company studios right after the audition, which turned out to be a disaster. They told me that although I was exactly what they were looking for, their resident tenor had decided not to retire after all. Oh well, they did offer to pay for my airfare, which I nobly accepted.

At the ballet company, I found Jess doing his barre exercises with the corps de ballet. Jess always looked his most seductive in ballet clothes.

"Oh, I just happened to be in the neighborhood, so I thought I'd drop in and see how you're doing," I said airily, containing my urge to embrace him.

I told him about my audition with the opera company, trying to make it sound as if that were my only reason for coming. But I don't think I convinced either him or myself.

"What are you going to do now?" Jess asked.

"Well, I guess I'll go back home," I replied glumly.

"Without taking me to dinner?" Jess said invitingly.

We ate in a homey white stucco house on the King's Gate that had been converted into a restaurant. The sun was still shining brightly at ten o'clock at night, and the only reason I knew the time was that my watch said so. For six months of the year, Norway is blessed with twenty-four hours of daylight, which it gives up for an equal six months of grey at the start of winter.

I had a strange dish consisting of broth, cereal, and beef, a unique Norwegian specialty. I had never chanced upon it before, nor have I since then, and I can understand why.

"Are you happy here, Jess?" I asked as the gruel made its way very slowly down my gullet, much like molten lava, carving its way down a mountainside.

"I'm doing my thing, and it feels great."

"No regrets on having left Stuttgart?"

"Steve, if I waited the full three years, I'd be an old man in this business. Most all the kids in school were in their early teens."

"How did you get the job?" I asked, now putting out the fire in my belly with a draft of cold Norwegian beer.

"I heard they were auditioning, and I just went for it."

"But you're in the corps de ballet, not a featured dancer."

"Yeah, but I got a better chance here than in Stuttgart. They're all stars there. Besides, I like the people here."

"Yeah, I know. I see them strolling down the Karl Johans Gate in their jeans and boots."

"And they have blue eyes and blond hair," Jess added dreamily.

"Then you prefer kippered herring to knockwurst?"

"Steve, do you have to be so crude?"

"It's my Jewish wit, Jess," I said, wiping my mouth with my napkin. "Well, I'm glad I got to see you and that you're okay and happy."

Jess looked at me strangely for a long time.

"What's wrong? Did I say something else crude?"

"No, I was just thinking," he said pensively.

I let the moment pass, and I can remember Jess's next words as if it were yesterday.

"I was thinking," he said, *"why don't you stay here?"*

"In Norway?"

"Yeah."

"What would I do?"

"Well, we could get a big house, and we could be together."

"And what would I do here?" I persisted, not believing what I was hearing.

"Well, I'd be dancing . . . and you could start a business. Or sing. Or anything. You're good at getting things started anywhere. And we could begin a new life together."

I was speechless. I never thought I would hear those words from Jess's mouth. Mine, maybe. Here was this boy that I had pursued thousands of miles on innumerable occasions. And now he was offering me the prize at the end of the journey.

I was so overcome with emotion that I couldn't think straight. Everything I had always wanted: a beautiful boy, a home together, an artistic lifestyle, doing my own thing. So what was wrong? It was Professor DeLoache offering me a scholarship to Yale all over again, when I couldn't bring myself to leave my mom and brother.

"Jess," I said, forgetting the business, "I have a wife and two children."

"Yeah, I know, Steve. You always had a wife and two children. And it didn't stop you before."

"But I never really deserted them. I mean, Norway! A little farther and we'd be in the Arctic Circle."

Jess poured himself another glass of red wine. He never did bother with beer.

"Well, Steve," Jess said solemnly, "don't say I didn't make the offer. This time it's you who's running away."

"I'm not running away, Jess. I'm just going home."

* * *

The plane landed at JFK late Saturday evening, and all I wanted to do was go to my house on Seventy-first Street and see Joanne and the kids.

"Who is it?" Joanne's voice came through the intercom.

"It's Steve."

"I thought you were away. What do you want?"

That floored me.

"What do you mean, what do I want? I'm home. Open the door, Joanne."

No response. No buzzing on the intercom. And then I could hear footsteps on the stairs. Suddenly the door opened.

"What makes you think that this is your home?" Joanne said icily as she stood firmly in the doorway, dressed only in a robe.

"'Cause I pay the bills," I said with a tight smile.

But Joanne wasn't in a joking mood. "A home is where you live, not a place where you pick up your mail. Or is that not what you're here for?"

"Come on, Joanne, I've just come back from Norway; and I want to see you and the kids."

"The kids, who may or may not remember you, are asleep. And that's where I'm going. You can see them in the morning." Without pausing for breath, she continued, her voice now taking on a hard cutting edge, "You never told us where you were going and when you were coming back. Did you expect us to stay up every night, waiting for you, Stephen?"

"I told you I was going on an audition trip, Joanne," I said with as much restraint as I could muster.

"And I'm sure you auditioned lots of people."

I let that one pass. "Actually, Joanne, I wanted to spend the night with you and see the kids when they wake up."

Joanne was now screaming. "What makes you think you can come here anytime you feel like it and just jump into bed as if you never left? I'm not one of your little playmates!" And with that she slammed the door.

I stood out in the cold for a long time. There was no doubt that Joanne was hurt and wanted to hurt back in the only way she could.

Well, there was always the Baths, I thought, trying to cheer myself up. It was Saturday night, there was still time to make the show, and for sure, Pablo would be there.

* * *

My pulse quickened as I entered the club, hearing the opening strains of "The Continental" bouncing off the mirrored walls. Ted and Scotti were to handle the show in my absence, and I wasn't quite sure who was performing tonight. All I wanted to do was to find Pablo, sit in the audience with him, and just enjoy the show. That would be a first.

Well, it didn't take me long to find Pablo. There, seated in the front row was not only my Pablo, but on his lap was Tanya, the queeniest little Spanish boy in the club, notorious for picking up straights.

"Ladies and gentlemen." Ted had started the show. "Steve Ostrow and the Continental Baths"—Ted always put it that way—"are proud to present the one and only . . . Holly Woodlawn!"

What! I thought. Holly Woodlawn was the town's most infamous transvestite who owed her superstar status to having been a product of Andy Warhol's Famous Factory. She had recently been featured in Warhol's classic film *Trash* but had let the title go to her head, forgetting her humble beginnings as Harold Dunhaki from Brooklyn.

I had no objection to a class drag act like Charles Pierce or Gypsy but had always resisted putting Holly on as she was usually more stoned than Mount Rushmore, although in form she could be alluring and had quite a following. I had caught her act in Reno Sweeney's and must admit that her rendition of Fanny Brice's classic "Cooking Breakfast for the One I Love" was outrageous. Ted, who had an affinity with drag queens, having worked for the inimitable Gypsy for many years, had used my absence to sign Holly on. But Gypsy was a reliable performer who knew how to work a crowd into a frenzy, much like Dame Edna Everage. With Holly, one never knew what to expect; and I didn't like surprises, at least not on stage.

Well, Holly came on, walking—or I should say stumbling—to the piano and, with a glass of champagne in her hand, waved genially at the audience. And they did applaud, many identifying with her tragic persona.

Holly acknowledged the applause and then managed to seat herself up on the piano à la Dietrich in *The Blue Angel*. Then, before singing a note, she collapsed onto the piano, the champagne glass slipping from her fingers and crashing on the floor as Joey Bishop started the drumroll.

The drumroll rolled on, but Holly didn't roll over. Seeing that neither Ted nor Scotti knew what to do next, and not wanting this travesty to go on any longer, I ran onto the stage and, picking up the mike from the floor, said, "Ladies and gentlemen, let's hear it for Holly Woodlawn! She's been rehearsing this act for years."

Somehow I got the curtain to come down. After removing Holly, we went on with the rest of the show, a sedate, by comparison, evening of songs by the magnificent Morgana King, who saved the day.

The gay press had a field day with this incident, accusing me of being a prude and not letting Holly continue. I suppose they were right on both counts; but perhaps if I had not intervened, Holly would never have gotten up to write her own story, *A Low Life in High Heels*.

My homecoming was not exactly what I had expected. That night, alone in my room—having left Jess for the last time, Joanne having rejected me, and Pablo having taken off with Tanya—all I could think about was, *Will I ever find where home really is?*

Bloomingdales Continental Towel

ELEANOR STEBER
Live at The Continental Baths

(Recorded October 4, 1973)

With impromptu remarks by the artists and Mr. Ostrow

Chapter 41

Winter Is Nigh

The winter was spreading its icy tentacles deeper and deeper into the heart of the city, the weather reflecting the somber state of the economy. Retail sales were at a standstill after a halfhearted Christmas spurt. The city now was polarized into a poverty class and a traditionally well-off class, with the middle class swept away by an economic maelstrom. Unemployment was at the highest in the city's history since the Great Depression. Crime was rampant. No one was safe anymore. The impoverished and underprivileged formed groups that roamed the city, looting and mugging anyone unfortunate enough to be in their way. There was no convenient war to mobilize the youth and create jobs manufacturing weapons of destruction.

The decades of political corruption had finally laid the city's coffers bare, and even John Lindsay's earnest efforts to make a clean sweep were impotent as the gridlock of recession took hold.

Slowly but inexorably, the city caved in until finally the unthinkable did happen: New York City, the foremost financial center of the world, faced bankruptcy.

The Continental had succeeded because it had fulfilled a need, a desperate aching need at the time, but now smaller establishments were filling those basic needs much more efficiently. Those who were at the low end of the spectrum went back to the old Everard and St. Marks Baths, where sex was all that was offered but cost little and were accessible to all. The beat culture flourished, as did the scene at the docks, the trucks, and the warehouses, where it was clandestine, dangerous, *and* cheap. All the things that we no longer were. The Continental through its disco and shows had given a sheen of glamour to a gay population that had finally found its way out of the closet. But the stylish gays and the trendy swingers who followed their lead were now queuing up at the

Palladium, Les Jardins, and Studio 54 when they wanted to dance, only coming to us during the week for serious business.

Whole areas of the Baths' vast acreage were often vacant, creating an eerie no-man's-land. Now that cabaret and disco were flourishing throughout the city, the lines for tickets to the shows were also shrinking as it was no longer kicky to sit on the floor or in a towel when you could go to the newly elegant city venues, *if* you had a buck.

It was time to try something new.

* * *

I have often been accused of being a male chauvinist pig, and no doubt with good reason at times. So, I thought, why not recognize that not only guys were queer but an awful lot of girls were just as bent?

The lesbian movement was not as strong in New York back then in the seventies as it is now, and there were only a handful of venues that catered to daughters of Sappho's persuasion. What few there were were mostly dykes-in-leather bars. They were off limits to gay guys and were actually classified as dangerous for any other type gender.

Cheryl and Pinky, my stage tech hands, had been lovers for years.

"What about a ladies' night for lesbos?" I asked as we sat at the Continental bar one day, peeling peanut shells.

"You're sick, Steve. You wanna freak out the guys? Some of them have never seen a vagina since they left the womb."

"Hold on, Cheryl," I said defensively. "I was thinking of giving over one room area on a Monday night, which is hairdressers' night anyway, and letting *real* girls in."

"What would they do?" piped Pinky.

"I dunno . . . what *do* girls do?"

"Well, they don't suck cock, I can tell you that."

"Thanks, Cheryl, I kinda figured that out."

"Look, Steve, why don't you give it a try? You've done everything else."

"Thank you, Pinky. Will you guys help?"

"We'll spread the word and hold your hand," they promised.

"Oh, Cheryl, I didn't know you cared!"

The first Monday night arrived, and so did the girls, timidly at first, and then with more determination.

I had sectioned off the famous room 50 area by the pool for their exclusive use. The sauna and steam room of course were mixed for the evening. By 10:00 PM, women had stopped arriving, and those that were in house were sitting around the snack bar tables drinking tea. Gossip flowed with the tea, but nary a girl ventured into the steam room or sauna. Whereas the guys were busy sucking and fucking, the girls spent the night sipping and talking the hours away.

"Well, you tried it, and it didn't work," Cheryl said sympathetically back at the bar a week later as she deftly dipped a fresh teabag in the pot. "We're just not as promiscuous as you guys are. We like to find a partner and just be together doing girlie things, don't we, dear?" she said, pouring Pinky a cup of tea.

We tried holding "ladies' nights" for three months, but the only games the girls would play were canasta and mahjong. The experiment was a bust.

It was becoming all too clear that the Continental was a dinosaur too big to survive the ice age of economic change. As the revenue shrunk, we were forced to cut payroll and lay off help, giving them residence in the Baths in compensation.

Jacob Starr had been sick for years now, and even his son-in-law Allen had been replaced by a superefficient cost-cutting management committee. If the old man had been around, I would have renegotiated the rent, which was eating us alive. As it was, we still had two years to go on our original ten-year lease.

A new Mercedes I had bought to replace the Caddy had long since gone, as had the Fire Island house, which I sold at a loss to keep up interest payments to Eric Marks and take care of Joanne and the kids. Even 14177 had to go as the extra $300 a month was now critical, and so I found a small apartment for myself in the Beacon Hotel, over the same theater where I had presented Josephine Baker.

Never one to watch over details, I had no idea where our finances were until my accountants Ernie and Helen sat me down one day.

"Steve, you can't survive through the winter," Ernie said sepulchrally.

"You're facing bankruptcy," Helen pursued.

"I've faced worse before. How much money have we got in the bank?"

"Enough for one month of operation at the current rate of business, without paying the rent—which is two months in arrears."

"After eight years, that's all we have?"

"Don't forget the legal bills, the police payoffs, the Fire Island house, 14177, trips to Europe, Canada, chauffeurs, horses, Mercedes-Benzes, Cadillacs—"

"Stop!" I interrupted. "I get the point!"

To clear my head, I went out to walk the desolate streets. *Maybe I should have run for mayor,* I thought.

Snow was now starting to fall seriously. Sometimes in life, there is a combination of events, any one of which taken singly would seem insignificant. But seen together, they can lead to dynamic change.

Just such a combination of events was about to occur.

As I made it back to the Baths, I went down the famous mirrored staircase and surveyed the scene of a thousand past vibrations. What an incredible era it had been! I thought of all the lives that had been touched and changed by this basement paradox.

I must have been in a very reflective mood as I didn't hear my name being paged over the intercom until Manny tapped me on the shoulder.

"Steve, you've got a phone call."
I grabbed the telephone.
"Is this Steve Ostrow?"
"Yes."
"It's Montreal calling person-to-person collect."
"Hello, Steve, it's Sonny Steinberg."
Sonny was Maurice "Sonny" Steinberg, my Montreal attorney.
"What's up, Sonny? Run out of dimes?"
"No, but I'm not going to foot the bill while they track you down in the steam room. I just thought you'd like to know that the Sauna Neptune was raided last night, and the owners have shut it down. I know you were raving about it on your last trip . . . sounds like your kind of thing."
"Wow! That was fast! They've only been open a few months. See what you can find out, Sonny. Contact the owners and get back to me ASAP."
"Will do. How's the wife and kids?" Sonny had visited Joanne and me last year in New York City.
"Everybody's great, Sonny. Get the facts; maybe we'll all move out to Montreal."
"Leave it with me."

* * *

While I was mulling over this new development, I was paged again, this time by Helen in the back office.
"Yeah, what's up, Helen?"
"Steve," she said, "you better come right up."
Helen didn't say a word as she passed on a registered letter from the Hotel Ansonia board of trustees.

> Dear Mr. Ostrow. Consider this a formal notice of eviction as you are in default of your lease agreement. Unless the arrears of rental are brought to date, together with the next month's rent, we will be forced to institute foreclosure proceedings against you for all sums due, and to commence dispossessory action requiring you to vacate the premises. You have thirty days to satisfy your obligations. Please be advised that in any case of default on your part, all furniture, fixtures, appliances and improvements affixed to the premises will be deemed to be the possession of the landlord and as such may not be removed. Yours truly, the Ansonia Board of Trustees.

In the old days I would have received a call from Jake Starr, who would have barked at me over the telephone, after which we would have come to some amicable arrangement. But those days were over. The once-desolate basement property was now prime real estate, improved as it had been over the years with an up-to-date electrical, plumbing, and air-conditioning plant, for which I was still paying thousands of dollars weekly to Eric Marks.

Even so, I knew the board would not be considering action unless they had someone hot after the premises.

"Helen, see if you can find out where old man Starr is."

"I thought he died," Helen answered as she looked up some telephone numbers.

"He's too ornery to die. Find out where he is, no matter what you gotta do. Pretend you're Miss Moneypenny."

"Yes, James."

* * *

The voice on the other end of the line did indeed sound as if it were not of this world. But weak as it was, there was no mistaking the old man's growl.

"So what's up, Steve? I'm too sick. I don't get involved anymore in the hotel." The voice was weak but discernible.

"I just wanna know, Jake—who's after the Baths' premises?"

"What makes you believe I would know that?"

"The same way that I know there's a god in heaven."

Silence and then a faint chuckle.

"Vell, I'll let you know about that for sure soon." I could hear the old man's cigar-scarred lungs wheezing as he managed to gasp, "Levenson and Gordon."

Barry Levenson and Hy Gordon were well-known promoters, much the same as me. But their specialty was straight swingers' clubs, a new seventies phenomenon.

I arranged to meet them at the Baths to feel out their intentions. Surprised at how much I had already guessed, they confirmed that they wanted to build the biggest swingers' club in the city—and what better premises than the Continental, with its pool, glitz, and reputation? It was made to order for them, and they would save millions if they had to construct it themselves at today's prices. They were planning to call their new club Plato's Retreat.

"We've got the dollars and the backers, and we're ready to roll," Hy Gordon said cockily.

"Yeah, but I've got a ten-year lease with two years to go," I countered.

"Not if the Ansonia throws you out for nonpayment of rent."

"Do you know how long it would take them to legally dispossess me? I've got the best lawyers in town. And besides, I could throw the company into Chapter 11 and stick it out for years. You'll be passé by then."

"Look, you've had your run," Levenson said nastily. "Why don't you get a haircut and find yourself a job?"

It was clear that we weren't going to come to any understanding at that meeting. But for thirty days at least, I was still in possession, and so I had the upper hand.

* * *

A few days later, I heard from Sonny in Montreal about the Sauna Neptune's owners. "The two guys who own it are scared shitless," he told me. "They don't want to go to jail, so they're boarding the place up even though they've got a ten-year lease."

Sounds familiar, I thought.

"Can they get out of it?"

"No, because they personally guaranteed everything. And they're up to their ears in building development costs that they still have to pay."

"So they're stuck," I said.

"Like a wounded pig," said Sonny. "I mentioned you, and their lawyers think they would grab at any kind of deal that could get them off the hook."

"Set up a meeting. I'll take the next flight up."

"You bet. You coming alone?"

"Yes. I usually do these days."

Sonny was straight, so I doubt if he got the innuendo.

"Okay," he said, "we'll grab some dinner, just the two of us."

I was right; he didn't get it.

I took the next flight up and sat down with the Sauna Neptune guys, who looked as if they'd already been tried and hung. "We're up on charges of prostitution, narcotics, and allowing sex with minors on the premises," Lorne said.

Interesting, I thought, *no homosexuality allegations*. As the story unfolded, it was a classic example of poor management. The two business novices who had made their money in interior decorating thought that a good idea was enough.

They had built the club and then given all management control over to young gay kids while they stayed off the premises and counted the money. They had no idea what was going on in their own business. In the meantime, it had become a haven for illicit narcotic sales, commercial prostitution, and pubescent teenagers. No wonder the bubble had burst.

"Well, I can't help you with any of that, fellas," I said. "I assume you have the best legal representation available. But perhaps we can talk a deal that may help you keep your heads above water while the prosecution tries to put a noose around them. After all, you're going to have a lot of legal expenses—take it from me."

"What can you do for us?" they asked, as if I was their last hope. They were very aware of my reputation. The Canadian gay papers had always championed gay rights and had glorified me as the American hero à la John Wayne who had single-handedly ridden into the east and wrested New York gays from oppression. The Continental Baths was an international legend, thanks to Bette and the thousands of tourists that had come from all over the world to pay homage at the gay mecca.

Well, I thought I'd better cut a deal fast before they find out that the Tubs are going down the tubes.

"Look, I'll get your club open," I said, testing the waters.

"How?" they both chorused.

A plan was starting to form in my mind. "I'll bring in my own staff from New York to get it rolling. All moneys that come in will go to my management company. You guys will get 10 percent of the net income—that is, after all running expenses are paid."

"Suppose there's no money left?" Andre, the elder of the duo, asked.

Pretty shrewd, I thought. *He's figured out that net income means after I decide what and who gets paid.*

"There probably won't be for the first year till we catch up all your back bills and till we get volume up again. But you'd have to pay all of that yourselves, even with the club closed."

"When do you have to know?" Andre asked.

"Now. I'm a busy guy, and I won't come back here to the North Pole till next Christmas if there's no deal."

"We have just one question," Lorne said. "What happens if you can't get it open?"

"Then you're no worse off than you are now, are you?" I said.

After a final exchange of glances, the two French lovers stood up and shook my hand.

"Let's do it."

All parties were to converge at Sonny's offices the next day for signing. It all went off without a hitch, and now the ball was in my court: put up or shut up. Somehow I had convinced everyone—including myself—that I could pull this off. Just how, I'd have to figure out later.

Armed with contract in hand and dressed in my Cossack fur, I went off to do battle with the Montreal police. The French boys had given me the name of the officer in charge of the raid, and it was to his office that I went directly after announcing myself at the front desk.

Introducing myself as the owner of the Continental Baths in New York City, I explained that I was planning to take over the Sauna Neptune, bringing in my own managerial staff but employing dozens of Montreal locals to operate the club. Montreal was also suffering from the economic slowdown in New York City, and jobs were at a premium.

"And what type of clientele do you propose to cater to, monsieur?" the inspector asked.

"It would be a men's social and health club," I replied.

"You know, of course, that homosexual acts are illegal in public places in Quebec."

Ah. Now we're getting to the point, I thought.

"Monsieur *L'inspecteur*, we would be a men's health club. Now according to the latest Kinsey Report, 10 to 16 percent of all males are either homosexual or bisexual at some time in their lives. There is no way that we can exclude them."

"Pray continue, monsieur."

"My question is this: if I reopen the Sauna Neptune, will you close it down because there may be homosexual acts committed in private behind closed doors? Because if so, I might just as well pack up my bags and leave now." The cat was out of the bag.

"Monsieur Ostrow, the Montreal police have no problem with homosexual acts committed in private by consenting adults. And a room rented by an individual is considered to be his private domain, as is his home. We do not intend to go peeking behind closed doors. We will not, however, permit any homosexual—or any other sexual—act to be committed in the public view such as in corridors, public rooms, lavatories, steam rooms, saunas, et cetera."

"And is that what happened at the Sauna Neptune?"

"You may draw your own conclusions."

"I understand the charges were prostitution, narcotics, and the admittance of minors," I said. "Suppose I guaranteed you that none of those offences would be committed at the Sauna Neptune under my control?"

"Then you would have no problems, Monsieur Ostrow. But . . . how can you guarantee that?" the inspector queried, twirling his mustache and looking very much like Hercule Poirot.

"I would like *you* to do that for me," I said.

There was stunned silence from the police officers in the room. Finally the inspector stated, "That would be quite impossible, Monsieur Ostrow. The police department's budget would not permit that."

"What I mean is, I would like your off policemen to patrol the premises in three shifts, twenty-four hours a day, to ensure that no illegal acts take place. As I'm sure you know, it is common in the United States for police to take jobs as security officers in their own time."

"That is common here too," he replied. "And you are willing to undertake this expense?"

"Yes. Not only that, but I would like to have your men in uniform at the time so there's no hanky-panky from the clientele. Is this possible?"

We struck a deal, and with that I was back in business. After enjoying a coffee with my new police friends, who would now further the cause of gay liberation in Montreal, I walked out of the station into the crisp winter air singing "Stouthearted Men."

Chapter 42

The Last Dance

Back at the Continental, I couldn't help noticing the paint peeling from the walls, the ceiling pipes leaking, and the dank smell everywhere, none of which would have been apparent if the old hordes of towelled predators had been teeming through the halls. But like an endangered species, their numbers had diminished, giving those still surviving a strange aura of futility.

I gazed upon what had been the towel capital of the gay world. Funny how everything in my life that I thought would go on forever—my marriage, Freedom Finance, my relationship with Jorge, and then with Jess—had all come to an end.

Was it now time for the Continental? Only this time, the end would come by my own hand. What to do?

I now had the possibility of a whole new future in my contract with the Sauna Neptune. But how could I leave the Continental to die? I knew I could overcome the financial problems, find new ways to operate, consolidate, cut, create.

But even as I was trying to recapture the past, to rekindle the spark in my mind, I was stepping over bodies passed out in the hallways. The smell of acid and the acrid taste of angel dust permeated the place. Stoned-out bodies were crashing into me as I walked. Needles and syringes littered the halls. The hard-drug era had hit New York City, and it was not a scene that I could live with. The Baths had been turned into a battleground, with resident gangs ripping off customers to buy a hit or a fix. What had been a fantasia of love, art, and beauty was now a reflection of the depths of despair and depravity that the city had sunk into. This was no longer Steve Ostrow's Continental Baths.

I knew then that it was over for me. It was time to move on.

I summoned the two swingers promoters, Hy Rubin and Barry Levenson, back to the Baths with a proposition.

"Tell you what I'll do," I said. "How would you like to take over my lease? You'd get immediate possession."

"That's the general idea," Levenson said suspiciously. "What's your angle?"

"An obtuse one, far beyond your comprehension," I said. "You take over the lease and all notes and obligations still owing on the club." *Are you listening, Eric?* I thought. "Including the arrears on the rent. And the place is yours."

"You're crazy!" Rubin exclaimed.

"That may be, but it's not the issue. Either that, or you can wait two years or find yourselves another spot." I knew that nothing like the Continental existed anywhere else in New York City, and to build such a club at current day's prices would have been prohibitive.

"Immediate possession?" Rubin asked.

"Give me two weeks to get my boys out."

The two men conferred for less than ten minutes while I lit my proverbial pipe.

"Ten days."

The pipe lit, I blew a perfect smoke ring into the air and watched it dissipate.

"Deal."

Next, I called a meeting of the entire staff, who assembled on the disco floor. I took the stage in my familiar emcee role, only this time I had a sad announcement to make: "The Continental will be closing in ten days."

I could see the panic in everyone's eyes. Where would they live? Work? Play? The Continental had been home and family for many of them since coming out.

"I am going to open a club in Montreal, Canada," I went on. "This is a new undertaking, and I can't guarantee anything. But any of you who want to come with me are welcome. Your airfare will be paid, and you can live at the new club till money comes in for payroll. To those of you who don't choose to come, I understand, and my thanks for all your effort and loyalty in the past. Those of you who do choose to come—well, brothers, all I can tell you is that Montreal is an exciting city. But be prepared to freeze your nuts off. Who's in for the ride?"

Joe, Gus, Chula, Manny, Al, Scotti, and Paul—the Magnificent Seven—one by one, they left the others and joined me on the stage.

"Gentlemen, I thank you. Start knitting sweaters. We leave in ten days."

* * *

Nine days had passed. It seemed they took longer than the nine years that the Continental had been opened.

"How are we doing?" I said to Helen and Ernie. We were having our final wrap-up session in the back office.

"Well," Helen said, "all payroll has been cleared, all trade invoices paid, and all taxes are to date." And with that she sat back in her swivel chair for perhaps the last time.

"What about you guys?"

"Look, Steve, if we take our money, that's the bottom of the barrel. How are you going to get to Montreal?"

"I wanna go clean, fellas. Clear it up."

"Okay," Ernie said resolutely.

"What about Eric Marks's notes and the lease payments?" I asked.

"All transferred to the new company, Plato's Retreat," Ernie replied.

Eric had been resigned to the Continental's closing and had been happy to get Plato's on the hook for all the Continental's construction work. I had turned all my other enterprises—Uptight, Tiger-Mite, Hi-Lite Wines and Liquors, and Super-Rite Food Markets—over to their respective managers on notes to be paid to Eric, as there were huge amounts still owing on their construction.

Eric had seemed quite despondent at our meeting when I told him what I was doing. But it was more, I think, from losing a friend than any concern he had over the money. Eric's wife, Ina, had started up a chain of yoga studios and had written a best-selling book on the subject. She was now a quite prominent guru figure and was seldom home. Eric's only daughter had long since broken away from Eric's despotic household, and he was alone, a poor frightened man whose millions had never brought him happiness.

"Steef, all I come home to now is my dog. What good is all the money?"

"Call me anytime, Eric. I'll be there for you."

"Ya, ya," Eric said stoically. "Come with me, we go for a ride in the plane." Eric had his own Piper Cub Turboprop plane and delighted in taking people on rides. Only now there was nobody to take.

"I've got to get back to the club, Eric, and get everything in place," I said apologetically. "I'll take a rain check."

"Ya, ya, Steef, go, go. Good luck." He dug his hand into his pocket. "Here, take some money."

"No, no, Eric. I don't know when I can pay it back."

"So what else is new?" he said, squeezing $5,000 in $100 bills into my pocket.

"Thanks, Eric. Stay in touch. Give my regards to Ina."

"Ya, ya. You'll probably see her before I do."

* * *

"Well, guys," I said to Helen and Ernie, "anything left in the bank?"

"Two thousand dollars, and that's it," Helen said.

"Okay. Take that, and whatever else comes in tomorrow, and divide it all up with the employees we're letting go."

"Whatever you say, Steve. But how are you going to pay the airfares to Montreal?"

"We'll seal about that," I said.

The only thing of value that hadn't been sold was my Alaskan seal fur coat. It had been my friend now for many years and had been looking forward to the Montreal snow. But alas, feeling like Colline in act 4 of Puccini's *La Bohème*, in which he hocks his coat to buy the dying Mimi medicine, I made the trek to a pawnshop. You don't get much when you hock things; but I did get $3,000, which would get us all to Montreal.

With tickets in hand, I made my last stop in New York, at Joanne's. Since the last separation, we had become good friends again. The kids were used to my comings and goings, but they always knew I was around the corner. That corner would now be La Gauchetière and Ste Catherine, a bit out of the way.

We all kissed and hugged, and then I took Joanne aside. I had kept her up to date on what was happening at the Continental and my plans for Montreal.

"Here, Jo, take this so I know you guys are okay for a while," I said, pressing the $5,000 from Eric into her hands. Then noticing her bare finger, which had always borne the black opal ring I had had made for her when things were going well in our marriage, I exclaimed, "Where the hell is your ring?" It was a rare twenty-point black opal surrounded by thirty-two white diamonds and set in platinum. Joanne never took it off, even to wash the dishes, which was a no-no, as black opals are very fragile. "You broke it!" I accused.

"No, Steve, I pawned it." And putting her hand in her jeans pocket, she pulled out $5,000 in cash and gave it to me. "Here, take this so I know *you* guys are okay for a while," she said, mimicking me. I couldn't help remembering what Joanne's mother had told me fifteen years ago. *Joanne is highly strung,* she had said, *but if she loves you—as she obviously does—then you have a friend for life.*

And so it was that on the tenth of February 1977, in a blinding snowstorm, eight raunchy New Yorkers boarded an Air Canada Jet for a steamy mission in the frozen North.

And with that the fabulous Continental era came to a close. Little did we know the adventures that awaited us and how all of our lives would change forever.

In seven short years, we had helped emancipate a minority no less oppressed than the blacks and Jews who populated the city. But they had never been legislated against for just being *who* they were. Discriminated against, yes, but it wasn't illegal to be black or Jewish—at least not in New York City. But it *had* been illegal to be a practicing homosexual. In addition, almost single-handedly, we had brought glamour back, reinvented the disco, resurrected cabaret, and spawned or nurtured the careers of the likes of Bette Midler, Barry Manilow, Laura Kenyon, Melba Moore, Peter Allen, Manhattan Transfer, Patti LaBelle, Morgana King, and countless others.

In those seven years, almost three and a half million guests visited the Continental, its vibrations felt worldwide. But if the Continental were to be remembered for one thing only, I would like it to be "love": the dignity of loving yourself for who you are and the right and delight of sharing that love with those who would.

> And I'll take love from where it comes, and that's where I will go
> And I will offer anyone me to get to know
> So don't look back
> And don't attack
> Just let whatever be
> And maybe you and I
> Together can be we

Epilogue

Three months later, what had been the Continental Baths reopened as Plato's Retreat, a straight version catering to the swinging '70s. After three years of operation, the club was closed by the federal police. In the summer of 1979, Hy Rubin and Barry Levenson were each sentenced to five years in prison for tax fraud.

Disclaimer and Acknowledgment

Disclaimer

All the events depicted in this narrative actually happened. Any resemblance to characters living or dead is strictly intentional. Some of the names have been changed to protect the guilty.

Acknowledgment

To my soul mate Charles Wong, thank you for your caustic wit, impeccable grammar, nimble fingers, and refusal to accept anything but the highest standard of literary excellence, without which my humble talent would never have been able to pen this epistle.

Ostrow's List

Joey Iannone, my manager at the Continental, and his lover Gus moved to Upstate New York to raise and show dogs. Gus died of AIDS some years afterward.

Frankie Knuckles, my DJ at the Continental, has gone on to be one of the world's most in-demand recording mixers, his talents in demand in New York, Chicago, Miami, South Africa, Australia, and Europe.

Ted Hook, my PR man at the Continental, went bankrupt after opening his own restaurant, Ted Hook's Backstage. Ted died of AIDS in 1995.

My brother **Marshal** retired after a long and productive career in the New York City Civil Service. He and his wife, **Sully,** lived in a retirement community in West Palm Beach, Florida, for many years until his death in 2002.

Don Scotti, my brown-eyed little star of *Saturday Night at the Baths* who began as a personal secretary et al., has disappeared from the face of the earth; and all attempts to locate him have failed. Scotti, if you're reading this, pick up the *fuckin'* phone! Since writing the above, I have rediscovered Scotti. He is alive and well in Los Angeles and in the motion picture business. *Saturday Night at the Baths* has been made into a DVD and is selling extremely well. All net profits from the DVD that come to me will be used for AIDS research in the name of Chula DeJan.

Scott, my son, and his wife, **Jennifer**, are busy raising kids in a little town in California where the population is so small that their efforts make front-page headlines as they alter the census.

Maria, my daughter, is now a computer scientist for Boeing in California and is happily married after three rehearsals.

Peter Allen is the subject of a blockbuster Australian musical based on the bio *The Boy from Oz*, written by Stephen Maclean. Peter's own show *Legs Diamond* was a flop. Peter died of AIDS in 1992. *The Boy from Oz* has now gone international with Hugh Jackman now playing the lead role.

Patti LaBelle came to Australia on a concert tour last year. She picked me out of the audience at the Sydney Hilton saying, "Steve baby, you haven't changed a bit." Patti can still sing, but she's lost her eyesight.

Bette Midler and **Barry Manilow** are still strutting their stuff. Bette has just finished a forty-city concert tour of her show "Kiss My Brass," and Barry has signed a sixty-million-dollar contract with the Las Vegas Hilton! And it all started at the Tubs.

Joanne and I divorced through her mother's insistence. Joanne then became a chaplain with the LAPD and was fast becoming the patron saint of Los Angeles prisons when she was stricken with terminal breast cancer. I went back to the United States to stay with her in a hospice. She died Easter Sunday 2001. We had become closer than we ever were.

Chula died of AIDS in 1985. I send flowers to his mother every year on his birthday, the eleventh of May.

Eric Marks flew out in his own plane to visit me in Montreal as soon as I opened the Sauna Neptune. He was preoccupied over an impending tax audit. On his return to New York City, he hit a telephone pole and was decapitated. He was still holding over $1.5 million in notes from the Continental at the time.

Barry Slotnick went on to become one of New York City's most respected attorneys. He and his wife and children lead a semiorthodox Jewish life, and Barry is a celebrity in his own right.

What was formerly the **Continental Baths**, and then Plato's Retreat, is now a parking garage in the Ansonia Hotel.

Jess Jimenez lives alone in the CBD in Sydney, Australia, and conducts stretch classes at the Hyde Park Club, where I work out daily. Jess was struck by a car two years ago and will never dance again, but he is surviving and teaching movement!

Jorge de La Torre, my glorious Peruvian, lives on as a legend in SoHo, New York. I have not seen him in over twenty years. We were to meet on my sixty-eighth birthday, but that is another story.

Me

After building the Montreal baths into a highly profitable enterprise, it was commandeered by the Canadian Mafia when Premier Levesque did away with bilingualism in Quebec in 1978. Chula and I left to live in San Francisco, where I sang with the San Francisco Opera for seven years. At the same time, I built the largest male escort service in the United States, the Golden Boy Agency. In 1984, we were raided by the San Francisco Police Department and closed down. I then moved to Germany, where I sang in the Stuttgart Opera House and was employed by the US government and the USO to put on shows for the eight hundred thousand NATO troops and their families living in West Germany.

In 1987, I traveled to Australia to visit Jess, who was dancing with the Australian Ballet. I never left.

I sang with the Australian Opera for eight years and then, after a bout with laryngeal cancer, set up the Sydney Academy of Vocal Arts. I now teach singing and am also an education officer for the AIDS Council of New South Wales and project officer of MAG, the Mature Age Gay Men's Group in Sydney, which I founded in 1991 and which is now the largest gay organization in all of Australia and the largest of its type in the entire world!

One night, after Chula had died, I went out into a little park near where I now live. I looked up at the starry night and found the brightest star there. I knew it was him. I was lonely and tired. It had been a long trip. I asked the star to send me a soul mate, someone I could love. And he did.

I wasn't going to tell you about all of the above until my next book, *The Best Is Yet to Come*. But both my agent and my editor insisted, saying, "There may never be a next book. And even if there was, no one might read it." I'll leave that to you.

*The Best Is Yet to Come has now been written, and I can be reached on sostrow@bigpond.net.au.

Index

A

Aberdeen, Robert 178
Advocate 33, 153
After Dark 119
AIDS 66, 219
AIDS Council of New South Wales 221
Allen, Peter 74, 76, 220
American Ballet 153
amyl nitrate 14, 64, 65
androgynous look 108
angel dust 14, 65
Anna Regina. *See* King, Joanne English
Annenbergs 59
Ansonia Hotel 11, 31, 45, 65, 101, 187, 220
APA (American Psychiatric Association) 14

B

Baker, Josephine 165, 166, 167, 169, 170, 171
Baths language 38
Beacon (theater) 169
Beacon Baths 176
Beacon Hotel 203
Béjart, Maurice 161, 162
Bel Canto Opera Company 19
Beneficial Finance Company 17, 23
Beretta, Joanne 174
Bohème, La (Puccini) 19, 20, 212
bondage 86
Bonicom (inspector) 40, 41, 42
Bricktop 166, 167, 168
Brown, Helen Gurley 59, 69
Brown, Howard 14
Buckley, David 176, 177, 178

C

Calloway, Cab 85, 163, 165
Cantrell, Lana 85
Cardin, Pierre 57, 58
"Chella Mi Credo" 19
Cherry Grove 72, 107
Chula 116, 165, 166, 181, 182, 183, 210, 220
Cohen, Noel 128, 147
Collins, Pat 104, 105
Combs, Earl 59, 73
consensual sex 35, 63
Continental Band 51, 63, 101, 165
Continental Baths 13, 16, 30, 31, 34, 50, 52, 53, 68, 143, 165, 168, 189, 190, 207, 209, 220
Continental disco 46, 107
Coward, Noël 86
Cranko, John 160, 161
Cross, Barry 17, 33, 113, 141
Cunningham, Billy 51, 52, 60

223

D

Daily News 121
Decadence 153, 154, 159, 178
DeLoache, Benjamin 15, 16
Dick 42, 43
Die Meistersinger 78
discipline 86
Divine Miss M. *See* Midler, Bette

E

Edwardian look 87
enticement and entrapment 41, 62, 63
Esterel, Jacques 57
"Esultate" 78
Everard Baths 27, 29, 201

F

Fanciulla del West, La (Puccini) 19
Fire Island 71, 72, 74, 78
Flamingo, the 107
Forum 119
Forum of the Twelve Caesars, the 58, 133
Freedom Finance Company 23, 24, 71
Fusco, Michael 107

G

Gabe. *See* Gabriel
Gabriel (assistant manager) 23, 30, 31, 32, 23, 30, 31, 32, 33, 34
Garage, the 107, 145
Garland, Judy 53, 108
gay culture 13
Gay Liberation Rally 60, 63
gay mecca 113, 140, 207
gay press 34, 37, 41, 119, 121, 151, 198
gay world 117, 125, 209
Germany 78, 162, 221
Giametta, Michael 33, 153
Golden Girl. *See* Payne, Freda

Greenwich Village 30, 38, 44, 62, 63, 84, 89, 133, 155, 178
Gregory, Dick 99

H

Hair 14, 38
Halliday, Lorne 183, 206
Hampton, Dawn 172
Harlettes 109, 112, 114
Helen (accountant) 43, 54, 80, 121, 122, 203, 204, 211
Henry Street Settlement 15
Hi-Lite Wines and Liquors 133, 211
Hollywood 145
homosexuality 14, 29, 35, 62, 63, 183, 194, 206
Hook, Ted 84, 141, 163, 219
Hopkins, Linda 87, 93

I

Iannone, Joe 88, 89, 90, 219
Ice Palace 107
Il Pagliacci 78
Improv, the 49, 51

J

Jagger, Mick 69, 87, 108
Jewish Men's Hashiva Club, the 12, 32
Jimenez, Jess 104, 105, 107, 119, 125, 128, 133, 134, 153, 159, 160, 193, 195, 196, 220
Josephine's (restaurant) 166

K

Kahn, Ben 49
Kahn, David 119, 120
Kaiserslautern 78, 79, 81
Kent, Walter 25, 27, 30, 31, 32, 33, 34, 54, 176

Kenyon, Laura 172
Khedouri, Franklin 178
kike 99
King, Jeanne Reed 21
King, Joanne English 20, 21, 24, 29, 34, 38, 40, 44, 53, 62, 73, 81, 94, 95, 96, 105, 131, 196, 197, 212, 220
King, John Reed 20, 21, 78
King, Morgana 163, 198, 212
King Morgana 85

L

LaBelle, Patti 84, 99, 212, 220
LaBelle Patti 85
LaFlamme, Andre 183, 207
Lauritz Melchior Heldentenor Foundation 31, 193
La Baker. *See* Baker, Josephine
Leary, Timothy 14, 46
Les Jardins 107, 145, 202
Levan, Larry 107
Levenson, Barry 205, 209, 215
Levesque, Rene 221
Linda (swinger) 184, 185
Lindsay, John 13, 62, 190, 201
Loft, the 145
LSD 14, 65
Luft, Lorna 85, 173

M

Mafia 14, 35, 124
Magnificent Seven, the 203
Manhattan 15, 24, 142
Manhattan Transfer, the 172, 212
Manilow, Barry 60, 61, 63, 108, 109, 113, 220
Manny (towel boy) 39, 40, 97, 203, 210
marijuana 65
Marks, Eddie 45, 47
Marks, Eric 127, 140, 203, 211, 220
Marks, Rosalie 44, 47
Matawan, New Jersey 24

Mature Age Gay Men's Group 221
McCall, Carl 62, 175
McNally, Terrence 127
Melchior, Lauritz 31, 146
Mercer, Mabel 166
Met. *See* Metropolitan Opera Company
Metropolitan Opera Company 16, 190
Michael's Thing 33, 153
Midler, Bette 50, 51, 52, 53, 60, 61, 62, 63, 76, 154, 155, 156, 220
Mitchell, Joey 51, 60
Montreal, Canada 57, 58, 181, 182, 204, 206, 207, 210
Montreal police 207, 208
Moore, Melba 85, 99, 212
Mount Morris Baths 100

N

National Gay Task Force 14
New York City 29, 33, 35, 38, 41, 42, 45, 46, 49, 63, 65, 76, 78, 85, 87, 99, 103, 108, 129, 151, 175, 176, 184, 201, 209
New York City Ballet Company 178
New York City Council 13
New York City Department of Health 45
New York Daily News 53, 153, 190
New York State 23, 25, 31
New York State Department of Sales Tax 122
New York Times 25, 75, 121, 156, 160, 169, 190
nigger 99
Nureyev, Rudolf 69, 132, 133, 134, 136

O

Ohrbach, Richard 46, 70, 71, 96
Olivor, Jane 134, 153, 173
14177 97, 104, 116, 128, 139, 203
Orgy Room 28, 47, 52, 90
Oslo, Norway 193, 194, 195, 196
Ostrow, Marshal 16, 21, 135, 219

Ostrow, Steve 17, 19, 21
  businessman 32, 40, 190
  business empire 133, 211
  family 34, 38, 39, 53, 80
  gay relationship 57, 125, 128, 133, 134, 151, 166, 183, 209
  sexual encounters 59, 120
Otello 78

P

Pablo (Puerto Rican youth) 184, 185, 186, 197
Palladium, the 202
Payne, Freda 143, 144, 145
PBS (Public Broadcasting Station) 153
Pedro (bath attendant) 97, 153
Physique Pictorial 17
Piaf, Edith 134, 153
Pines, the 72
Plato's Retreat 205, 211, 215, 220
Post 121
Poutassa 173
Puccini 19, 212
Purple Office 42

Q

Quaalude 14, 105
Queen Yanna 157, 158

R

Rabb, Joseph 188
raids 41, 42, 43, 44, 61
RCA Victor 188, 189, 191
Reed, Rex 53, 153, 190
Reiss Park 16, 45
Ritz, The 127
Rolling Stone 119, 176
Rose, The 74, 83, 154
Ross, Diana 108
Roth, Lillian 134, 163
Roth Lillian 85

Royal National Norwegian Opera, the 193
Rubin, Hy 205, 209, 215

S

sadomasochism 38, 65, 85, 86
Saint Laurent, Yves 57
San Francisco Police Department 221
Saturday Night at the Baths 181, 219
Sauna Neptune 181, 204, 206, 207, 208, 209
Schliesser 57
Schmidt, Wilhelm 79
Scotti, Don 74, 97, 128, 144, 148, 153, 178, 210, 219
sexual experimentation 59
sexual freedom 38, 125
sexual liberation 65
Shepperd, Ellen 178
Slotnick, Barry 91, 123, 154, 155, 156, 220
"Sonnet to a Prude" 151, 153
spic 99
St. Mark's Place 28
St. Marks Baths 28, 100, 201
Starr, Jacob 11, 12, 32, 45, 96, 203
Steber, Eleanor 187, 188, 189, 190
Steinberg, Sonny 204, 206
Stokes, William Earle Dodge 146
Stone, Caleb 153, 178
Stonewall riots 13, 63
Strauss, Levi 147
Streisand, Barbra 53, 108
Studio 54 202
Stuttgart Ballet 160, 161
Super-Rite Food Markets 133, 211
"Sweet Marijuana" 114
S and M. *See* sadomasochism

T

Taylor, Elizabeth 108
Tenth Floor, the 107, 145
Tiger-Mite Health Food 133, 211

Tommy (hairdresser) 90
Torre, Jorge de la 56, 57, 58, 59, 70, 73, 221
Torres, Liz 50, 51, 52
Trash 198
Tubs. *See* Continental Baths

U

UNESCO 167, 168, 169, 170
Uptight Boutique 59, 73, 87, 133

V

Valentino 69
Vaughn, Sarah 85, 99, 121, 122, 123, 124, 163
Vesti La Giubba 78
Vietnam War 175
von Furstenberg, Egon 59, 69, 159

W

Warhol, Andy 59, 69, 118, 119
Warhol Club 118
West Side Detention Center 40
Whiting, Margaret 85, 163
WINS 101
Women's Wear Daily 119, 174
Wonder, Stevie 68
Woodlawn, Holly 198
Wrangler 147

Y

Yale University 16
Yale University Repertory Theatre 127
"You Gotta Have Friends" 63

Z

Zimmerman, Fred 40, 71, 92

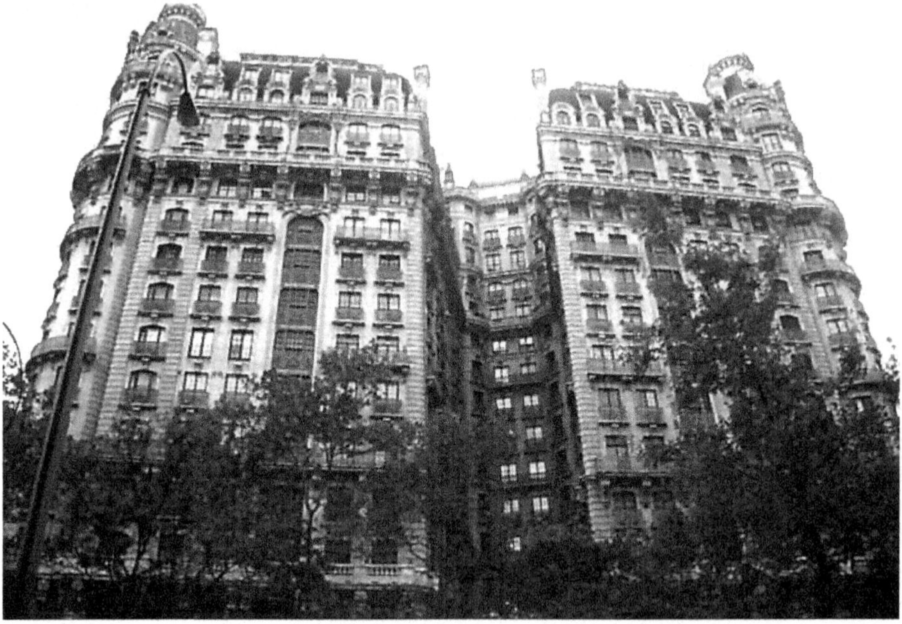

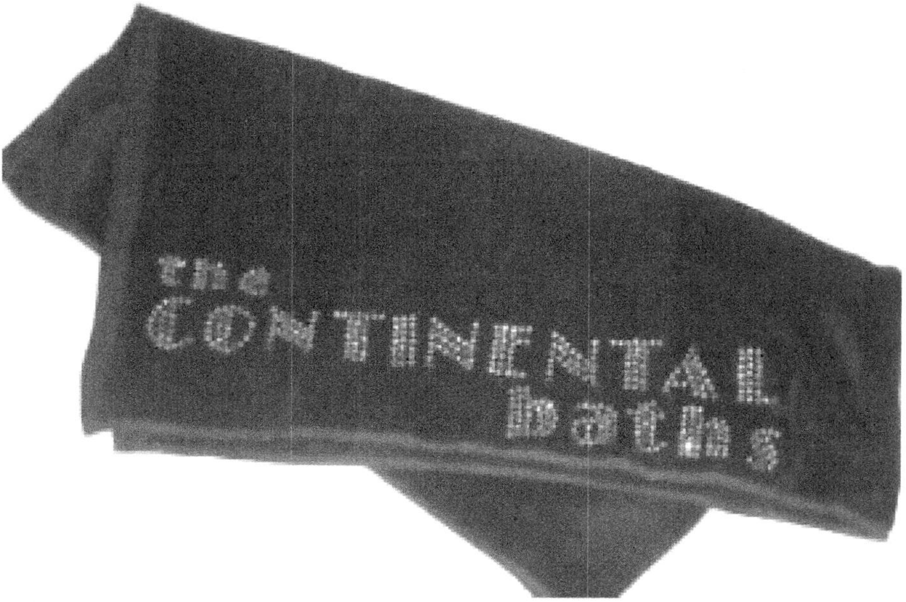
the
CONTINENTAL
baths

Me and Ted Hook

Made in the USA
Middletown, DE
27 March 2022

63243897R00129